Mr. Chairman

THE LIFE AND LEGACY OF WILBUR D. MILLS

"Kay Goss' biography is an insightful look into th˰ ˡˢ˰ ˰an I held in high
regard. When I was a junior member ˰˰The W˰˰˰ Committee, I
appreciated the time he took ˰˰˰˰˰˰ ˰˰˰˰ ˰lls served his
country well and I learned a l˰˰

–George H.W. Bush, 41st Presiden˰ ˰ ˰˰ ˰˰ ˰ House
Committee on Ways and Means when ˰

"A uniquely American story, Mr. ˰˰˰˰man tells how a boy from small town
Arkansas became one of this country's most powerful leaders."

–United States Senator Mark Pryor, Senior Senator from Arkansas

"As my college professor, Kay Goss inspired my belief in politics being the art
of the possible. As the author of the definitive biography on Wilbur Mills,
the powerful and accomplished chairman of the House Ways and Means
Committee, she will inspire yours."

–James L. "Skip" Rutherford III, Dean, University of Arkansas Clinton School of Public Service

"Biographer Kay Goss captures the greatness and the human frailties of
Wilbur Mills, the most powerful and highly respected member of Congress
during my tenure there, when I was honored to earn his friendship."

–Congressman John Paul Hammerschmidt, Retired

"This biography of the legendary House Ways and Means Chairman, Wilbur
Mills, brings a great man and superb Member of Congress to life for those
who never had the great privilege of knowing him. I hope it will be widely
read by the many, who unlike those of us who served on the Hill in the 1960s,
missed the great privilege of knowing him."

–Lee Williams, former Chief of Staff to J. William Fulbright, Chairman of the United States
Senate Committee on Foreign Relations

"For political junkies, Kay Goss' biography of Wilbur Mills is a gold mine.
Moreover, it is a fascinating journey into the inner corridors of those who
most shaped our nation's political landscape during the mid-Twentieth

Century; Mills' engagements with Rayburn, Kennedy, and Johnson are particularly memorable. An entire generation our nation knew Wilbur Mills as its premier "economic statesman", a legislator who virtually controlled Washington's fiscal nerve center. Just as Chairman Mills mastered our nation's Tax Code, Kay Goss has mastered her subject. She has examined the Mills public record in remarkable detail, combining it with a vivid portrait of the man, his larger political philosophy, his humanity, and his vulnerability. And, her handling of his early years gives us a delicious serving of Southern politics at its most readable. While her treatment of Mills reflects caring and admiration, Goss never sacrifices candor or historical accuracy; her assessment rings true, and that is what makes this biography of such special value.

–David Lambert, former Sr VP, New York Stock Exchange and Clinton Appointee to FAS, Italy

"Wilbur Mills was a talented populist with a keen sense of business and understanding of economics who cared deeply about the people and the well-being of the nation. His views on taxes, trade, Social Security and other public policy, combined with a mastery of the workings of government, especially the complexity of Congress, were sought after by politicians, academics, pundits and Wall Street alike. Chairman Wilbur Mills' input was oftentimes the key to achieving the consensus essential to a national policy for the people and nation he loved and served."

–Bill Alexander, Member of Congress from Arkansas First District, Retired

"Kay Goss has special and personal knowledge of Wilbur Mills, both 'The Chairman' and the simply human. She shares it with us wonderfully. Mr. Mills provided steady help and hope for ordinary working Americans and for those in need beginning in 1934 with what was in effect a 'County Medicaid' program while serving as County Judge in White County, and later the massive strengthening of Social Security and creation of Medicare and Medicaid, which he shepherded through Congress as Chairman of Ways and Means. His good deeds live on in the memories of those who watched and in the lives of those receiving these services today!"

–James Guy Tucker, Former Arkansas Governor and Congressman

"Sympathetic in tone, analytical in style, this comprehensive narrative of one of Arkansas's greatest contributors to United States' history is essential reading for anyone interested a better understanding of modern American history"

–C. Fred Williams, Professor Emeritus, UALR

"This timely biography of the late Congressman Wilbur D. Mills reminds us of the days when Arkansas's congressional delegation was second to none in knowledge, commitment, and clout. Kay Goss has performed a service to the people of Arkansas, and indeed the nation, in reminding us that this small southern state produced outstanding national leaders long before President Bill Clinton was even born."

–Tom Dillard, founding editor-in-chief of the Encyclopedia of Arkansas History & Culture.

"A richly detailed inside look at one of Arkansas's most fascinating political figures and a trip back to a time when Southern Democrats essentially ruled the United States Congress. Kay Goss explores the talents, excesses, struggles, and triumphs of one of the most powerful public figures of his day and tells how he and his colleagues in Arkansas and in the Congress worked the levers of power to create a safety net for many of the most vulnerable of their fellow Americans."

–David Stricklin, Head, Butler Center for Arkansas Studies

"Wilbur, by the way, was of the two most able guys I ever served with. The United States Tax Code is an incredibly complicated document, but Wilbur knew every comma in it. He was also a power, and had been Chairman of Ways and Means since 1958."

–Tip O'Neil, retired Speaker of the U.S. House of Representatives, in his memoir, Man of the House

"In my 30 years in Congress, I never knew any other member that I respected as a legislator more than Wilbur Mills. He was always fair and respectful of other Members irrespective of their party affliation or philosophy. Under his chairmanship, the Ways and Means Committee always functioned on a non-partisan basis. The only criteria was 'Is it good or bad tax policy?' What I learned in my experience with Wilbur Mills profounded affected me and helped me to be far more effective when I became Ways and Means Chair in 1995. Your book does him a well-deserved justice, and will be a real benefit to future members of Congress, as well as scholars."

– Bill Archer, former Ways and Means Chair

"Wilbur Mills was a man of enormous skill and intellect who made significant contributions to the prosperity of this nation, benefitting generations of Americans to this day. And Kay Goss has captured it all—from his humble roots in Arkansas to his many accomplishments at the pinnacle of power in Washington D.C.—it's all here. Goss presents a comprehensive profile of Mills' long and distinguished career of public service, while chronicling without compromise the human side of the man as well—the man his constituents, colleagues and Presidents called "Mr. Chairman".

ROB LEONARD, former General Counsel for the Ways and Means Committee and now a senior partern at the prestigious law firm AKIN GUMP in DC

Newly Elected Congressman Mills.

Mr. Chairman

THE LIFE AND LEGACY OF WILBUR D. MILLS

KAY COLLETT GOSS

PARKHURST BROTHERS, INC., PUBLISHERS

LITTLE ROCK

www.parkhurstbrothers.com

Parkhurst Brothers books are distributed to the trade through the Chicago Distribution Center, and may be ordered through Ingram Book Company, Baker & Taylor, Follett Library Resources and other book industry wholesalers. To order from Chicago Distribution Center, phone 1-800-621-2736 or send a fax to 800-621-8476. Copies of this and other Parkhurst Brothers, Inc., Publishers titles are available to organizations and corporations for purchase in quantity by contacting Special Sales Department at the location given on our website. Manuscript submission guidelines for this publishing company are available at our website.

Printed in the United States of America

First Edition, 2012

2012 2013 2014 2015 2016   10 9 8 7 6 5 4 3 2 1

Library of Congress Cataloging-in-Publication Data

Goss, Kay Collett.
Mr. Chairman : the life and legacy of Wilbur D. Mills / Kay Collett Goss. — First edition.
pages cm
Includes bibliographical references and index.
ISBN-13: 978-1-935166-49-8 (trade paperback : alkaline paper)
ISBN-10: 1-935166-49-2 (trade paperback : alkaline paper)
ISBN-13: (invalid) 978-1-935166-50-4 (e-book)
ISBN-10: (invalid) 1-935166-50-6 (e-book)
1. Mills, Wilbur D. (Wilbur Daigh), 1909-1992. 2. Mills, Wilbur D. (Wilbur Daigh), 1909-1992--Influence. 3. Legislators--United States--Biography. 4. United States. Congress. House--Biography. 5. United States. Congress. House. Committee on Ways and Means--History. 6. Budget process--United States--History--20th century. 7. United States--Politics and government--1933-1945. 8. United States--Politics and government--1945-1989. I. Title. II. Title: Mister Chairman.
E748.M625G67 2012
328.73'092--dc23
[B]
2012038204
ISBN: Trade Paperback   978-1-935166-49-8   [10 digit: 1-935166-49-2]
ISBN: e-book   978-1-935166-50-4   [10-digit: 1-935166-50-6]

The printed edition of this book is printed on wood pulp fiber, a renewable resource which is fully recyclable.

This book is printed on archival-quality paper that meets requirements of the American National Standard for Information Sciences, Permanence of Paper, Printed Library Materials, ANSI Z39.48-1984.

Cover design: Wendell E. Hall
Text design: Charlie Ross
Editors: Roger Armbrust,
                                              Ted Parkhurst

Proofreaders: Barbara and Bill Paddack
Acquired for Parkhurst Brothers, Inc., Publishers by: Ted Parkhurst

122012

Dedicated to

Susan Laura Collett Goss,

the fabulous daughter of the late Gene Goss and mine,

as well as the goddaughter of Wilbur and Polly Mills,

whom she first referred to as "My Mills."

Susan carries forward the legacy of service,

answering the call to serve the public

and help people every day.

At her suggestion, this book

is also dedicated to the memory

of the late Speaker of the House,

Thomas Phillip "Tip" O'Neill, Jr.,

who had planned to write the Foreword to this book.

Acknowledgements

With deep gratitude to the hundreds of people who provided the information, anecdotes and perspective necessary to fashion this biography. I want to express special deep gratitude to the many people who provided enormous encouragement, extraordinary insight, and valuable information to me over the years.

First, my amazing daughter, Susan Laura Collett Goss, knows better than anyone how many hours and how much work has been invested in this book. Special thanks go to her for making it possible with her advice, forbearance, and understanding. Thanks also to the late Gene Goss for his keen insight, carefully crafted from covering Mr. Mills as anchor for KATV News for five years, from serving as his congressional chief of staff for the last 14 years of his tenure, and from the 15 years they were friends afterward until Mr. Mills' death.

Thanks also to the wonderful Mills family—especially daughters Martha and Becky; brother and sister-in-law, Roger and Virginia Robbins Mills; and sister and brother-in-law, Emma Gene and Charles Yancey.

Thanks also to the late Speaker of the House Tip O'Neill, the late chairman of the Ways and Means Committee Daniel Rostenkowski, and the late President Gerald R. Ford for their encouragement, assistance, and perspective.

Many professional historians, colleagues, and leaders provided inspiring and enabling support, including the Arkansas Humanities Council, the Arkansas Historical Association, Arkansas Historical Quarterly editors, the University of Arkansas Press, the Arkansas Studies Center's Encyclopedia of Arkansas, the History of Arkansas Medicine Associates, Devonalu Perry, the late Bill Huddleston and Fran Flener, Jeanne Wayne, Victor Ray, Ted Boswell, the late Warren Bass, Dave Parr, the late Jack Files, Sam Boyce, Dwane Treat, the late J. W. "Red" Morris, Brown Dodd, J. R. Thomas, the late Dan Garner, the Arkansas History Commission, the Carl Albert Center on Congress, the John F. Kennedy Presidential Library, the Lyndon B. Johnson Presidential Library, the Sam Rayburn Museum and Library, the Harry S Truman Presidential Library, the Gerald R. Ford Presidential Library, the Washington Post, the New York Times, the Arkansas Gazette, the Arkansas Democrat Gazette, and the Searcy Daily Citizen.

I was blessed to have the best possible publisher, adviser, and editor, so special thanks go to Ted Parkhurst, as well as to Roger Armbrust for making the first scrub.

I give these special folks all the credit for all the successes and take all responsibility for any oversights or mistakes.

– K.C.G., 2012

Contents

Author's Note

One of the founding fathers was George Mason of Virginia, a delegate to the Philadelphia Convention in 1787, who described the U.S. House of Representatives as "the grand repository of the democratic principle of the government." He observed that members of the House should "sympathize with their constituents, should think as they think, and feel as they feel; and, for these purposes, should even be residents among them."

With that thought in mind, the founders provided in the U.S. Constitution that the premier power to raise revenue originates in the House of Representatives. Therefore, the first committee created by the first Congress was the Ways and Means Committee. It was designed to keep the "power of the purse" as close to the people as possible.

The person who served longest on that committee and who served longest as chairman was Wilbur Daigh Mills of Kensett, Arkansas. In that role, he designed the major tax, trade, highway, unemployment compensation, social security, disability, and health care legislation of the twentieth century.

Mills' tenure as chairman was often called the era of progressive tax legislation, with the repeal of the unpopular excise taxes, cuts in personal rates, the closing of loopholes, and the creation of a minimum tax in 1969 aimed at rich people who previously had been able to avoid taxes entirely.

About the time President Clinton was elected, Robert McIntyre of the Citizens for Tax Justice was quoted in the *Arkansas Democrat-Gazette*, as saying that if Mills' tax code had been in effect, the richest 1 percent of Americans would be paying another $70 billion in taxes.1

The power of Congress has swung like a pendulum over the centuries. The peak of presidential power under Abraham Lincoln was followed by a surge of congressional power after his assassination, causing Woodrow Wilson, a political scientist at the time, before becoming governor of New Jersey and later president, to write in his book *Congressional Government*, that congressional committees were "lord proprietors." However, during the personality cults of the twentieth century (Theodore Roosevelt, Woodrow Wilson, and Franklin Roosevelt), Congress was weak and overshadowed.

After Roosevelt's passing and the passage of the Legislative Reform Act of 1946, Congress began regaining power. At this time, Mills was a rising star in Congress and a few years from becoming Ways and Means chairman. He was a part of a new generation in Congress, 40 years younger than Robert Doughton of North Carolina, the chairman of Ways and Means at the time, and compiling the second longest tenure.

The power of Congress increased until the congressional reform acts of the

1970s. Thus, Mills was a congressional legend while I was a student of political science at the University of Arkansas, pursuing bachelor's and master's degrees in political science and history, doctoral studies at West Virginia University, and teaching public administration and political science at three of Arkansas' institutions of higher education.

Richard F. Fenno, Jr., then the academic icon of congressional research, called on political scientists for participation and observation-oriented research on members of Congress. He described them as widely discussed, but narrowly understood, even though they were often the lead subjects of compelling stories in newspapers and television. Nevertheless, they were only infrequent subjects of political scientists' books, and even more rarely described from close contact or observation.2

To write a book about the life and career of perhaps the most influential committee chairman in congressional history could be a decades' long project. I am reminded of Sonny West, who said of the writings on Elvis Presley, "It takes a lifetime to sum up a person's life."

So, although this is not a complete biography of Wilbur D. Mills, I do want to share the highlights of my research to this point. As the biographer of Marilyn Monroe observed, "the biographer's task should be a constant series of surprises." I certainly experienced that. I hope you will as well.

Kay Collett Goss
Washington, D.C.
September, 2012

Foreword by
Senator Dale Bumpers

Kay has captured and shared a great Arkansas and national political story, covering not only the remarkable political life of one of Arkansas' favorite sons, but also his compelling personal and professional lives as well.

The early potential of Wilbur Mills was obvious to all in his day. The myriad accomplishments of his 42 years in public service are brought to life very vividly in Kay's well-documented account. The challenges Wilbur Mills faced as he slipped into the disease of alcoholism and resulting controversy are dealt with forthrightly here, rekindling the reaction in the public's mind during those difficult months. Unfortunately, Mills' late-career difficulties dimmed the remembrance of some of his major achievements. We should not forget how instrumental Mills was in creating or extending Medicare, Medicaid, Social Security Disability, Social Security increased coverage and levels, tax reform, Interstates 40, 30, 430, 440, 630, the Little Rock Port Authority, Burns Park, Greers Ferry Dam, House support for the Arkansas River development project, as well as balancing the federal budget and paying down the national debt. In addition, he was instrumental in hundreds of other measures coming out of Congress, as well as thousands of case-management projects for individual residents of his congressional district.

The legendary stories from his years as the youngest county judge in Arkansas are told to this day by those thousands who benefited during the Great Depression from his hard work and daily devotion to his constituents.

I sincerely appreciate that this book balances those accomplishments, without ignoring Mills' troubles. Kay Goss has deftly weighed Mills' character and shown the complexity that was Wilbur Mills. She lets his example show that–no matter how high a person goes, how much he or she achieves–it is possible to fall *and then to recover magnificently* as Mills did when he went on to help others who suffer from addictions to rebound and rebuild. Wilbur Mills is shown here to be a case study in strength, in overcoming personal difficulties to strive again in service to individuals and society.

As Dwane Treat of Searcy observed on the day Mills died, "Wilbur was the Congressman for the Common People!"

Dale Bumpers
Little Rock, 2012
Arkansas Governor, 1971-1975
United States Senator, 1975-1998

Preface by
Senator David Pryor

I know of no one who could capture and put on paper the legendary life of Congressman Wilbur Mills as Kay Goss has done. Her patient and extensive research demonstrates her curiosity and long fascination with one of America's foremost legislative icons of our generation. From his value system acquired early in life in Kensett, Arkansas, the 29-year-old county judge of White County was elected to Congress by taking on and defeating the vested power structure of the local political establishment.

Some three decades later, I had the privilege of being elected to the U.S. House, representing the Fourth Congressional District. I was honored to serve with Congressman Wilbur Mills and have the rare privilege to observe him at "close range." Learning from him in the House was a unique opportunity, one in which I place great value.

Only a handful of members of the House and Senate called him "Wilbur." To most of us, he was "Mr. Chairman." No legislative tactician grew to understand better or in more detail the myriad complexities of the federal government–especially our country's tax code, its intricacies and how our tax laws affected every American business owner and worker alike. In addition, his enormous impact on health programs, most notably Medicare, and social issues remains a hallmark of his service.

The tremendous respect Chairman Mills enjoyed among his colleagues in the House translated into support from both Democrats and Republicans. It was said that during his years chairing the House Ways and Means Committee, a roll-call vote was needless, as the chairman governed his committee by reason and ultimately consensus.

I valued our relationship, the lessons he taught and the generosity of his priceless time so kindly given to a young and sometimes far too restless member of the House from his home state.

In today's toxic national capital, Wilbur Mills' calm, measured and respected voice would carry great weight and bring credit to a tarnished institution.

Kay Goss has made a fine contribution by reminding us once again of Wilbur Daigh Mills and the unique public service he gave to Arkansas and America.

Mr. Chairman is a must read for all who love Arkansas and American history.

David H. Pryor
Little Rock, 2012
Arkansas Governor, 1975-1979
United States Senator, 1979-1997

Wilbur Mills, age about thirteen months. This and all other photos courtesy of the Mills family unless otherwise noted.

CHAPTER 1

BOY WONDER
1909-1933

Wilbur Daigh Mills was nearly declared dead as a "blue baby" in the family home at Kensett, Arkansas. It took the experienced eye and touch of an African-American midwife, Josephine Rodgers, affectionately known as "Aunt Joe," to save him. Dr. Tapscott, who delivered him on May 24, 1909, thought him dead. "Give me that baby," Aunt Joe demanded. She took him into another room. Soon, a newborn's loud cry filled the home.

Ardra Pickens Mills, 27, and Abbie Lois Daigh Mills, 24, were inspired in 1904 when Wilbur and Orville Wright made their successful airplane flight at Kitty Hawk, North Carolina. A. P. Mills suggested naming their baby boy "Wilbur Orville." Abbie thought that was a little much and decided on Wilbur, adding Daigh, her maiden name.

Wilbur's family heritage was Scottish on both sides. His mother's father sat on Abraham Lincoln's lap as a youngster in Illinois in the early 1850s, while Lincoln was a local leader; so says family legend. In late life, Wilbur's granddad remarked about the roughness of Lincoln's face and his moodiness.

The Mills family came to America very early, during South Carolina's colonial period, migrating eventually to Tennessee, Mississippi, and then to Arkansas. Genealogical research, still in progress by Wilbur's older daughter, has gone back to James Granderson Mills, born in 1815 in North or South Carolina.

Wilbur spent summers with his grandfather, James A. Mills, who had a store in White County, Arkansas, first in Higginson and then in Plainview. His grandfather was one ancestor known to drink alcohol on a regular basis, one glass of bourbon every night before bedtime. Wilbur's mother referred to it as "grandfather's medicine," taken to help him sleep. Wilbur's father drank moonshine in the privacy of his store's backroom, but gave it up, becoming uncomfortable with the habit.

Wilbur's father was the third of six children, born April 20, 1882, near Abbeville, Mississippi. He married Abbie at the Gleason Hotel in Little Rock, Arkansas. His brother, James Hugh Mills, born September 1, 1893, was a Poinsett County (Arkansas) county official during the 1940s.

Life in Kensett, a quiet little town near the Little Red River, was an open book. Wilbur dreamed of the world beyond, while always maintaining his personal and voting residency in Kensett, as well as his bank account, his church membership, and his home.

His brother Roger never left Kensett. His sister Emma Gene moved to a plantation near Marianna, an hour's drive east. Two of Roger's three children stayed in White County, a son, Bill (a Methodist minister and former state representative and chancery judge), in Kensett; their late daughter, Sandra Kay Mills Coleman, in Searcy; and a son, Roger Q. Mills, Jr., in nearby Conway. Emma Gene's children live in Little Rock (Ann Yancey Ferrill) and Clinton, Mississippi (Mary Yancey Clayton). Wilbur's daughters, Martha Sue Dixon (a former library official) and Rebecca Ann Yates (a former high school physics teacher) live in Connecticut and New Jersey, the first members of Wilbur's immediate family to move from Arkansas. His six grandchildren live in Colorado, Hawaii, Connecticut, and New Jersey, all adhering to the family service legacy, ranging from tax attorney, professor and researcher to former staffer for the U.S. Olympic Committee.

Wilbur's father began his career as a teacher, was promoted to superintendent, started a country store, and eventually became a partner in the local bank. Much of his lending, however, was out of pocket, so to speak–through the store. For example, he loaned the school district enough to get started each year until property taxes were paid on October 10. Through the store, he loaned to people with poor or no credit. He could work out terms to best accommodate his customers, especially those who could not qualify for bank loans. There were no federal credit worthiness rules on stores, as there were on banks, so he could accommodate special circumstances and sometimes irregular payment schedules.

During the Great Depression, when dozens of farmers owed him money and couldn't pay, Mills' father forgave debts and let people start over, turning financial bills into moral debt. He wound up owning the Bank of Kensett outright, as well as a good deal of surrounding farmland, even though he didn't really want it, saying, as Roger Mills remembered, "I don't want to be 'land poor.'"

The senior Mills became a legendary local leader of Southern politics, boss of his part of White County. Thus, Wilbur grew up on wings of business and politics, standing on a stool behind a teller's window until he was tall enough to see over the counter, and counting votes at precinct boxes.

In Wilbur's mind, his father was not just Dad, but a legend bigger than all others. Wilbur Mills admired Edmund Burke, Thomas Jefferson, Abraham Lincoln, Sam Rayburn, Harry Truman, and Joe T. Robinson; but his father was his life's main hero and model guide.

Long after the senior Mills' death–until his own–Wilbur's conversation was sprinkled with affectionate references to his revered father. Wilbur was called "Son," by his family. When he went off to Hendrix College in Conway, he asked everyone, except his father, not to call him "Son" anymore. Roger remembered, though Wilbur never once mentioned it, that their father many times called Wilbur "Sweetheart," even on an evening when Wilbur made it home long after their father's established curfew. His father threatened to punish Wilbur when he came home. Instead, he said, "Are you okay, Sweetheart?"

In adult life, even after going to Congress and smoking up to three packs of cigarettes or cigarillos a day for 60 years, Wilbur never let his father see him smoke. However, he did not lie to his father, who had promised his children a $1,000 reward for not smoking. When A. P. was about to write him the reward check, Wilbur refused it, confiding that he didn't deserve it. A. P. was surprised– and respectful.

As a teen, A. P. Mills had moved from Abbeville, Lafayette County, Mississippi, to Arkansas to attend Beauvoir College (owned and operated by a Mr. Spence) in Wilmar. Shortly after, he graduated from Draughon's Business College in Little Rock. Finding work in Oklahoma–teaching school–he met Miss Abbie Daigh, a postal clerk in Oklahoma City. A. P. returned to Arkansas, where his own father, also a merchant, was living in Higginson. A. P. split cross-ties and was hired eventually as school superintendent of Kensett, earning $50 a month for an eight-month term. A. P. Mills and a partner founded Mills and

Wilbur Mills in elementary school, fourth from left in the second row.

Brock General Store for extra income, necessary to raise a growing family. After a year and a half, A. P. bought out his partner and renamed the store A. P. Mills General Store in 1908. He did it with $500 savings amassed by Mrs. Mills from her income as a postal clerk in Oklahoma City.[1] He ran the store until his death in 1958, then his son Roger operated it until it closed in 1992.

In time, A. P. owned and operated a cotton gin in addition to A. P. Mills General Store. He had become Kensett's merchant, banker, farmer, cotton ginner, and economic developer. He served on the city council, chaired White County's Democratic Central Committee, and was president of both the Bank of Kensett and the Kensett School Board.

A. P. Mills, often called "Apple Pie" by his children behind his back, admonished Wilbur regularly: "If you are going to do anything, do it right." Younger brother Roger remembers Wilbur at 11, standing on a box to reach the store's adding machine, keeping track of farmers' accounts. "He was always grown up, even as a kid."[2] He and his father worked hard to make the store expand. Wilbur revealed later:

> Business was certainly my father's calling and he worked long
> 12- and 14-hour days, and soon the store had sales of around
> $100,000 a year, even during the Depression. If his customers
> didn't make anything, payment would have to wait until later.
> Back then it was difficult, if not impossible, for a farmer to get
> a loan at a bank in our county. Merchants, like my father, were
> probably the only place to get credit. Borrowers would pay 10
> percent on what they owed regardless of how soon they paid off
> their debt. Dad also devoted much of his time and energy to the
> Bank of Kensett. While my father didn't start the bank, he did
> become a director, with about $2,000 worth of stock. He would
> say, "Any business that I'm involved in is not going to go broke."
> He put all of his savings into that bank to keep it from going
> under.[3]

Mills' mother was also actively involved in the store and community.

> My mother was a great asset in running the store, far beyond
> her $500 they used to buy into the business. Mother had a keen
> memory, which was very helpful because Dad did not. People
> would come in to pay a bill, and if the bookkeeper wasn't available
> and Dad couldn't think of their names, even though he had always
> known them, mother was always there to whisper their names
> in his ear. In those days, Mother was what you would call a good

"mixer." She got along well with everybody. She had a wonderful voice. She sang duet, with another woman in town, at church services, for funerals, and community events. In her later years, Mother would sit out in front of the store and greet everyone as they entered. She would also give out candy to children. In the first grade, I gave out candy to kids as well. It made me very popular with them and in trouble with Dad.[4]

Wilbur never did own any of the store or bank. His brother Roger managed the bank for many years. When his father died, Wilbur and his sister sold their inherited shares to Roger.

Wilbur's sister became Mrs. Charles Yancey. Her father-in-law owned a large plantation near Marianna, in Lee County, Arkansas, where she and Charles built their home. Mills recalled good-naturedly:

Emma Gene took great delight in tormenting me, causing me embarrassment. One such time was when I had some friends from college over for dinner. While we were around the table, Emma Gene came in to give her announcement, "Wilbur, Uncle Frank is in jail again ..." This, of course, was a joke intended to embarrass me in front of my friends, and it did. "Uncle Frank" was not in jail, though he might easily have been. "Uncle Frank" was my grandfather Wyatt's stepson. He was quite a bit older than I was and was quite an outlaw. He would always be talking to me about this, that, and the other, all of which were illegal. Practically everything he mentioned was outside the law. Emma Gene never seemed to tire of needling me with this "black sheep" of the family.[5]

As a small boy, Wilbur worked after school and during summers and holidays, assisting the store's customers, carrying their groceries, loading their wagons, delivering goods, being a general clerk, and keeping the books.

He also worked at the bank, family cotton gin and farms, learning all aspects of diverse business operations. His father was impressed with Wilbur's business acumen and leadership. His Dad cultivated Wilbur's natural curiosity and good judgment. Wilbur set attendance and achievement records in Sunday school at Kensett Methodist Church and in Boy Scouts.

So great was his Dad's trust in young Wilbur that the boy received a rifle for his 11th birthday. When Wilbur was only 12, his father asked him to drive his mother, brother, sister, and a friend on a family trip to Oklahoma for a visit, a journey over only dirt roads that involved, predictably, a few flats.

Wilbur held the longest continuous membership at Kensett Methodist

Church, joining as a boy and continuing with monthly contributions deducted from his checking account at the Bank of Kensett, until his death. When he first went to Washington, he attended Metropolitan Memorial Methodist Church on Nebraska Avenue. Dr. Edward G. Latch, the minister, later served as chaplain of the House. Mills suspended his church attendance as work and personal pressures increased, though he could preach a sermon as easily as make a political speech. He would often say that he did not want to hear "a preacher complaining about what people were doing, including me, so I'd just drink on Sunday, because I didn't have to work."

At a moonshine still in rural White County, Wilbur had his first drink when he was 12 years old. His last drink came 54 years later at the Waldorf-Astoria Hotel in New York City.

As a boy working at the store, Wilbur had noticed that some farmers would frequently buy 20 hundred-pound bags of sugar. He wondered: "How could their wives make that much jam and jelly?" His father instructed him, "We sell sugar; we don't inquire into its use. So, don't be blabbing about it, Son!"

Meanwhile, Wilbur's mother, a strong Prohibitionist, hosted Women's Christian Temperance Union meetings in her living room. Years later, while Wilbur was White County judge, he had to rule on whether White County would be wet or dry. He ruled in favor of dry, because residents had voted "dry" in a local referendum.

A. P. Mills was a caring and compassionate person. When a tornado hit Judsonia, he provided food and low-interest loans to victims, and served on a county committee to restore the town.

When Wilbur was nine, he launched his dream to become a member of Congress, with the encouragement of Congressman William Oldfield, U.S. representative from Arkansas' Second Congressional District. Oldfield made an impressive mentor. He was a member of the Ways and Means Committee, a Batesville attorney, and a Spanish-American War veteran. Once a year, Oldfield reported goings on in Washington to A. P. Mills while holding Wilbur in his lap, patting him on the head, and telling A. P. that Wilbur had the "makings of a very fine congressman" and future member of Ways and Means. Later, Mills suggested humorously, "Oldfield, being an able politician, probably gave all proud parents throughout his congressional district the same compliments." However, Mills took it seriously and played "U.S. House of Representatives" in his own back yard, instead of robbers or cowboys and Indians. Mills always served as "The Speaker." Some of his playmates were girls, so there were female members in Wilbur Mills' "Congress" long before his friend Hattie Caraway of Jonesboro, Arkansas, became the first female elected to the United States Senate. The kids would set up "The House" by laying boards of two-by-eight lumber across milk kegs so everyone would have a seat.

Wilbur attended Kensett Public School from first through ninth grades. The school was a large, white two-story building, eventually torn down in the early 1920s. One of Wilbur's favorite teachers was Miss Essie Henson, older sister of Polly Billingsley, his future wife. His father, then school superintendent, moved Miss Henson up in her teaching assignments, so that she was teaching whatever grade Wilbur was taking. After acing his seventh-grade exams, he immediately asked to take eighth-grade exams, passed easily, and was promoted from seventh to ninth grade.[6] In 1922, at age 13, Wilbur began commuting three miles to Searcy, county seat of White County, population 2,836, to high school, securing accredited courses in preparation for college. He wore bib overalls every day.[7]

After graduating top in his class a few weeks before his 17th birthday, Mills enrolled in Hendrix College. The Methodist liberal arts institution was in Conway, Arkansas, 45 miles southwest of Kensett. His mother selected the college for its high moral standards, strong discipline, and academic excellence. The student enrollment at Hendrix in 1926 was 336–255 men and 81 women.[8]

Mills was already planning to go to law school after Hendrix and to seek a seat in Congress. All of his academic schedule and extra-curricular activities were selected with his goals in mind.

Mills got off to a very good start. In February 1927, during his second semester, he became assistant business manager of the *Bulldog*, the student newspaper. The managing editor and a future Methodist bishop, Aubrey Walton, taught young Wilbur to smoke. They became lifelong friends.

Mills often discussed the first time he drank alcohol at Hendrix. It was during his first semester. Three large football linemen, each over six feet tall and weighing over 200 pounds, came to his basement dormitory room, which he shared with two roommates during the fall of 1926. They asked, "Which one is Wilbur Mills?" He stood up in the corner where he was studying and proudly said, "I am." They said, "Come with us. We've got something we want you to do upstairs." On the way up, they told him they had picked him out to take on the college's cognac drinking champion. He was surprised.

Mills said he did not dethrone the champ. He did take about three drinks, became quite drunk, and missed classes for two days. Dr. Thomas Starling Staples, dean of men, Dr. Green, and Dr. Reynolds believed his absences were caused by flu.[9]

During spring semester, Mills joined the college dramatic club, where he starred in plays. Fine reviews followed his performances for the remainder of his Hendrix days. He was preparing for a lifetime on the public stage.

In 1927, Mills also served as business manager of the Franklin Literary Society. He took part in the freshman declamation contest, open session, and annual banquet. At the end of his first year, Mills was nominated by Aubrey Walton to become business manager of the *Bulldog*. The newspaper observed that Mills had shown himself to be "an ardent and efficient worker and salesman."[10] To organize for the coming year, *Bulldog* staff dined in style at the Hotel Revilo in Conway. The banquet tab of $500 was paid from the surplus Mills had amassed selling ads.

In early March 1928, a visit in Little Rock with his former roommate, J. W. Best, led to Wilbur's first adult experience in politics. Mills met future Congressman Brooks Hays, an attorney for Pyramid Life Insurance Company, and a friendship of mutual respect was struck. Hays, then 30 years old, served as an assistant state attorney general, and told Wilbur he was planning to run for governor. Mills, only 18 and underage to vote, promised to work in the campaign.

In 1928, Wilbur's family friend, U.S. Senator Joseph T. Robinson of Lonoke and majority leader of the Senate, was chosen as Democratic presidential candidate Al Smith's running mate. Wilbur, during these early impressionable days, saw his chance to become a national leader by mastering as many issues and policies as possible, making as many friends as possible, and putting forth a dedicated effort.

In April 1928, the Franklin Literary Society had its annual banquet at Hendrix's Tabor Hall, introducing a startling and pleasing innovation in entertainment: a circus. Gordon Young, who later married one of Wilbur's college girlfriends, Elizabeth Gregg, and was later appointed and confirmed as a federal judge at behest of Mills and Senator John L. McClellan, was the circus' ringmaster.[11]

Then that summer, Mills kept his political promise. Hays, a decided underdog, ran against incumbent Governor Harvey Parnell. The primary was August 14, five days after Hays' 30th birthday. Parnell was re-elected with a plurality—94,396 votes to 59,426 for Hays.

Mills came close to carrying Kensett Township for Hays against the established machine, which included his own father. Young Mills served as Hays' driver from Searcy to Jonesboro.[12] To show his strong support publicly, Wilbur had a large Hays campaign poster mounted at A. P. Mills General Store Doing so, Wilbur directly contradicted his father's policy of not taking sides at his place of business. The predictable paternal lecture was a thing to behold.

In the general election that year, Mills worked for the Al Smith-Joe T. Robinson national ticket. The Democrats carried Arkansas, but lost nationally to Herbert Hoover.

In September 1928 at age 19, Mills began his junior year at Hendrix. His schedule included an honors reading class, initiated for three top students: Mills, with his best friends, Elizabeth Gregg of Pine Bluff and E. J. Butler of Forrest City. They read in the library in lieu of attending classes, reporting for a three-hour session on Saturdays with Drs. Thomas Starling Staples and

William Curt Boothman. The lengthy syllabus covered the period from the fall of the Roman Empire to modern western civilization. One of Mills' papers was on "The Rise of Towns."[13]

Mills took all mathematics courses offered, earning an A+ in each.

Butler and Mills were paired against the Southern Methodist University debate team in Dallas for competition in 1929, taking the negative side of "Resolved, the parliamentary form of government is superior to the presidential form."[14] They won 3-0. According to the *Bulldog*, Mills and Butler debated a team from the University of Mississippi in April, losing by a very close decision. In May, following their successful Southern Methodist University tourney, they traveled on to Austin College in Sherman, Texas, winning 2-1; and to Southwestern University, Georgetown, and Tennessee, where they also won.

The debate team traveled by train. Mills originally memorized his presentations, but eventually felt comfortable departing from prepared texts. It was excellent preparation for a future stump speaker.

After debate at Southwestern University (now Rhodes College), the *Memphis Commercial Appeal* quoted Mills and Butler and included their pictures. Soon, Mills received a fan letter from a young lady in Blue Mountain, Mississippi, inviting him to come for a visit. Mills and his brother Roger drove to Blue Mountain.[15] Coming home, they had a flat tire. Arriving at a filling station for tire repair, the Mills brothers found themselves surrounded by several older men, standing around the garage area, seeming quite cool, almost hostile. Asking the garage owner about the hostility, Wilbur learned that the locals thought he and his brother—well dressed and from out of town—were revenue agents. When they identified themselves as college students just passing through, reception warmed immediately. The men invited Wilbur and Roger to help themselves from a stash of moonshine nearby. Declining with thanks, the brothers headed toward Hendrix, laughing about the encounter.[16]

Also, Mills debated at Maryville College in Tennessee and at Centenary College in Louisiana, taking the negative side on "Resolved that nations should adopt a plan of complete disarmament excepting such forces as are needed for police purposes."[17]

Mills was stricken with an acute attack of appendicitis and underwent surgery on a Sunday afternoon in early January 1929. Soon out of immediate danger, his condition suddenly worsened due to side effects from ether, a regular anesthesia of the time. The event resulted in his contracting pneumonia, for which he was hospitalized for another two weeks. Brother Roger hurried from Hendrix College to the hospital in Searcy in his Model A Ford. After Wilbur's surgery, Roger sat up all night with his brother who was in severe pain. Roger remembers that he jokingly guessed at that time that Wilbur lingered in the hospital due to admiration for his nurses.[18]

By his senior year, Mills had a busy social life, with a girlfriend in Kensett, one at Hendrix, and several at Arkansas State Teachers College (now the University of Central Arkansas and, like Hendrix, located in Conway). As he explained, campus rules and restrictions at ASTC were less strict than at Hendrix.

In December 1929, Tau Kappa Alpha, the debate fraternity, was reorganized. Mills, "popular senior from Kensett," was elected president. The fraternity had been inactive since 1927. Prompted by the strong student leadership of Mills and strong faculty sponsorship of Dr. 0. T. Gooden, other Hendrix debate students joined Tau Kappa Alpha. Three seniors, in addition to Mills, (E. J. Butler; Johnnie Wallace, a niece of Arkansas Governor Charles Brough; and Kessinger Norwell) joined; Sterling Melborn was the lone junior; sophomore members were Guy "Mutt" Jones (later an Arkansas state senator), Noble Gill and Donald Nelson, all prominent eventually in Arkansas public affairs.

In early 1930, debate teams were again formed. Mills appeared on KTHS radio in Hot Springs to discuss the importance of college debates, significance of assigned topics, and designated issues.[19] That spring, the Mills-Butler team won all its debates. Mills finished second in his senior class and was named salutatorian. The valedictorian was Johnnie Wallace.

In 1953, Hendrix College awarded Mills an honorary doctorate of laws degree. In 1963, he was named a distinguished alumnus. On the Hendrix board of trustees, his connections and wisdom proved beneficial to the small liberal arts college. In 1975, the Wilbur D. Mills Center for Social Studies was dedicated. The building now houses his official papers, including a reduced replica of his congressional office, as well as a bust of him by sculptor Hank Kaminsky of Fayetteville. In 1975, he was removed from the board of trustees, after public display of the disease of alcoholism. The board appointed Betty Bumpers. In 1976, Mills donated his office furniture and his official public papers to Hendrix College. In 1977, after he retired from Congress, Hendrix College, sponsored by Hendrix board member and sustaining contributor Richard Butler, Sr., of Little Rock, joined with other institutions and individuals in Conway and Faulkner County to thank Mills for his public service and leadership. In 1982, Mills returned to Hendrix's Mills Center to deliver a major address on economics and tax policy.

In the summer of 1930, after his 21st birthday and Hendrix graduation, Mills threw a cocktail party, possibly Kensett's first, at his home. His parents, who were traveling at the time, were horrified when they learned of the event, remembers Roger.

Mills also bought his first poll tax that summer, as he first became eligible to vote in the 1930 election. Governor Harvey Parnell ran for re-election and Brooks Hays opposed him again, losing by a larger margin than in 1928. However, with skillful support of Mills, Hays once again did very well in Kensett, even though established political leaders, including A. P. Mills, supported Parnell, the incumbent governor.

A. P. Mills believed Wilbur had a good mind for business, with priceless experience. His confidence was put to the test during the summer of 1930:

> I had just graduated from Hendrix College and was preparing to go to law school. Dad took Mother, Roger, and my sister, Emma Gene, to Canada to visit my mother's relatives. They had a tremendous wheat farm, with about 150 people working for them. Dad, Mother, and all were gone for about eight weeks. I was left in charge of the store and bank. I was 21, and even though Dad had confidence in me, he had left instructions on how to deal with accounts.
>
> There was a terrible drought in 1930. The crops were burning in the fields. Farmers who used to make a bale of cotton on one or two acres now needed five acres. It was a horrible year. Dad had told me of arrangements he had with farmers, the amount each was to pay, and how much we would furnish them. Even though Dad had instructed me, I cut way back on everything that they were to get. Of course, I didn't cut out their tobacco and snuff, I couldn't do that. If they were supposed to get $300 worth of groceries, maybe they got $50 or $60 worth. I cut them back to practically nothing. He had told me that I could loan up to $700,000, but I approved only $250,000, saving Dad from losing several hundred thousand dollars. We lost some money, but not all that we would have.[20]

Later that year, Mills left for Harvard Law School, to concentrate on corporate law. His father waited with him at the train station until the scheduled midnight departure, still trying to talk him out of becoming an attorney. He wanted his son to become a businessman—a merchant or a banker, arguing one could meet a payroll, create jobs for people, create capital, and be in charge of one's own life. Becoming an attorney, he said, would cause one always to be dependent upon "being hired." Many attorneys were going broke in Searcy during the Depression. His father even offered to purchase the Bank of Searcy, estimating he could buy it from Tom Watkins for $75,000. Mills was determined to prepare for a public career. Since Mills had always been at the top of his class academically, Harvard Law School was a natural choice for a young man seeking the best legal education and determined to become a congressman.

Two classmates from Hendrix (E. J. Butler and Albert Graves of Arkadelphia) also chose Harvard Law School. Other friends from Arkansas at Harvard included Ed Lightle of Searcy, later a state senator and owner of Lightle, Raney, and Beebe law firm, as well as Shuford Nichols, Howard Stebbins, and Buddy McHaney, all of Little Rock.

"I remember when we first arrived, the dean sat everyone down," Mills said. "He told us to look to our right and left, that two out of three of us wouldn't be back next year. I didn't look because I knew he wasn't talking about me. E. J. Butler did leave after one year and went on to finish at Vanderbilt."[21]

Mills resided in an off-campus rooming house for boys on legendary Lowell Street. His lunches cost 50 cents and his dinners 75 cents at a restaurant. His father gave him $2,000 for room, board, and tuition each year at Harvard from the sale of his interest in Fones Brothers, a large wholesale hardware firm at Little Rock.[22]

Harvard was "just a constant grind" to Mills.[23]

> Coming from the South, life in Boston was very difficult for me. We were kidded a bit because of that. They would want to know how a bunch of yokels from Arkansas could ever have made it to Harvard. Massachusetts was more conservative back then, but I didn't find it as friendly as the country. Down South you would speak to someone and they would speak back. In the North, if you would say something to someone who didn't know you, they would stare at you like you were crazy. I remember, once, walking down the street talking to everyone that passed by. One man turned around and watched me for two blocks like I was some sort of a madman. Finally I quit doing it; I didn't want to stop all the traffic.[24]

One of Mills' housemates was Johanas Karl Zahn Detlock, who later became president of Mercedes-Benz Corporation.

> Johanas came down to Kensett after my first year at Harvard for a visit. He had completed his studies and was preparing to return to Germany. I will never forget his telling my mother that his girlfriend was going to meet him in Spain and they were planning a leisurely return to Germany. Mother caught on right quick that they were going to be in the same bed. She said she hoped that I hadn't picked up all of his bad traits.[25]

Mills did not drink a lot at Harvard. Yet he was cognizant that the Coast Guard confiscated Canadian liquor from rumrunners and stored it at the Port of Boston. He and his classmates would sometimes pick up liquor there.

Mills lamented always being unlucky in getting small bottles. Also, he remembered local proms and partying with girls from Ratcliff College who came to Harvard. Once, he and friends got a chaperone drunk on four or five glasses of their "punch," so she'd pass out and they could dance with the girls. Once, he remembered drinking so much "purple passion" (grape juice and bath tub gin) that he fell down while dancing, pulling his date down on top of him. He often remarked, "I guess she was glad at least that I didn't fall on top of her."[26]

Among Mills' other classmates were Fred Scribner of Maine, who became under secretary of the Treasury, and Gerald Morgan, White House legal counsel, both under President Dwight Eisenhower.

Among his many distinguished professors was Felix Frankfurter, appointed by President Franklin Roosevelt to the United States Supreme Court in 1939.

While Mills was at Harvard, his longtime friend from Kensett, future hall-of-fame catcher Bill Dickey, was playing with the New York Yankees. Dickey invited Mills to spend some of his spring breaks with him in New York. When describing the catcher's renowned skills at bat, Mills would say that Dickey could hit the ball "a country mile."[28]

They double-dated, enjoying dining, dancing, and Broadway plays. Dickey introduced him to Lou Gehrig and Babe Ruth. Babe Ruth's nickname for Mills, ironically for a Harvard man, was "Peapicker."

Later, in campaigns when young Mills was questioned about why he had gone out of state to Harvard Law School instead of the University of Arkansas' law school, he would quip good naturedly that he wanted to learn how to talk to President Franklin D. Roosevelt.

Again in 1932, Mills was recognized as a local political power back home when he was selected to be on the welcoming committee for Senator Huey Long of Louisiana. Long came to Searcy during his highly publicized 10-day swing through Arkansas on behalf of Senator Hattie Caraway. Their joint appearance in White County, dubbed the "Hattie and Huey" show, was on August 3, 1932, at the east entrance of the Searcy courthouse. Mills noted that when Huey arrived in a long black car with three bodyguards at his hotel in Searcy, he was hot, uptight, and irritable. Discovering Senator Long might enjoy "moonshine," Mills delivered from a local still he'd known since childhood. Afterward, Long rallied to the satisfaction of a crowd of 15,000, speaking glowingly of Hattie and his own "Share Our Wealth" program.[29]

In 1932, Hattie Caraway became the first woman elected to a six-year term in the U.S. Senate. That year also marked a change for the country as a whole, with the election of Franklin Roosevelt and his "New Deal." "My first presidential vote was cast for FDR. In a state hit so terribly by the Depression, his 'New Deal' offered hope that the people of Arkansas needed."[30]

Mills abruptly returned to Kensett, ending his Harvard studies in March, 1933, before graduating. Wilbur became a teller at his father's bank. In fact, his father met him at the train and gave him the bank keys, so he went to work immediately, even before going home. Banks were under tremendous pressure because of the Great Depression. When not at the bank, Wilbur would sit in on circuit court hearings to learn the judicial process in Arkansas. Nights, he read Arkansas law in order to pass the Arkansas bar exam. Soon he was named cashier of the Bank of Kensett. After passing the bar exam, he practiced criminal law. He thoroughly enjoyed "going to trial and getting them off." For the rest of his life, he loved criminal law, reading mysteries, and watching "Perry Mason" and "Matlock" on television.

Only one year after his return, he declared himself a candidate for county and probate judge of White County, Arkansas.

Wilbur Mills stands at the cashier's counter, Bank of Kensett, August 24, c. 1931.

CHAPTER 2

YOUNG POPULIST LEADER
1934-1938

White County was in dire straits. Most people were unemployed. The county was in debt. Diseases were spreading: tuberculosis and pneumonia. Mills' father made sure the Bank of Kensett stayed open and sound; the A. P. Mills General Store, remained fully stocked and the credit policy was lenient. Business was at a standstill; a feeling of panic gripped the nation. The October 1929 stock market crash had shattered most Americans' prosperity. Small businesses and factories closed. Workers lost homes; farmers, their farms. An estimated one out of four workers nationwide had no job. In White County, it was more like one out of two.

The economy collapsed. National income fell by half. Five thousand banks closed their doors. Nine million deposit accounts vanished in thin air. Before dawn on presidential-inauguration morning, Governors Herbert Lehman of New York and Henry Horner of Illinois suspended banking in their states. When the New York Stock Exchange opening bell was about to ring, Richard Whitney announced it would not open. In Chicago, the Board of Trade closed its doors on a business day for the first time since 1848. After trying unsuccessfully to get his successor to join him in stopping these actions, "We are at the end of our string," President Herbert Hoover murmured, "There is nothing more we can do." [1]

Mills had come home when Roosevelt became president on March 4, 1933.

The new administration reopened banks, established a Civilian Conservation Corps, abandoned the sacred gold standard, enacted a Federal Emergency Relief bill, passed the Agricultural Adjustment Act, Emergency Farm Mortgage Act, Tennessee Valley Authority, Truth in Securities Act, Home Owners Loan Act, National Industrial Recovery Act, Glass-Steagall Banking Act, and many pieces of landmark legislation. The sense of imminent national peril, followed by a sweep of reform legislation, created an excitement of change that moved Mills. He was anxious to become a part of the New Deal.

Roosevelt had won 57 percent of the vote, defeating Hoover at 39.6 percent, earning a solid mandate. The tottering economy had set the stage for the most extraordinary burst of legislative achievement in the nation's history.

In 1933, Democrats in the House outnumbered Republicans 310 to 117; in the Senate, 59 to 36.

Roosevelt's first goal was ending the banking crisis. A wave of bank failures in February had frightened the public. Depositors rushed to withdraw their money for fear banks would all fail. Roosevelt declared a "bank holiday," closing all banks on March 6. A. P. Mills refused to close the Bank of Kensett. On March 9, Congress passed the Emergency Banking Act. The new law allowed government inspectors to check each bank's records and reopen only those banks in strong financial condition.

The Bank of Kensett was quickly sanctioned. Within a few days, half the nation's banks reopened. They held 90 percent of the country's total deposits. Their reopening did much to end the nation's panic.

The Glass-Steagall Banking Act of June 1933 provided further protection for investors. It gave the Federal Reserve Board more power to regulate loans made by banks and created the Federal Deposit Insurance Corporation (FDIC), insuring bank deposits up to $2,500. In July 1934, FDIC insurance was raised to $5,000.

While working at the bank, Wilbur continued to prepare for public service. He planned a campaign for White County judge. He would promise to cut his salary the first year, and take no salary the second if he were unable to balance the county's budget and pay off its $15,000 debt. Mills would explain, "I was just a fool kid!" Forty-five years later, Mills described this as "a platform created by immaturity."[2]

Also, the "fool kid" was preparing to take on a seasoned, respected county judge, Foster O. White, Sr. In an election year framed by a historically adverse economy, all incumbents were vulnerable. A record low had come in 1933 when local estimates listed 4,627 unemployed men in White County.[3]

Also, since Arkansas had defaulted on its highway bonds, incumbent county judges lost access to state road funds. In contrast, the Works Progress Administration became available to Mills, after he became judge. Senator Joe T. Robinson and Governor Marion Futrrell gave him full authority over WPA funds for White County. Mills used those funds to build roads, bridges, and highways. He saw investment in infrastructure as creating jobs, providing a foundation for economic development, and enhancing quality of life.

In early January 1934, local candidates began announcing for election to county offices. White, the 52-year-old incumbent, a very well-liked, respected official, had served for 16 years. His established reputation was for "building bridges, grading county roads, putting in culverts, making impassable roads good roads." The Searcy *Daily Citizen* specifically assessed his administration as one having "a good record."[4]

Following Mills' announcement, Cul Pearce, father of Cal Pearce of

Springdale, formed the White County Taxpayers Association to cut back county costs by initiating a new salary act, a popular county initiative of the period, adopted in Phillips and Union counties in 1932.

Mills had talked with leaders in Kensett and other White County communities before deciding on his candidacy. The White County leadership, including Mills' father, all told Wilbur that Judge White was "a political fixture in White County," a friend to whom they were indebted. Basically, they indicated that he appeared invulnerable.[5]

However, Mills recalled:

> The judgeship was the most important office in the county. The county organization wanted me to go to the state Senate or state House of Representatives. They probably could have handed me either position on a silver platter. They couldn't understand me doing what I did. They wanted to know what I had against incumbent Judge White. I told them that I didn't have anything against him. I just wanted to be county judge. I thought that this office was the stepping stone to Congress that I needed.
>
> There was a great amount of pressure exerted on me not to run for Judge White's seat. In the beginning, everyone, including my father, was against me. Dad even told me he wouldn't vote for me. He was very close to Judge White as he was part of the county organization.
>
> I didn't have any political allies when I began running against Judge White. I was running against the county political machinery. I had to make my allies. Fortunately, I was known in the county because of the respect folks had for Dad.[6]

On May 23, 1934, the Searcy *Daily Citizen* carried the surprise announcement: Mills was declaring himself a candidate for White County judge.[7] The day after his announcement on May 24, Mills celebrated his 25th birthday, reaching the constitutional minimum age for a county judge. The local paper described Mills as "a young man of fine attainments, from a business, professional, and social standpoint. He has a bright future and his friends and supporters believe he possesses all of the qualifications necessary to fill the responsibility of county and probate judge."[8]

On May 26, Mills went to a political meeting in Floyd, where folks told him, "You are too young and unmarried, both big political problems." He told them jokingly, while he acted as though he was more and more depressed, "I will solve one of those problems."[9] On May 27, as planned for some time, he married Gertrude Clarine "Polly" Billingsley, also of Kensett. Formerly county examiner and assistant to the county school superintendent, she had to test teachers to ascertain qualifications for teaching. She refused to appoint someone the establishment wanted and she lost her job. Perhaps this spurred Mills to take on the establishment. Polly had many contacts among members of school boards in rural areas of White County. Mills had been accompanying her to pie suppers throughout the county, prior to his candidacy and their marriage.[10]

Mills' oldest daughter indicates that Polly Mills was considered by Wilbur to be his greatest political asset throughout his 42-year political career and their 58-year marriage.

With the campaign slogan "Give a Young Man a Chance," Mills waged a vigorous hand-shaking campaign. He stressed he would put the county on a cash basis in his first year, or he would not accept a salary in his second.

Mills laughed about it later. He said, "That was quite a wild rash promise I made. I don't know whether anyone believed I could do it. I finally got to the point myself that I was in doubt."[11]

His black-on-white campaign card carried the message "Vote for Wilbur D. Mills of Kensett Township for County and Probate Judge. Economy and a square deal for all is my motto. Primary election, August 14, 1934. Your support solicited."[12]

When Mills challenged veteran Judge White to a series of debates in each of the county's townships, some felt it was an awful mistake. The series became a legend in Arkansas political history. Many thought they were like the Lincoln-Douglas debates of 1868, a series of seven outdoor, oratorical contests, each lasting three hours. The Mills-White debates were also outdoors, slightly shorter, much more numerous. Mills opened the first at McRae with a 30-minute presentation, discussing Judge White's deficit spending and other issues. White followed with a one-hour-and-20-minute presentation, including denials and defense of his record. Mills finished with a second 30-minute presentation, citing county court orders and public notices.

Judge White had a tremendous voice and was a lay preacher. He had a good record, and was very popular. Mills had a friend who spent six weeks going through county records with a fine-tooth comb.

Mills' father, as the debate heated up, became angered by something that White said about Wilbur, so he financed his son's entire campaign. He wanted him to have plenty of financial backing, but he did not want him beholden to anyone.

At the end, consensus was that Mills won the debates. He presented a positive program of change and frugality, supporting a salary act to take county officials off the fee system, separating sheriff and collector functions, and eliminating road commissioner positions.[14]

Mills observed of White, "He was quite a speaker, and I'm sure he felt fully qualified to handle an upstart; but I think I got the better of the debates and people began thinking maybe I had a chance to win. That made me work harder. I organized all the young people, and got mothers for me and people who wanted to see their sons do something in life; [I] made quite an appeal to them." Mills involved many who had not previously participated, teaching his leaders how to organize precincts and influence indifferent voters.

Mills checked periodically with his township leaders. Just a few days before the primary, he asked how he was doing. Most said, "We are having a hard time throughout the county, but doing pretty well here locally."[15]

"I saw all the voters," Mills recalled. "I used to think I knew everybody in White County. I guess I did come pretty close to that. I knew their names, their complete backgrounds. Who married whom, their grandmothers and grandfathers."[16]

Mills once tried to bluff a farmer into thinking he could look at a mule's teeth and guess its age. When he was far off the mark, "The farmer shook his head and said: 'Son, never try to pretend something you don't know.'"[17] It was a good political lesson Mills applied throughout his public service career, usually knowing more than people would guess and more than he would claim.

Mills learned another lesson when he went to see James A. Neaville, Sr., of Griffithville to ask for his support. "He was so nice to me that I came back and told Dad that he was all for me, but Dad said, 'No, Son, he just called me to say that he was very sorry that he was already committed to Judge White, but he will help you win half the vote.'"[18]

Mills won about half the vote in Griffithville; Neaville kept his promise. On Election Day, August 14, 1934, Mills dramatically edged out White, with a surprising tally of 2,457 votes to 2,100.[19] Mills learned another important political lesson from a close neighbor who reported to him that she had voted for him even though he had not asked her for her vote. He replied, "I didn't think it was necessary." She said, "That is my point."[20]

Soon after Judge Mills took office, he recommended former Judge White for a position as district engineer for the Highway Department's Batesville office. White became one of Mills' biggest supporters in the 1938 congressional race. Mills later assisted White in securing a better job with the federal Farmers Home Administration. However, in 1942, Mills believed White supported his opponent, O. B. Robbins. In 1944, White supported Circuit Judge Marcus Bone of Independence County against Mills' re-election.[21] White's grandson, Jim Guy Tucker, Jr., succeeded Mills in Congress and on the Ways and Means Committee; Mills talked to Speaker Tip O'Neill, in 1977, on Tucker's behalf. Tucker ran for U.S. Senate in 1978 and governor in 1982, eventually became lieutenant governor in 1991 and then governor of Arkansas in 1992, succeeding President Bill Clinton in the latter office.

Mills made state history in becoming the youngest county judge in Arkansas and the only one with a Harvard law school education.

During his first meeting with the quorum court, members were hostile.

> They beat me on my man that I wanted for road commissioner.
> The man they selected had been for Judge White and became a
> very close friend of mine and everything worked out fine. At first,
> they didn't want to agree to my man for school superintendent,
> though they eventually did. They all resented me because I won
> the election. Judge White was a saint to them. It made things very
> difficult at first.[22]

In the spring of 1935, Mills, a strong soil conservation advocate, established and chaired the White County Terracing Association. Donald Moore served as secretary; J. E. Lightle, as treasurer.[23] The association provided White County farmers with terracing machinery and experienced operators at little cost. Mills acquired funds for it through the Arkansas Rural Rehabilitation Corporation. Under the program, farmers paid only operating costs for a McCormick-Deering diesel tractor and an Adams terracing machine. At the outset, farmers signed up 1,400 acres to be terraced. The program's success was apparent. White County's major economic activity was agriculture, including cattle, cotton, strawberries, and soybeans.

Some federal funds became available in 1935 for infrastructure projects to create jobs. When Judge Mills took office, there were 2,000 miles of county roads, with only 250 miles graveled and none paved. There were bridges and culverts to be maintained and repaired.[24] Senator Joe T. Robinson gave Judge Mills special authority over the Works Progress Administration's funding for White County, securing an impressive number for White County. For example, 50 miles of county roads were graveled in 1936 alone. Mills set a state record: nine separate WPA projects under way simultaneously. Though there was a great need for these WPA jobs, Mills had difficulty getting some of his constituents to accept them because of their fierce sense of pride and independence, even in economic hardship. The pay for these was minimal–$13 for a 40-hour week. To this day, WPA roads provide 1,000 miles of basic highway and byway infrastructure routes for the county. Although statistical data on unemployment is not available for the Depression era, estimates for the U.S. ran from 20-22 percent and much higher for White County.[25]

❧❧

Charles Murphy, Sr., of Murphy Oil fame, was chairman of the State

Highway Commission. He and Governor Marion Futtrell supported road building efforts, allowing Mills to add all the highways he built–nearly 1,000 miles–a historic record for Arkansas counties, to the state highway maintenance system.[26]

Many residents survived only through Judge Mills' active generosity. When Circuit Judge W. D. Davenport appointed Mills, as a public defender, to represent poverty-stricken citizens in court, he noticed Mills won every case. But Mills downplayed his success by saying, "All the people on the jury were put on WPA by me or had a member of their family who was."[27]

A contemporary official in the county clerk's office remembers Mills performing his first wedding ceremony. Justices of the peace, by law, charged $2.50 for weddings, an attractive source of income for some during the Depression. A few justices stayed around the courthouse every day for a chance to conduct business. During his campaign, Mills had promised several couples that he would marry them without charge. When a couple came by his office to take him up on his campaign pledge, he stepped across the hall quickly to the county clerk's office, asked Floyd Bradberry for a copy of the official wedding vows, read them carefully, and returned to his office, where Mills said, "Please join right hands. Do you take this man to be your lawfully wedded husband? Do you take this woman to be your lawfully wedded wife? I, therefore, under the laws of God and the State of Arkansas, do hereby pronounce you man and wife." Bradberry served as a surprised witness to "the world's shortest wedding ceremony."[28] Mills performed 165 such ceremonies during his four-year tenure. His sister, Emma Gene, commented, "I believe I'd get a minister to perform another, longer, ceremony before I'd go to bed with a man."[29]

Mills was a pronounced agent of change for White County:

> I decided to clean out the money changers from the courthouse.
> There were three or four people who were buying script. You
> could go in with a 10-dollar county check and they would give
> you seven dollars and a half for it. They would then take it and
> sell it to the Missouri Pacific Railroad or some big corporation
> for eight dollars and a half. These people would then turn it in
> on their taxes at 100 cents on the dollar. They made a good living
> doing that. I ran them all out of the courthouse.[30]

On May 15, 1935, Mills took an important step toward fulfilling his campaign promise to balance the county's books. He issued a court order for "reissuance and reclassification of county general (5 mill) fund warrants, and cancellation of such claims and warrants that the court may find to be illegal or invalid, for purpose of determining outstanding debt."[31] Additionally, he required all outstanding warrants to be returned to the county within 90 days, that is, by August 1, 1935. In this way, about $3,200 was removed from the books because formerly outstanding warrants were never presented. They were perhaps lost, or their owners were dead, for outstanding script covered a period going back to 1925.[32]

Mills passed and implemented a model salary bill (as supported by the White County Taxpayers Association and Cul Pearce) and dramatically reduced his own annual salary from $3,600 to $2,000. A position of road commissioner, with a lowered salary of $1,800, was approved as "custodian of all road machinery, equipment, tools, materials, and supplies belonging to the County."[33] Mills took the circuit court clerk off a fee basis and placed him on a salary of $2,200. Likewise, he took the county clerk off a fee basis, with a salary of $2,000. The offices of sheriff and collector were separated. The county's outlay for feeding prisoners was reduced from $1 to 50 cents a day per prisoner. The county collector was put on a salary of $2,100; county treasurer, a salary of $2,000 with no fees.[34]

When all official and employee salaries, as well as expense claims were paid, half the remaining surplus was transferred to the common school fund, distributed throughout the school district, just as other such funds were distributed. The other half went into the county general fund,[35] saving the county an estimated $16,000 a year.[36]

This local action was in line with national efforts in 1932 and 1933. The Economy Act of June 1932 reduced members of Congress' pay from $10,000 to $9,000. The salary was again lowered in 1933 to $8,500 and gradually brought up to $10,000 by 1935.

Mills centralized purchasing, putting it on a competitive bid basis. Any county official in need of stationary, books, or other supplies, had to requisition them from Mills, who would buy them from the lowest bidder. One of the so-called "peddlers" who called on him was Hugh Patterson, who later became publisher of the *Arkansas Gazette.*

The competitive bid process was not required of counties by state law until the early 1960s when a "Young Turk" reform move led by then-state Representative (and future Governor and U.S. Senator) David Pryor of Camden and Virgil J. Butler of Batesville. Butler had served as Mills' campaign manager for his first congressional race.

By the beginning of his second year, Mills had wiped out the debt of $30,465. Mills was able to fulfill his promise, and at the end of his first year he had cash on hand of $5,462.74.[37] White County was in the black for the first time in anyone's memory, especially remarkable given the economic depression.

The budget Mills proposed for his own office was less than any other county constitutional officer. For the first time in many years, justices of the peace

(74 were present and voting) were paid an allowable fee for their attendance, indicating both Mills' respect for grassroots representation and White County's improved financial status.[38]

A resolution was passed congratulating Judge Mills for his success. The *Daily Citizen* praised his "efficient manner" and observed: "This is the first time in many years that citizens of White County have been able to cash county warrants as soon as they were issued."[39]

Mills' early proclivity for balancing budgets reflected a career-long goal, and his father's admonitions: "Don't ever pay rent or interest."

In June 1936, Mills discussed his ideas regarding "Women's Place in Politics" before 250 women attending the county council at First Methodist Church in Searcy, urging them to pay their poll taxes and vote in elections. He observed, "Community standards have always been improved through the influence of high ideals women hold for their communities and homes," and commended them for "studying economic problems and assisting in solving those problems." Additionally, he pointed to the "great opportunity" to "help county officials realize their ambitions of making White County an ideal place for the youth of the county."[40]

Mills practiced some law while administering White County government:

> There was one time when I was defending an insurance company in a disability suit, the jury turned against me. I had a big $5,000 fee; that was big in those days. I suppose I rated that because of my reputation. A fellow had become disabled due to a back injury. They brought him into court on a cot; he couldn't move. He would just lie there; he wouldn't even blink his eyes. Everybody thought that he was disabled for life. He was suing the insurance company because he had a policy with them to provide him with $150 a month if he were to become disabled.
>
> We had two experts, doctors from Memphis and Little Rock, who said that there wasn't anything wrong with him. A local doctor, who happened to be the doctor for all 12 men on the jury, said that he had an injured back. The doctor thought his back was injured and was being honest about it. Of course, members of the jury were going to listen to their doctor. They weren't paying any attention to our Memphis and Little Rock doctors. The jury was only out for about 15 minutes. One juror asked the foreman if he thought I had received my fee. The foreman said that I was smart enough to get my money ahead of time. They figured, this being the case, it wouldn't hurt me if they found in favor of the plaintiff,

which they did. My eyes popped when the verdict was read. I couldn't believe my jury was going back on me. They all said they didn't think it would hurt me. I said, "Hurt me, hell, you destroyed my reputation!" When the Shea and Gould law firm called me to come to New York in 1977 to offer me an Of Counsel, I told them this story, and that they probably shouldn't hire me because I lost a case even at the hands of a jury, all of whom had received jobs with my help.[41]

Jack Holt, Sr., of Harrison ran successfully in 1936 for state attorney general. Before announcing, Holt asked Mills to manage his campaign. Mills was inclined to do it, and checked with his father. He suggested Wilbur ask Senator Robinson, who advised him to stay out of other candidates' races, while being a candidate himself, especially if he ever wanted to run for a higher office. Accepting Robinson's advice, he did not manage Holt's campaign but worked very hard in seeing to it that Holt carried White County.[42] Also, Mills, along with the sheriff, sent out letters to organization leaders supporting Carl Bailey for governor.

When Mills announced his intention to run for a second term that year, the *Daily Citizen* predicted no opposition, calling him in "close touch with people."[43] Mills initiated the formation of the White County Tuberculosis Clinic, in conjunction with the White County Medical Society, county nurse, and the Works Progress Administration. The clinics were partially financed by sale of Christmas seals, with the Arkansas Tuberculosis Association, providing clinicians and local doctors who contributed their time liberally. Mills said, "With thorough-going cooperation ... there is a chance of victory over tuberculosis within the lifetime of this generation." The first round of tests reflected this need—43 children were tested without charge, 19 of whom were found to be infected.[44] Dr. Angie Hassell, father of Lanny Hassell, implemented the project. Mills was determined that his constituency would receive every means known to medicine to cope with the ravaging disease. According to historians, White County had more treatment lodges (called Burr cottages) in use than any other county in the eight states which comprised the New Orleans Regional Public Health Agency.[45]

The annual meeting of the White County Quorum Court, November 9, 1936, was more positive than any other in the county's history. The *Daily Citizen* reported "no contests of any kind, no public speeches ... unusually harmonious."[46] After the meeting, members enjoyed the judge's hospitality, including an invitation to the American Legion building for a dinner served by the Women's Home Demonstration Club. Mills paid for the dinner personally.[47]

For the 1937 county budget, the quorum court appropriated funding for new services installed by Mills, including $2,330 for county court paupers (those who could not afford the fees and were declared paupers by the court); $2,400 for the county health department; $100 for the orphan children's home; $700 for tuberculosis care; $500 for the state sanitarium; and $200 for a tuberculosis cottage.[48]

Mills' budget expenditures in 1937 reflected a bold new direction in social programs, providing general health and medical care to those who could not afford it, as well as a significant new welfare program. Judge Mills worked out a system, a forerunner and microcosm of Medicare-Medicaid, which he later designed for the nation. Mills had the quorum court appropriate $5,000 to assist those unable to afford adequate medical care. He asked doctors to forego fees. He asked druggists to provide medicine at cost. He asked Mrs. O. C. Wakenight at the hospital to charge only $2 per day for those in need.[49] People needing medical financial assistance initiated the process by contacting their local justice of the peace, who then presented cases to the judge. Mills helped them all. Many years later numerous White County residents told how Mills helped their family during desperate times, including as late as his funeral in 1992 and in sympathy notes to his widow and daughters. State turnback funds were only a little more than one-fourth of the county's budget, only $2,826.27 during 1937's first quarter.[50] These new programs and services had to be funded locally. Local taxes were not increased under Mills' administration. His conservative fiscal practices and careful cash management made the programs possible. Mills matured under his father's watchful eye. Once Mills told his father that he planned to take golf lessons. The senior Mills, obsessed with productivity, said, "If you are going to exercise, why don't you do something productive like raise a garden?"[51]

According to Forest Waller, a Mills successor as White County judge, "What made Wilbur an outstanding county judge was his business-like manner in conducting affairs of the office . . . Mills was careful in selecting county employees, picking qualified and loyal employees. All county residents, regardless of their social and economic status, were treated kindly and fairly."[52]

A typical day in Judge Mills' life, described by C. P. Lee, Jr., in the *Arkansas Gazette*:

> A man in overalls asked, "Could the judge give one a job on the county roads." The judge said, "No."
>
> Another asked, "Could the judge let an aged invalid have more morphine?" The judge said, "Yes."
>
> Then came a justice of the peace asking, "How might I determine legality of voters in a school board contest? How can I handle those who refused to show a poll tax and said they had one?"

"Have them sign an affidavit to that effect," said the judge briskly, "That clears justice, but it won't clear them if they sign it falsely." The visitor departed, satisfied.

In came a young girl, nicely dressed. "A job, please; any kind of job. Out of work, since December." The judge sympathized and said, "Perhaps."

A farmer told the judge that his wife was in the hospital in need of an operation, and he had no money. Into the telephone spoke the judge, and the man departed happy.[53]

Lee observed, in conclusion: "That, I learned, is why he is so highly respected. Every man is satisfied; he knows that the county is now a business, only occasionally a charity, and that it is being run like a business."[54]

The third generation Perrin Jones, Jr., longtime editor of the Searcy *Daily Citizen*, observed that Mills was always a "foot-washing politician."[55] Walking down a street or working a crowd with him was a happy experience, seeing him remember everyone he had ever met–their children, their grandparents, and their past problems, exhibiting genuine care and concern for all.[56]

Mills visited all of White County's country stores on a regular basis, sitting on the floor so that older folks could sit more comfortably on stools. In the winter, stools circled around the stove. These visits were the centerpiece of his communication with constituents.[57]

Mills had learned to "hunker on the courthouse steps, to roll his own Bull Durham cigarettes, and to chew tobacco without turning green (at least until he got out of the donor's sight)."[58]

Mills liked to visit with former Arkansas Congressman Stephen Brundidge, who had served from 1897 to 1909, asking him about Congress, gaining insight. Brundidge died in early 1938 at age 81, while Mills was a congressional candidate.

Arkansas' senior senator, Joe T. Robinson, died in July 1937, setting off a series of political events that would bring profound changes to Arkansas politics, and to Mills' political career. Mills speculated that, if Senator Robinson had not died, Roosevelt would have appointed him to the Supreme Court. Roosevelt attended Robinson's funeral, as did Mills and his father. The policies, politics, and programs of Judge Mills' administration were populist and progressive.

One of America's dramatic political odysseys had begun. These early years as county judge (the county's chief administrative office) reflect Mills' public philosophy and personal views, even more clearly than his years in Congress. His legislative tenure was more driven by the need to achieve a consensus around each policy issue, rather than in forging programs of his own preference, and in making direct decisions for immediate implementation.

Mills' experience as county and probate judge steeled him for his future congressional leadership as a guardian of the common American, and "the most brilliant fiscal mind since Alexander Hamilton."[59]

Wilbur Mills the proud father.

Wilbur Mills' parents and sister are in the front row. In the back row, Wilbur (on the right) sands beside his brother, Roger.

CHAPTER 3

FRESHMAN CONGRESSMAN
1938-1942

Mills, always planning to run for Congress, had an open congressional seat in his home district and some humorous advice. Grandfather Mills, a local merchant at Plainview, Arkansas, told him: "I know you are going to want to go to Congress. I also know you will win. So, you'll run into a lot of Republicans; but you'll never see a Republican, no matter how wonderful, who is as good as the worst Democrat."[1] Mills bipartisan approach wasn't exactly what his grandfather jokingly advised.

In late 1937, Senator Robinson had died without warning. Mills' own popular four-term Democratic Congressman John E. Miller of Searcy–quiet and soft-spoken, providing courteous attention and polished manners, without exciting oratory and drama–became Robinson's successor. A congressional seat–in Mill's own district–was open.

When Governor Carl Bailey was named by the Democratic State Committee as the party's nominee to succeed Robinson, many key people opposed the selection method. Among the dissenters were Pulaski County Sheriff (and later Governor) Homer Adkins, Congressman Miller, Senator Hattie Caraway, and R. Max Allison of Batesville, along with Senator Robinson's widow. They, in turn, led a statewide petition process. A rump convention, attended by over 2,000 self-appointed delegates, nominated Congressman Miller as an independent against Governor Bailey.[2] Miller did not mind risking his career. His 1936 re-election had been a tough one with a close result against Roy Richardson of Lawrence County. Richardson, a locally elected prosecutor, vowed to run again in 1938. Miller told Mills afterward to get himself ready to run because Miller would not seek re-election. Mills remembered saying, "Well, let's see what happens. You'll change your mind." With Miller's successful Senate candidacy, Mills had the green light to run for his home congressional seat.

Mills traveled to 66 counties in 1937 in Miller's behalf, winning him wide support, while refining his own speaking ability, expanding his contacts, and preparing for his next step in Arkansas politics. Miller beat Bailey by over

20,000 votes of the over 100,000 cast statewide.

Miller carried White County by a lopsided 2,703-262, the first time Miller had ever won his own and Mills' county by such a wide margin. Immediately, Judge Mills proclaimed the afternoon of October 21, 1937, as a special White County holiday honoring Miller. Mills asked future Mayor Lawton Grubbs of Searcy to chair homecoming ceremonies and designated then-Congressman (and later U.S. Senator) John L. McClellan of Sheridan as keynote speaker.[3]

On Miller's homecoming day in Searcy, Roy Richardson, prosecuting attorney of Lawrence County and very strong 1936 Miller opponent, announced his candidacy for Congress to succeed Miller. Later, another hopeful, Jerry Screeton of Hazen, rented a suite at the Grady Manning Hotel in Little Rock. He later said, "It was three days before I realized Wilbur had a suite above me."[4] Screeton was very well known around the district because, as a member of Miller's staff, he dispensed Miller's patronage. Finally, Screeton met with A. P. Mills, who pointed out that Judge Mills was most interested in the honor of office and its potential for service, and speculated that Screeton was more interested in the political process and the very prestigious $10,000 salary. Screeton eventually decided not to run for Congress, supported Mills, and became his first administrative assistant, a job also carrying a salary of $10,000.[5] He and Mills became strong allies, bridge players, and fast friends for life.

Judge Mills declared himself a candidate for Congress on December 1, 1937. The *Daily Citizen* supported him with a strong front-page editorial, calling him "one of nature's noblemen."[6]

Only Mills and Richardson remained in the race. A third candidate, Representative W. M. Thompson of Batesville, filed, but never campaigned. On June 15, 1938, Mills officially began his first of 18 campaigns for Congress—13 without opposition.[7]

A few weeks later in Newport, Roy Richardson opened his second and last campaign for Congress with a generous introduction by Fred Pickens, Sr., a local Democratic leader who considered running himself. He indicated that he had opposed Richardson in 1936 because he believed "Miller should be re-elected but now the seat is open."[8]

He called it "Richardson's time" and pointed to Richardson's stand on issues: for Roosevelt's farm program, increased assistance to the aged and to those unable to secure a living, extension of credit to all individuals through the Reconstruction Finance Corporation, and the reservoir plan for flood control.[9]

Roy Richardson was an accomplished speaker, and reputed winner of a national oratorical contest in Philadelphia. Likewise, Mills was capable of moving political oratory and discussion of public policy, and a successful debater at Hendrix, Harvard, and county judge campaigns.

In this 1938 race, Mills became the first candidate to use a loud speaker in his congressional district. He had a steel contraption built for him to hold a microphone, freeing hands for gesturing, and he could turn from side to side, for eye contact with all. His friend Sam Atkinson of Conway, later appointed postmaster by Mills, traveled everywhere with him. According to Mills, although Sam's wife wanted to be "wined and dined," as well as to go dancing, Sam journeyed every step of the campaign trail. Mills would say, "Sam idolized me. We idolized each other."[10] Sam's son, Richard B. "Dick" Atkinson, later served as chief justice of the Arkansas Supreme Court in the 1980s.

Mills' issue stands were reflected by his campaign platform:

Old Age Assistance–"Old-aged Arkansans are entitled to as much compensation from the National Treasury as are the old-aged of New York, regardless of inability of Arkansas to match federal funds."

Education–"Education is a national issue and must be treated as such. Boys and girls of our rural communities are entitled to the same opportunities as boys and girls of larger cities. Federal subsidy plus local supervision offers a sound solution to our school problems."

Rural Electrification–"Cheap rural electricity will bring a new era to farm life and must be obtained either through efforts of public utilities or through projects similar to the Tennessee Valley Authority (TVA)."

Flood Prevention–"The program of reservoirs and dams is a step in the right direction. Efforts tending to speed up this program must be made."

Soil Conservation–"Soil erosion is the farmers' greatest problem. Every effort through legislation must be made to conserve our remaining farm acreage through increased CCC [Commodity Credit Corporation] efforts and increased crop rotation. Fertility of the soil will be the measure of our future national prosperity."

Agriculture–"Farm earnings must be put on an equal basis with capital earnings and labor … through increased farm subsidies and crop control. Arkansas will progress only as its farmers prosper."

War–"Blood is more precious than gold. Aggressive warfare should not be tolerated. Legislation to conscript the rich man's dollar the same as the poor man's son during war will do much to stop war."[11]

Mills made 50 forceful speeches during his vigorous campaign across the 12-county district, conveying strong persuasion in simple language, all before advent of television and electronic media. Then, such oratorical rallies were an entertainment/art form. It was not unusual for Mills to attract thousands even in rural areas, though he put together his own speaking engagements rather than going to ready-made crowds at fairs or other public events.[12]

A large majority of the district's newspapers endorsed Mills.[13] There were no radio stations. Newspapers and public appearances were the only means of reaching voters. "But in those days they would come out to hear candidates and they liked debates," Mills said. "'Pour it on! Pour it on!' I'll never forget that. You'd always hear it in the audience. They liked good debates with a lot of humor. I don't think campaigning has changed all that much. The successful candidate is the candidate who is the best salesperson."[14]

Judge Mills, toward the end of the hard-fought campaign, went to Dalton in Randolph County, where a political rally was being held near Richardson's home. Upon arriving, he discovered his opponent was already speaking. As Mills made his way to the first row, where other speakers were sitting, Richardson wound up his speech by saying, "I am sick and tired of White County demagogues who tried to rush up this election, but to show you what a big person I am, I'm going to introduce my opponent to you. Wilbur D. Mills is a fine young man from Searcy and some day he will serve in Congress—when I am through with it. Let's welcome young Mr. Mills."[15]

Mills happily took the microphone and presented his full platform, his specific stand on each major issue in his best oratory. Afterward, Richardson, still feeling extremely confident, rose to the microphone again. This time, he said, "Now, just to show this young man how nice and hospitable we are in this part of the state, I am asking all of you gentlemen who plan to vote for me to come forward at this time and shake young Mr. Mills' hand and make him feel at home."[16]

There was a very long pause because "while they may have been leaning toward the local candidate, they were not inclined to embarrass his opponent." So, Richardson asked again for all of his own supporters to come forward to shake Mills' hand. Again, not one person moved. Then, Judge Mills took the microphone to soften the situation: "I suggest that all of you come forward so that we can both shake all your hands." The crowd rushed forward. When the votes were cast, Mills carried Dalton precinct, as well as Randolph County.[17]

Mills challenged his hometown by saying he would not accept a position in Congress unless he carried Kensett unanimously. He challenged Richardson to say the same thing about Dalton. Observers understood that Mills was serious and Richardson's hometown support was questionable.[18]

The final tally of votes cast was 23,415 for Mills and 18,141 for Richardson. White County supported their favorite son by more than a five-to-one margin and Kensett cast a unanimous vote of 246 for Mills.[19]

For the first and only time in White County election history, an opposed congressional candidate carried every precinct.[20] Mills described his $17,000 campaign as more than his total $10,000 per year congressional salary. "My father thought we had bought the world."[21] Again, A. P. Mills insisted on financing the campaign himself, so that the new congressman would not be beholden to anyone. Mills, however, said later that his father lobbied him regarding a highway going through Searcy, so even fathers have special interests.[22]

The three other Arkansas congressional races in 1938 saw close results–Congressman E. C. "Took" Gathings won by 58 votes; Congressman Clyde Ellis, 82 votes; Congressman W. F. "Bill" Norrell, less than a majority. On the other hand, Congressmen Fajo Cravens and David D. Terry won easily; Congressman Wade Kitchens was unopposed. John L. McClellan lost his Senate bid to incumbent Hattie Caraway.

Therefore, there were five new congressmen from Arkansas. Only Terry and Kitchens were incumbents. Congressman Terry of Little Rock, the delegation's dean and member of the powerful House Appropriations Committee, had been elected in 1932, thus, little seniority existed in the delegation. Then, in 1942, Terry ran for the Senate against John L. McClellan and lost, leaving the House, beginning Mills' rise to dean of the delegation.

On August 16, 1938, White County gave Mills a warm homecoming, its largest political event, with thousands of enthusiastic supporters in attendence.[23]

It was at this function that Lawton Grubbs, chairman of White County's Democratic Committee and lifelong friend of Mills, as legend would have it, took "the silver spoon from Judge Mills' mouth" permanently, by reciting Mills' lifelong hard work from earliest boyhood to his newest status as Arkansas' "boy wonder," elected to Congress at age 29, youngest from Arkansas.[24]

Shortly after Richardson's defeat, he threw a huge fish fry in his home county for Mills, with 3,000-4,000 people attending. Mills enjoyed strong support from that area for the remainder of his public career and for his entire lifetime.[25]

Senator John E. Miller took Mills to Washington early, so he could get his office assignment and meet whomever he would like. Mills asked to see President Franklin Delano Roosevelt and Vice President John Nance Garner.

Garner of Texas, longtime member of the Ways and Means Committee and eventually House speaker, had become vice president in 1933 with Roosevelt. He had served five years as vice president when Mills was elected to Congress, and 30 years as a member of the House. He was, far and away, the leading Southern politician.[26]

When Mills first met him, he told Garner, "I came here to see you, Mr. Vice President, because I want to find out what I have to do to stay here as long as you have." However, Mills didn't take all of Garner's advice to heart–like destroying every copy of every floor speech he would make. Garner told him, "No matter how good the speech is when you make it, 10 years from now, it's not that good." "I always thought my speeches were good and I was proud of them," Mills remembered.[27] But he did follow some of Garner's instructions, such as staying in touch by phone, letter, and personal visits with people in his home district, taking good care of casework, answering correspondence immediately, and spending as much time as possible in his district.[28]

Miller also introduced Mills to President Roosevelt, who said, "Well, John, we are not only electing them younger every year but also better looking."[29]

Mills drove his new car to Washington and back for that initial trip. Senator Miller and Jerry Screeton went with him. His car didn't have a heater, still considered a very expensive option in those days, so Miller continuously wrapped and rewrapped himself in newspapers for warmth during the 21-hour drive. Mills recalled, "He looked like a mummy." When they checked into their motel, they turned their space heater on as high as it would go and fell asleep. They were awakened suddenly during the night, when the wallpaper cracked from high heat, with a gunshot-like sound, bringing frightened responses. In fact, Miller darted hurriedly out of the room outdoors in his pajamas.[30]

The speaker of the House at the time of Mills' election was Representative William B. Bankhead of Alabama. He had become speaker in 1936. Sam Rayburn, Garner's friend from Bonham, Texas, was chairman of the Interstate and Foreign Commerce Committee and majority leader since 1937.[31]

Mills often laughed about how audacious he had been when Rayburn mentioned that Mills' cousin lived in Rayburn's district. Mills had corrected the legendary "Mr. Sam," saying, "No, he is just my second cousin; he is my father's cousin."[32] Rayburn took an immediate liking to Mills and made him his protégé.

Mills asked Speaker William Bankhead (father of the actress Talulah Bankhead), always in his office during noon hour and accessible, questions about Congress. When Bankhead died in 1940, Rayburn became speaker. John W. McCormack of Massachusetts became majority leader. The two remained in those posts for 22 years, until Rayburn's death in 1962, at which time McCormack became speaker.[33]

Wilbur Mills (l.) visits with his parents in the Mills General Store, Kensett, AR, c. 1935.

✷✷

Three days after Christmas, Mills and his pregnant wife left Arkansas for Washington, where they would maintain a second home for more than 53 years. Mills was, at 29, the second youngest U.S. House member.[34]

"On my first or second day as a congressman, I was standing behind the rail in the House chamber having a cigarette when to my surprise, 'Mr. Sam' came up to talk to me. I was in awe of him and the other House leaders. I had read about them in newspapers from the time I was very young. I was flabbergasted that Sam Rayburn himself would take time out to talk to me. Not only was I a freshman, but I was only 29 years old."[35]

He quickly gained a reputation for diligent attention to minute detail, bringing him into great favor with Rayburn. Shortly after being sworn in, Mills was named to the House Committee on Banking and Currency, which considered all legislation affecting banking and money policies, and where strong drives arose to change the money standard and inflate currency. According to Mills, up to that point, "the committee had been heavily dominated by Eastern congressmen representing Wall Street interests."

Mills and Albert Gore, Sr., of Tennessee joined populist Congressman Wright Patman of Texas on the committee. Mills often said, "I was particularly glad to have this committee appointment because my section needs increased representation on this group, more perhaps than any other committee in Congress, where I can speak for Arkansas on matters affecting currency. I proposed to express the desire of my constituents in matters affecting currency."

Mills was also extremely youthful in appearance. After he had been in Congress about six months, Congressman Will Whittington, a senior member and chairman of the Flood Control Committee, stopped Mills and said, "Boy, get me a copy of the billing report." Mills dutifully went back behind the rails, got a copy and brought it back to him.

> He thanked me. I didn't think anything more about it. However, about three or four months later he discovered that I was a member of Congress and apologized. I told him not to. I thought I was just doing what newcomers did.[49] What Sam Rayburn did was to appoint two fellows, senior members, to look after me, and told me that. He said, "I'm appointing Gene Cox and Lindsey Warren to chaperone you through the first few months of your tenure." They called me every day practically about whether or not I needed help in answering a letter ... Gene Cox was on the Rules Committee and Lindsey Warren, you know, in 1940 was appointed comptroller of the General Accounting Office by

Roosevelt.[36]

On one of their first nights out, Mills and his wife Polly were going to the Earl Theatre, first having dinner at O'Donnell's. Mills had a couple of glasses of Jack Daniels bourbon. She had a couple of pink ladies, became ill, and spent considerable time in the women's restroom. He finally asked a female staffer to go check on her, so he could take her home. He recalled, "Dang, she could get so sick so fast!"[37]

They didn't attend Washington cocktail parties. He would say his bass voice was so deep, it was very hard for him to make himself heard and he would become hoarse from trying. On March 12, 1939, their first child, Martha Sue, was born and named for Mills' grandmother, Martha Craig Mills. Two years later, their second daughter, Rebecca Ann, was born on June 19, 1941.

Awhile after having these "two pretty daughters," Mrs. Mills asked him if he wanted to try again for a son and, as he remembered, his response was: "No, we'd probably have a third daughter."[38]

One of Mills' earliest legislative efforts was supporting a farmers' parity program, restoring farm products to price levels comparable to those in 1909-1914, but it was successfully opposed by urban members.[39]

Early in 1939, Congress voted to extend the Federal Housing Administration (FHA) program to July 1, 1941, appropriating an additional billion dollars. Mills specifically urged Arkansas bankers and prospective home builders to take full advantage of the small loans to improve homes and buildings. The FHA insured these loans up to 90 percent. Mills said: "The bankers of my state should take the opportunity to make loans because they were guaranteed by government and interest rates were higher than that under bonds–5 percent under Title II, and 9 percent under Title I."[40] FHA usage in Arkansas through 1938 was $12,136,079 in insured loans, funding 12,786 home improvement projects and 2,578 home ownership loans for $4,666,469 and $7,469,610, respectively.[41] Mills pushed usage: "I hope prospective home builders will see fit to avail themselves of the opportunity offered by government in guaranteeing their payment of loans for construction purposes. The new money made available should stimulate return of money from stagnation into useful production and create additional employment."[42]

Mills kept in extremely close touch with the people back home. He spent as much time as possible in the district, and read each of its newspapers, as well as statewide papers. As he learned of births, deaths, marriages, achievements, anniversaries, events, and graduations in all of the district's communities, he was in touch immediately by personal letter, enclosing relevant government publications.[43] He conducted himself as if he were up for re-election every single day.

Mills said: "I wanted to do away with depressions, stop wars, and prevent anything bad from taking place. I had this vim and vigor and feeling that I could do it. It didn't take long to realize that I couldn't." [44]

Mills spoke out frequently on trade issues, defending the trade agreements program after anti-Roosevelt administration forces filed tables showing an increase of agricultural imports for the first five months of 1939, compared with the same period of 1938. Opponents said increases were caused by trade agreements. Furthermore, they said, 12 of 27 items in the table, including wheat for milling and export, flaxseed, hides, skins, cottonseed oil, peanuts, cottonseed cake, and meal were clearly "outside of the trade agreement."

Mills declared:

> This necessity for padding indicates the difficulty the opposition
> has in making a case against trade agreements, even assuming
> that increased imports are bad ... and solely resulted from trade
> agreements. Not satisfied merely with this misrepresentation, they
> duplicate a number of items. For example, total meat products are
> given, then figures for various meat items, which represent the
> same thing. [45]

He cited cattle and said: "Imports under reduced duty are limited by quota, and rates of duty on more than half of the number shown were not reduced by trade agreements. Furthermore, imports permitted under lower rates of duty constitute a small fraction of domestic consumption." [46]

In response to this support, Secretary of State Cordell Hull wrote to Mills:

> I wish to tell you that my associates and I appreciate your
> interest in the defense of trade agreements during the present
> session of Congress. I am sure that the information given in your
> remarks, appearing in the Congressional Record, will greatly
> aid in clarifying some of the misunderstandings relative to the
> program. [47]

Banking and Currency Chairman Henry Stegall of Alabama and Mills were invited to the White House by President Roosevelt to discuss prospects for slum clearance legislation, supported by Roosevelt. When he asked the chairman for his prognosis, Stegall responded positively, "Oh, Mr. President, I think it'll pass." Roosevelt then looked at Mills, trying to remember his name. Mills helped him. The President said, "Oh, yes, Congressman Mills, what do you think?" Mills replied, "Well, Mr. President, I don't think it will pass." The President was not pleased. Mills persevered and repeated, "I don't think it will pass, Mr. President." The President was extremely defensive, "Did your constituents send you up here to have a defeatist attitude or did they send you up here to pass legislation?" The slum clearance legislation failed, but Mills learned that Roosevelt wouldn't take "no" for an answer.[48]

Mills was somewhat shy about trading votes at first. Speaker Will Bankhead was pleading against reducing an appropriation for the Farm Security Administration. Four Philadelphia members promised Mills they would vote against the cut if he would vote for a slum clearance bill. "Is it legal for me to make such a trade?" asked Mills. Bankhead replied, giving Mills a good horse trading lesson: "By all means it is legal; and anytime you can get four votes for something you're interested in for one vote you don't care about, make the trade."[49]

Mills, always fiscally conservative personally, saved $5,000 a year on his $10,000 salary. He was never motivated by money. He paid $125 per month for a furnished apartment during his first year in Washington.[50]

Soon, he wanted to buy a home. He located one allowing his regular payment of $125, and two female staffers offered to rent rooms, paying their regular rent of $75 each. Mrs. Mills turned down the proposed arrangement. In 1991, Mills estimated not buying the house cost him $1 million, as the house would be worth $700,000; plus he calculated he would have saved more than $300,000 in rent over those years.[51]

Early on, he learned one of his most important political lessons. President Roosevelt sought to repeal a prohibition of foreign arms sales after Hitler invaded Czechoslovakia. "I got 289 letters from people at home urging me to vote against that and one letter from a person, known as the town drunk in Newport, urging me to support it. I voted with Roosevelt, contrary to what my people advised, because I thought it was right. I thought I'd be a one-term congressman, because I had voted contrary to the feelings of my district."[52]

However, when he returned to White County, no one mentioned that vote. So, he asked them what they thought. "I'd heard from 288 out of the total population of the district who disagreed with that position. I learned early that the opposition will always let you know their views but very seldom do others even write to give you benefit of their viewpoint. "They told me they wanted me to do what I thought was right and not to have to constantly tell me what to do."[53]

Mills supported military preparedness. He secured millions of dollars in war facilities for his district, including an egg dehydrating plant. Three of five training facilities in Arkansas went to Mills' district (Jackson County, Lawrence County, and Prairie County). A manganese **beneficiation** plant in Independence County was established, using thousands of tons of ore for which there had been no market. He had the Bureau of Mines survey his district for zinc and lead deposits in preparation for war. He pushed new and expanded services, as well as increased benefits for veterans.

He pushed other areas of economic concern, such as flood control and power dams on the White River, increased financial assistance for the elderly, raised wages for labor when businesses' profits increased, and opposed labor racketeering.

No one challenged Mills for re-election to a second term in 1940. He used this opportunity to plot another type of campaign, hoping to achieve a part of his boyhood ambition—to become a member of the Ways and Means Committee, following his own congressman and role model, William Oldfield.

"I wanted to be on the committee, but I didn't know how to get on," Mills said. "I didn't know you were supposed to talk to the speaker or majority leader."[54]

Beginning his second term in 1941, the Democratic caucus had three vacancies to fill on the committee. Mills and one of his Northern colleagues on the Banking and Currency Committee, Walter A. Lynch of New York, organized a campaign, completely independent of the House leadership. Mills was to deliver Southern votes for Lynch and Lynch was to deliver Northern votes for him.

The two young renegade candidates lost to the established leadership's slate. "But we scared the stuffing out of them," Mills said later, laughing, indicating they lost by only a few votes. "I got more votes than Lynch, so he did a better job for me than I did for him."[55]

House Speaker Sam Rayburn asked why Mills had not advised him of his interest in Ways and Means, then assured him that the committee appointment would be his. However, when the next vacancy occurred, Mills stood aside for a Pennsylvania congressman, allowing him to retain the seat of a Philadelphia member who had died.

He continued his close relationship with the Farm Bureau at home and in Congress, praising its work. The Young Business Men's Club of Searcy conferred upon Mills an honorary membership in Future Farmers of America. Billy Bryan, vice president of the national FFA, made the formal presentation to Mills.

> Mills' first Congressional office was located in the Cannon House Office Building. Then, when Congressman Bert Lord, a Republican from New York State, died, Mills moved to the Longworth House Office Building, settling into a good office, even though it was located toward the back of the building and in the basement. The windows were about even with the ground:

> We had a few things to learn about being located on ground level. One evening one of the girls in the office left a window open. Someone walked in and took a radio from her and some things of mine also. We learned to keep the windows down. The longer I

stayed in Congress, the closer my office moved to the front of the building. When I became chairman, I got a very nice corner office on the first floor at the front of the building.[56]

His staff was small and there were few people on Capitol Hill in those days. Jerry Screeton was his administrative assistant/chief of staff.

> Those first few months, one staff member was almost too many. Maybe I would get one call a month from my constituents, or one every two or three months. I would do well to sign two letters a day. The slow pace allowed me to develop good habits that would pay off later. Twenty-five years later, as chairman, I would sign up to 600 letters in one day. I established a rule that everything that came in today had to be answered today. If we didn't get it done, we wrote them and told them we were working on it.[57]

As a young congressman, he didn't have any legislation to call his own until being assigned to Ways and Means. On the Banking and Currency Committee, he voted only for or against legislation offered by others, rarely having any say in drafting:

> It was utterly out of the question in those days to go on the Rules, Appropriations, or Ways and Means Committees the day you got to Congress. You had to be up there and had to be judged. You earned the right to be on these powerful committees.[58]

During this part of Mills' congressional service, he often had family members meet him at, or take him to Memphis, so he could fly to or from Washington. But many times he would drive straight through, stopping only for restrooms, gas, and food. His daughters remember not nearly enough stops.

In 1941, a major push occurred to prevent Arkansas from losing a House seat to Michigan under reapportionment after the 1940 census. The House approved legislation by Congressman E. C. "Took" Gathings, but it was tied up in the Senate by debate on a lease-lend bill. The Arkansas delegation, including Mills, went to the White House. President Roosevelt assured them, "I am all for you because the member from Arkansas will in all probability be a Democrat and the member from Michigan might be a Republican, and I'd rather have an Arkansas Democrat!"[59]

Assessing Roosevelt as a leader, Mills said:

> Roosevelt had an amazing capacity to try new ideas. If something didn't work, he was willing to go back to the beginning and try another angle. I'm sure that the Depression would have run its

course with or without the New Deal, but what the New Deal did offer, if not an economic cure all, was hope and a sense of taking control of our own destiny.[60]

Though Roosevelt was a leader on the world stage, many in Congress did not share his world view. Mills noted:

> In Europe and the Pacific, storm clouds of war were gathering, while America turned away. At the end of World War I, Congress passed the Pittman Act, prohibiting sale of material that could be used by a warring country, even if they paid in gold and used their own ships to export it. With the Pittman Act, we became totally isolationist. World War I had been won, and that was the war to end all wars, many thought. Roosevelt had been after Congress to repeal the Pittman Act for some time. We beat him on it as late as August of 1939. Then, we came back in October and repealed it by unanimous consent, because Hitler moved, as Roosevelt predicted, but we didn't pay any attention to him at first. Several members of Congress had gone to Germany that summer and had assured us that Hitler was not going to invade any country. They reported that Hitler was a peaceful man. However, Roosevelt had been correct all along, and the world was once again at war. Of course, our involvement was initially that of an ally to those nations at war with Germany and was limited to material support.

Mills' mother had run into his home from next door to tell him she'd heard a radio bulletin about the bombing of Pearl Harbor. "Oh, Mother, that's just another Orson Welles story you're listening to," he said. But when he turned on his own radio, he heard the news directly. He immediately headed back to Congress via an American Airlines DC-3 from Little Rock, anxious and worried during four scheduled airline stops between Little Rock and Washington. He would vote to declare war. [62]

The president described it as "a day which will live in infamy." The Congress, including Mills, voted 388-1 in the House and 82-0 in the Senate to go to war.[63] The one dissent was by Jeanette Rankin of Montana who had also voted against World War I—as well as opposing the War in Vietnam after her retirement.

Many people began making personal sacrifices to help the war effort. Harding College students gave up their National Youth Administration funds, asking that those monies be applied to defense. Mills wrote a letter to Dr. George Benson, their president, commending their effort. [64]

In the same spirit, Mills drafted legislation designed to prevent inflationary wage and salary increases. It set up a division of wage and salary control within the Office of Price Administration charged with preventing employers from granting increases considered inflationary, and of rescinding inflationary increases, previously granted,[65] as well as changing wage rates and overtime compensation, requiring an increase in ceiling prices established on any commodity, and requiring payment of a larger sum than contracted for items essential to war prosecution.[66]

Mills set October 1, 1941, as deadline for the administrator to determine whether a proposed wage increase was subnormal, or employees' cost of living had risen sufficiently to justify increases.[67] Once again, when he went to Ways and Means, he submitted it, just as he had during the House Banking and Currency Committee's consideration of price control—where it was defeated by only one vote—with a different, successful result this time.[68]

Mills sought Roosevelt's opinion in 1942, as to whether Mills should join the military. Roosevelt said he wasn't going to give Mills a commission, if that's why he had come to see him. Mills said, "No, Mr. President, I'm willing to go in as a private." FDR said, "Well now, have you ever had any military experience, any training?" Mills answered, "No, I've never been in the National Guard, never had any ROTC, or any of that, sir." "Well," FDR said, "You can go in and you'd be a chauffeur for some general or admiral at your age … I want to ask you something. Do you think that you'd be more important chauffeuring an admiral or general or voting to continue the draft as you just did? I'll just leave it to your judgment." The draft continuation legislation had passed by only one vote. "Everyone who voted for it could say that his was the deciding vote," Mills said.[69]

Mills was 32 and his draft board deferred him without telling him. He stayed in Washington and supported the war effort through passing appropriations and expediting policy. For a very long time, he doubted his decision: "I felt as if somehow I had shirked my responsibility to the nation. I didn't realize that I couldn't pass the physical if I had been called, as I later found out that I had a heart murmur that would have disqualified me from service."[70]

While Roosevelt impressed Mills, Rayburn won Mills' heart and influenced his life:

> He used to have parties in his apartment. He started inviting me to those parties my first year. Gene Cox and some of them would bring wild turkeys up from Georgia. There was a restaurant right across the street on Q Street and Connecticut Avenue where he lived. They'd always prepare meals and he'd have some of the senators, maybe 30 or 40 people there, only members of the House and Senate.
>
> Rayburn had tremendous leadership ability. The membership

trusted him. He'd never ask you to vote for something if he thought it would hurt you. He knew about as much about your district as you did yourself. He was never gruff, hard to get along with, or hard to know … I never heard anybody say anything against him, frankly. Everything I ever heard from members were expressions of affection, respect and all.[71]

In mid-April 1942, Mills announced his intention to run again for re-election. 0. B. Robbins, a Heber Springs banker and Ford dealer, declared his candidacy, making Mills' routing Highway 67 around Searcy and his lack of military service the main issues.[72] In reality, Mills discovered that his predecessor, Congressman Miller, had previously committed to routing Highway 67 around Searcy, but he was not inclined to put political heat on Senator Miller, so he accepted it.[73]

The campaign proved extremely volatile, at times insulting, with Robbins' innuendoes that Mills had avoided serving his country, and a Mills ad alluding vaguely to Robbins' heavy drinking. But, by race's end, every district newspaper endorsed Mills. On August 11, Mills won a mandate, carrying all but Fulton County. It was his fifth election victory. [74]

Mills continued to work very hard in Washington and at home. In the early 1990s, he noted:

> I went home every year when we weren't in session. I never took any vacation trips; I always went home. I visited with my people. The only way you can know what people want is to visit with them and find out. You have to react in Washington, when you vote, to reflect how they feel. How are you going to do that if you aren't around them and stay with them? It was my deal that you had to do it. I wanted to do it. I loved to be around them and appreciated that so much.
>
> I know once the *St. Louis Post-Dispatch* did a poll in my district. They said that 75 percent of the people didn't know a thing in the world about how I had voted on any issue; they didn't care; they trusted me. I took good care of them, they said.[75]
>
> There were some that said that I campaigned even without an opponent. I don't think that I would ever call what I did campaigning, but rather staying in close touch with my constituents and letting them know I cared. I used to send out letters of congratulations to all high school graduates, most brides and new mothers. I still see people who got a graduation letter from me 50 years ago.[76]

Soon after his re-election, on October 15, 1942, his lifelong dream of serving on the prestigious House Ways and Means Committee was realized, thanks to Speaker Rayburn, who began to groom Mills for future leadership.

Roosevelt appointed Congressman Arthur Daniel Healy of Massachusetts from the Ways and Means Committee as a federal district judge in Boston, creating a vacancy. Before it was known, before it happened, Majority Leader John McCormack of Massachusetts came to me and said, "Now don't you turn the speaker down on this one. You take it. You can represent Massachusetts as well as Arkansas." See, Massachusetts was giving up its spot. It was his old spot. They didn't have anybody on the committee, which was unusual. It worked out that I got it and got it unanimously then, no contest. I was on the speaker's list.[77]

61?

CHAPTER 4

RISING CONGRESSIONAL STAR
1942-1948

During the summer of 1942, the *St. Louis Post-Dispatch* signaled Mills' rising star status in its "Inside Report from Capitol Hill," quoting Leon Henderson, influential director of the Office of Price Administration, reprinted in many Arkansas newspapers and discussed throughout Arkansas and Washington political circles:

"Our tomorrows look brighter because of a growing group of young Southern congressmen such as Wilbur Mills, Hale Boggs, Al Gore and Mike Maroney . . ."

Sam M. Walton, founder of the world's largest retailer, Wal-Mart, was asked in 1990 how his home state of Arkansas had been represented in Washington during this early period. He observed, "Wilbur Mills was serving when I went to Newport and opened my first store in the 1940s. Mills was a young guy out of Harvard, educated and respected. Wilbur was as popular and as good as any congressman who ever went to Washington."[1]

In 1942, J. William Fulbright of Fayetteville announced as a candidate for the U.S. House of Representatives. The incumbent Northwest Arkansas Congressman Clyde Ellis was running unsuccessfully for the Senate against John L. McClellan, and then went to work as the first administrator of the National Rural Electric Administration. Meanwhile, Fulbright had been fired the year before this election, as president of the University of Arkansas by Governor Homer Adkins, because Fulbright's mother, Roberta, in 1940 had editorialized in her newspaper, the *Northwest Arkansas Times*, in favor of Governor Carl Bailey, who lost to Adkins. Fulbright was successful in his 1942 race for the U.S. House of Representatives.

Governors at that time controlled all state boards and commissions. Afterward, U. of A. law professor Robert A. Leflar drafted a state constitutional amendment to guarantee that governors would no longer have that kind of control. When Fulbright arrived on Capitol Hill, he spoke to Mills, by then on Ways and Means, regarding committee assignments for Democratic House members. Fulbright sought an appointment to the House Foreign Affairs Committee. Mills recalled questioning how he could serve Arkansas on that panel, but Fulbright was determined, saying, "That is my major interest and I assure you it will help Arkansas." Mills said, "Sure enough, he was right, because he put us on the map around the world."[3]

After one House term, authoring and passing the Fulbright Scholar program, Fulbright ran for the Senate in 1944, defeating Senator Hattie Caraway, and becoming a member of the Senate Foreign Relations Committee. He became a most respected world voice for the next 30 years.

Mills was approached about seeking the Senate in 1944. However, he was very close to Mrs. Caraway. He and Mrs. Mills often played bridge with her and her husband, and then with her after she was widowed. He would not consider opposing a friend, though he knew she was vulnerable. Governor Adkins, Colonel Barton, and former Governor Carl Bailey all urged him to run. Mills also was in his second year on Ways and Means, his boyhood dream. He was increasingly becoming a favorite protégé of Speaker Sam Rayburn, and subject of speculation for a future speaker of the House.

Hulon Green, a Ways and Means staffer in those days, indicates that Mills ran the committee from his first days on it. The chairman relied on him to do most of the research, lobbying of other members, as well as writing legislation.

Mills' first Ways and Means chairman was Robert Doughton of North Carolina. Not close to Speaker Sam Rayburn, Doughton sent Mills and New York Congressman Walter Lynch to Rayburn for information. Mills said, "It took me three to four years to get close to Mr. Rayburn." Rayburn was slow to trust and ran people through tests. However, Rayburn gradually became Mills' political mentor and surrogate father. Mills read Western novels and mysteries with relish and enjoyed Western movies and television shows, as did Rayburn. They had many similar interests, including whiskey, steak, political conversation, policy issues, country music, and playing poker (though not as much as President Truman).[4]

Mills often spoke of his relationship with Rayburn and Roosevelt:

> Mr. Rayburn and my father were born in 1882, Franklin
> Roosevelt, too. They were a little ahead of him, yet Sam Rayburn
> outlived my father a couple of years. My father died of a series
> of heart attacks in 1958, the year I was elected chairman of
> the committee. He lacked a week being 76 when he died. Mr.
> Rayburn and my father knew each other. My father had been to
> Washington and Sam Rayburn had been in Pocahontas, Arkansas,
> in my district one time. Went up to an area and made a speech.
> Got up there and you never saw such a crowd of people in your

life. The president couldn't have gotten that many. Sam Rayburn was one of the finest men I have ever known in my life. He had more common sense than I guess anybody I have ever met. He was a lawyer by trade, but always for the farmer and the working man. In the press he was often referred to as "Mr. Sam." I would never call him that, he was much older. I always used "Mr. Speaker." Rayburn's political philosophy and thinking was never too far afield from my own. Perhaps it was the other way around. For whatever particular reason, the speaker took me under his wing and continued to give me valuable advice throughout the rest of his life. I think his most sage counsel was also his most simple advice: He told me that if I ever wanted any influence in the House that I had to convince members that I knew what I was talking about. I had to master the subject matter within the jurisdiction of the committee that I was on and, if they thought that I knew more than they did, they would listen to me. He could see that I studied every piece of legislation coming before the Ways and Means Committee. My briefcase would be full every night with some bill or tax code to read. Rayburn always brought his constituents to see me about tax problems. That's the way I met dozens of Texas millionaires, mostly oil men and big farmers.[5]

Mills, however, was not as close to Roosevelt:

One of the first times I ever had a conversation with Roosevelt was when I was called to the White House from a conference on welfare legislation. I was not entitled by seniority to have been in it, but Mr. Doughton got some other Democrats to step aside so I could serve on the conference. That was in 1942. Now, I'd been to the White House and talked to him on other matters before, but this was the first time I was ever called specifically on legislation. The call resulted from the fact that I had offered a compromise in conference. Roosevelt had advocated a variable grant for welfare. The Senate wouldn't take it because Senator Robert A. Taft said it was contrary to his principles. They wanted to do nothing more in the Senate than to increase the total dollar amount of federal participation–$20 to $25, something like that–that didn't help. I suggested that we pay $10 of the first $15 in this compromise. I was called to the White House about it. The president was quite irate at my suggestion. He said that it was beginning a course of action that would ultimately lead to federal bankruptcy. He went on to explain it and said if it's $10 out of the first $15 this year, next year it would be $15 out of the first $20 and so on, and the next thing you know we'd take it over. Whenever we do, we'll not be able to finance the government if we have to shoulder the entire cost of welfare. He asked me if I wouldn't withdraw it. I said, "Mr. President, I can't. It's up to the Senate." I mean the House had already accepted it. I said, "If the Senate accepts it, I've got nothing to say about it, it's their move." "Well," he said, "there's nothing that's impossible." Anyway, we got back in conference the next morning, and before I could open my mouth, Senator Walter George said, "We slept on this and we're willing to accept it." So, it went into law.

Roosevelt was right about it because then-Senator Pat McCarran of Nevada got to offering this increase every two years. We went to $10 of the first $15, to $15 of the first $20, and finally got it up to where we were paying $34 out of the first $40. Roosevelt was so right about the precedent creating a problem later on. We were shouldering too much of welfare costs, many of us thought.[6]

Mills' first Ways and Means meeting was December 2, 1942. Congressman Jere Cooper of Tennessee, chairman of the committee's Trade Subcommittee, made his report on a controversial bill allowing the president "to facilitate … for effective prosecution of war, free movement of property, people, and information into and out of the United States."[7] Congressman Richard Duncan of Missouri moved to accept the report; Congressman John Boehne, Jr., of Indiana, moved to table. After a general discussion, a roll call was held on the motion to table. Mills voted against it, as did the committee by a vote of 13-7. He also voted to move the report out for public hearings.[8]

President Roosevelt had asked for extensive war powers.[9]

Roosevelt promised a 10-person Arkansas delegation, headed by Mills, the state's two U.S. senators, and three U.S. House members, that he would do everything he could to revive production on farm lands damaged by severe flooding. "We pointed out the immensity of loss to Arkansas and adjoining states, and the president seemed surprised to hear that it was so great," Mills remembered. Roosevelt was persuaded.[10]

TAXATION

In early 1944, Mills, not always siding with Roosevelt, voted to override a veto of a tax measure:

> The president blames Congress for complication of income tax
> forms, with which taxpayers are currently struggling. Everyone
> knows that these forms are prepared by the Treasury Department
> and not by Congress. The president spoke of delays by Congress
> in framing tax legislation. Perhaps he does not know that work
> by the Ways and Means Committee on the tax bill was delayed
> several weeks at the request of the secretary of Treasury so as not
> to interfere with his savings bond drive.[11]

The president argued that Ways and Means had not designed a tax measure that would raise adequate revenue, while seeking $10.5 billion in new revenue. Mills explained that could not be so "because the Treasury Department has never included Social Security tax receipts in its general revenue total."[12] Further, Mills said: "Congress should convince all concerned of the necessity for limiting revenue bills to actual needs of Treasury and for not using such measures as vehicles for social reforms or issues unrelated to taxation."[13] To Mills, taxation was strictly for purposes of raising revenue. The Revenue Act of 1943 was subsequently enacted, with the veto overridden by both houses.

From his beginning on Ways and Means, Mills was concerned about excessive federal spending, and committed to educating constituents about the need for controlling the federal deficit:

> I have often said that you could put the most liberal person in the
> world on the Ways and Means Committee and in six months they
> would become the most conservative in the world. Why? Well, we
> take money out of your pockets. Anybody who is going to take
> money out of your pockets is going to get conservative.[14]

Among the first major pieces of legislation after Mills went on Ways and Means was employer withholding of income taxes on wages, adopted by Congress in 1943. This law converted the income tax into the payroll tax it has been ever since.

In order to expedite funding for World War II, Mills designed a plan for withholding tax, providing discounts for taxpayers to encourage payment of the 1943 tax in full, and becoming current. Taxpayers would receive a deduction of 6 percent for payments of estimated 1943 income tax liability if paid on or before June 15, 1943; a discount of 4 percent, if paid on or before September 15; and a discount of 2 percent if paid on or before December 15.[15]

The committee voted for Mills' proposal 10-6; future chairman Jere Cooper of Tennessee, made the motion for support.[16]

Mills also saw taxation as vital in controlling inflation and a possible postwar runaway economy. Mills told his fellow members:

> To the extent that we pay as we go through taxation and hold
> down on borrowing, our economic structure will be sound after
> the war. We must "sit on the lid" by imposing controls on profits,
> on prices of farm products and raw materials, on manufacturers'
> wholesale and retail prices, on wages and salaries, on rents and on
> prices of services such as transportation and electric power.[17]

In 1945, Mills supported the first tax reduction since the 1929 stock market crash. He proposed removing 12 million low-income persons from the tax rolls, providing special tax treatment for World War II veterans, repealing a war-imposed 85.5 percent excess profits tax, repealing a $5 use tax imposed on boats, and freezing the Social Security tax at 1 percent of employees' pay and employers' payroll.[18]

After World War II, there was pressure to repeal excise taxes that had expanded to cover lipstick, refrigerators, air conditioners, and virtually every other consumer good demanded by middle-class Americans, their pockets flush with wartime savings. Although the war had ended, taxes continued. Mills often observed, "Once you pass a tax, it has eternal life!"

In 1947, Mills opposed congressional Republicans' efforts to cut income taxes 20 percent across the board. Rather, he agreed with President Truman's State of the Union address calling first for a balanced budget, and then for paying off the national debt, before reducing taxes. Mills said, "If the Republicans can show us how to lower taxes and to reduce the war debt at the same time, I'd like to be shown." Mills viewed the Republican proposal as help only for high-income individuals, and argued that it was not equitable, timely or sound.[19]

When congressional leaders were chosen to meet with the nation's governors and Treasury officials, Mills was one of three House leaders designated to go to Salt Lake City for the national summit on taxation. State officials wanted the federal government to refrain from imposing sales taxes, gasoline taxes, and cigarette taxes, leaving states with these exclusive fields. Mills agreed: "We want to see states strong. In order to be strong, states must be able to collect necessary taxes to discharge their responsibilities."[20]

FEDERAL BUREAUCRACY

Mills proposed, after January 1, 1944, limiting federal employees in civilian positions to 2.9 million—and that a reduction-in-force be mandated.[21] He served on the Joint Committee on Nonessential Federal Expenditures. They met only once a year to receive a report of how many federal employees would work in the coming year.

FEDERAL DEBT/DEFICIT

Throughout his career, Mills' main concern was a balanced budget with no federal deficit, a view toward prosperity and paying off the national debt. In a speech to the Searcy Kiwanis Club, Mills warned the federal deficit was not just the president's and Congress' responsibility:

> The people in general have a share in this responsibility since much of the money is spent in response to demands for local needs which require financing by federal aid.[22]

He also spoke at the Jackson County Courthouse in Newport to a five-county Farm Bureau meeting:

> Mr. Average doesn't mind billions being spent for war. He wants those fighting to have the best at the quickest moment; but he is concerned about rapid growth of the national debt, and, therefore, doesn't like waste and extravagance in government.[23]

HOUSE POLITICS

As the speaker's protégé, Mills was a regular at Rayburn's so-called "Board of Education," the House's influential, invisible institution. At the end of each day's session, Rayburn invited a select group of close friends to talk politics and "strike a blow for freedom." The "Board" met in Room H-118 on the Capitol's ground floor, a small place (12 feet by 20 feet) by Capitol standards. A long black leather couch lined one wall, where Harry Truman was sitting when the White House called to tell him that Roosevelt had died.[24]

Mills became very close to Truman during these get-togethers. Both had served as county judges as their first public offices. Both had Midwest and Southern origins. They were neighbors in their districts and Washington residences on Connecticut Avenue, NW. They were close friends. Truman often invited Mills to join him for early morning walks. Mills declined because he usually awoke at 7 a.m., while Truman finished his walks at about that time. Mills joked, "I walked around a lot in my apartment."

Among those often attending Rayburn's gatherings, in addition to Mills and Truman, were: Lyndon Johnson and Homer Thornberry of Texas, John McCormack of Massachusetts, House Parliamentarian Lew Deschler, Gene Cox of Georgia, Hale Boggs of Louisiana, Henry M. "Scoop" Jackson of Washington, Richard Bolling of Missouri, and Carl Albert of Oklahoma.

> Usually this would be about five o'clock in the evening. If it was earlier, we might spend an hour talking, but if it was seven or eight o'clock and we were anxious to get home, we wouldn't spend

too much time there.

The "Board of Education" wasn't a bipartisan group; it was the speaker and a select group of Democrats. To be included was a real honor. ... There were several permanent members who had their own keys to the room. We certainly knew we had arrived in the Democratic leadership when one of these keys was in our pockets.

Oftentimes, after the "Board" had adjourned, I would accompany the speaker to dinner because he was alone. He liked steak and one restaurant in particular, Martin's, fixed them to his liking. He always warned against taking a drink in public. He said if you take one drink in public they'll swear you're an alcoholic. Simply because you hold a public office, they will exaggerate what you do. He would take a drink or two in the "Board" room before going out to eat, never more than two, but he would never drink in public.[25]

Mills was there on April 12, 1945, when Vice President Harry Truman arrived after the Senate session. Lewis Deschler told Rayburn that Truman needed to return a call to the White House. "Steve Early wants you to call right away," Rayburn said. Truman mixed himself a drink and made the call. Early told him, "Come quickly and quietly." He didn't say why. Truman lost all his color and exclaimed, "Jesus Christ and General Jackson!" He told them he was going to the White House and to say nothing. Soon they all learned that President Roosevelt had died.[26]

In 1944, Rayburn had been asked by Roosevelt to run as his vice president. Rayburn drew a tough primary opponent, preferred the speakership, and suggested Truman. As members of the "Board of Education" gathered, he asked Mills if he had done the right thing. Mills responded, "I think you did."[27]

Mills kept rising on Ways and Means:

Mr. Doughton used to use me a lot to do things that he as chairman shouldn't be doing. I would check members on things, ahead of time, twist some arms for him. He was a neat person with a tremendous mind and tremendous influence in the committee. I don't know why he picked me up when I first went on the committee. Just like the time I was telling you in 1943 when I served on the conference—I had no right to be on it. But he went to the trouble of asking all Democrats ahead of me to step aside so he could have me on the committee. He wanted me to help him, he said. I was very devoted to him, very loyal to him. The fact is that I was considered, I guess, his "right arm." The committee gave me the degree of prestige that I wouldn't have otherwise had. I could speak for him, normally, to committee members. I was always offering amendments and things like that—compromises.[28]

In 1947, legendary William "Fishbait" Miller, a 14-year House employee, became doorkeeper. He had a list of best friends in the House lined up to nominate and second. John McCormack, majority leader, took a look at his list, tore it up, and suggested that Mills nominate him. Mills did and Miller won easily.[29] Miller always felt indebted to Mills.

SPECIAL PROJECTS

On June 22, 1942, Mills announced authorization of $3 million in funding and construction for an Air Force training school at Walnut Ridge (Lawrence County) in his district. The construction, supervised by the U.S. Corps of Engineers Memphis district office, resulted from special project work by Mills.[30] Currently, these facilities form the campus of Williams Baptist College and include Mills Avenue, a namesake.

Mills also announced government approval for a basic training Army aviation school near Newport (Jackson County). "The school was estimated to cost $12 million and could accommodate up to 700 cadets."[31]

INTERNATIONAL TRADE

Mills advocated a vigorous trade policy to promote America's products and productive world relations, extending reciprocal trade agreements in 1943. He showed these trade agreements had not deprived American producers of any right to litigate, and that trade should be viewed as a foreign policy issue: "World trade issues transcend national boundaries and concern all peoples throughout the world."[32] [33]?

Mills rejected the isolationist philosophy of many postwar officials, such as Senators Robert A. Taft of Ohio and Kenneth Wherry of Nebraska. He spoke adamantly on this point to the State Democratic Jefferson-Jackson Day Dinner in Little Rock on April 5, 1947, at the Marion Hotel, "That way leads to war and we have to protect gains of past years."[34]

Mills believed that the American people should stop thinking of war as inevitable and begin thinking of peace as inevitable. He told the Searcy Kiwanis Club in 1948, "We will not have a war with Russia because of the location of their industrial plants and Stalin's age. No man Stalin's age has ever sought conquest."[35]

He also believed that the Marshall Plan was vital and widely favored, "The consequences of failure to support low tariffs and free trade would precipitate a world depression and economic chaos which would make it extremely easy for Communism to infiltrate into European democracies."[36] The world leaders of his time who most impressed Mills were Winston Churchill and Madame Chiang Kai-Shek. He studied their speeches, writings, and global views. [37]

A strong advocate for farmers, Mills pressed for a bill to protect rice growers and opposed ceiling prices on strawberries. Mills' home county was one of the largest strawberry-growing sections in America, and another county in his district was called the "rice capital of the world." Mills sponsored legislation for rural electrification and for 90 percent of parity for all agricultural products for the postwar period. His efforts reaped huge benefits for the agricultural economy generally. Rice farmers prospered in his district to such an extent that Arkansas rice is eaten around the world today. Rice, along with poultry, still drives Arkansas' agricultural economy, especially for the rural counties of Mills' congressional district.

In a speech apparently written by his friend and advisor, Max Allison, Mills urged farmers to remain closely organized, and to keep in touch with Congress for benefits and support in the postwar period. He paid high tribute to agricultural agencies and farmers for successfully operating production programs of food, feed, and fiber for an all-out war effort.

RESOURCE DEVELOPMENT

Mills sought opportunities to promote recreation and tourism for his district, a part of his overall economic concern for the environment, conservation, economy, and quality of life.

On August 11, 1943, 125 businessmen of Greater Little Rock accompanied a congressional group touring Arkansas industrial areas. At a Hotel Marion breakfast, they heard Mills and Brooks Hays give optimistic predictions of industrial possibilities in the postwar period. "Industries, now engaged in war production, will turn to peacetime work," Mills said. "The state should not be satisfied with what it has, but should find what it can do and do it. If plans for development are made and the story of Arkansas' resources told, there is no need to worry about capital."[38]

A highlight of the tour, which included most of the state's $250 million war industries, was a demonstration at the huge Pine Bluff Arsenal. Experts exploded every type of bomb and shell the plant made.

In 1944, at Mills' suggestion, the House Flood Control Committee's $800 million postwar omnibus bill included a provision permitting the secretary of war to lease land surrounding government flood control, public power, and reservoir projects to fishing camps, boating facilities, and vacation resorts.[39]

In early 1944, Mills and Senator John L. McClellan introduced a bill providing for immediate postwar construction of improvements along the Arkansas and White Rivers, and for leasing government reservoir banks for recreational development by private citizens. Thus began a quarter-century, $1.3 billion program to construct the Arkansas River Navigation Project, which the U.S. Army Corps of Engineers completed in 1971. Members of the congressional delegation and C. Hamilton Moses, chairman of Arkansas Power and Light Company, spoke at Newport. Moses asked to drive Mills home so they could discuss Moses' opposition to these public projects, fearing they might include hydroelectric power plants to produce competing sources of electricity. By the drive's end, Mills had convinced Moses to reverse his position and support the proposals. Mills received a commitment from Moses to contact the House Flood Control Committee, letting them know of his change of heart since his earlier testimony opposing the projects.[40]

Mills assured Moses the government would build no power plants. Subsequently and ironically, Arkansas Nuclear One was built there by Moses' old company.

Mills was also a leading supporter of the Rivers and Harbors Act of 1946. Appearing before the House Appropriations Committee, he called flood control projects capital investments in the future. Mills pointed out that President Truman supported the Clearwater Project on the Black River, the Bull Shoals Project on the White River, and the Augusta-Clarendon Levee Project on the White River. An early disaster mitigation advocate, Mills made a benefit-cost argument, citing 143 floods from 1921-1943 in Batesville, Newport, and Clarendon. He said if the proposed projects had been in place all along, there would have been only 40 floods.[41] Mills urged Truman to request the Greers Ferry Dam on the Little Red River in Cleburne County. The president declined to do so at first.[42] Mills eventually won Truman's and congressional support. President John F. Kennedy came to Arkansas at Mills' request to dedicate Greers Ferry Dam on October 3, 1963, his last public dedication event outside Washington before his fatal trip to Dallas.

Mills returned to Greers Ferry in 1966 to place a bust of Kennedy and name the park for the late president. He also returned on October 1, 1983, and on October 1, 1988, to place wreaths on a memorial monument to Kennedy. On April 22, 1992, Mills made his last public speech there–just 10 days before his own death–at an Earth Day celebration event with Congressman Bill Alexander. A couple of years later, a bust of Mills, crafted by Hank Kaminsky of Fayetteville, was placed next to Kennedy's. The Mills bust was dedicated by Senators Dale Bumpers and David Pryor, Congresswoman Blanche Lincoln, and Ted Boswell of Bryant, who represented the Mills Memorial Foundation.

VETERANS AND MILITARY ISSUES

A strong supporter of veterans programs and military training, Mills introduced a bill providing that any diseases or injuries servicemen suffered within five years after discharge would be "presumed" as service connected. His bill, similar to one approved after World War I, also made servicemen, their widows, children and dependent parents eligible for disability compensation.[43]

Since the Soviet Union had plans to continue compulsory military training after the war, Mills advocated the same for the United States, calling it "equal preparation." At the same time, Mills warned against large standing armies, viewing them as potential causes of armed clashes. He fostered an acceptable compromise, requiring compulsory military training, but limiting it to 17 weeks for army basic training.[44]

After the war, Mills sponsored increased dependency allowances for disabled veterans, and a new formula to provide them with cost-of-living increases. A strong believer in the G. I. Bill, Mills said, "Our objective is not to find new ways in which veterans can claim federal funds; it is to find new ways in which the veteran will get opportunities to cut himself off from federal funds and live on his own, with an adequate income.[45]

Mills attempted in 1948 to eliminate the estate tax on veterans, losing 17-7 in committee.[46]

EDUCATIONAL OPPORTUNITIES

Mills supported federal help in educational efforts, long before federal aid to education became law. In 1945, he introduced legislation to provide that all equipment appropriated for education and training of defense workers, would eventually become property of schools, colleges, and universities where located.[47] In the House, Mills introduced the Senate version of a bill to establish the National Science Foundation (NSF), successor to the wartime Office of Scientific Research and Development. He was a key House leader in planning a strategy for its passage in 1947. Mills' bill specified that national defense would be secondary to scientific development and general education for civilians. (By the 1970s, NSF would become heavily involved in developing the Internet).[48]

HOUSE HISTORY

In 1945, Congress established a Joint Committee on Organization of Congress, resulting in the 1946 Legislative Reorganization Act. The number of committees was reduced from 33 to 15 in the Senate and 48 to 19 in the House, increasing the Ways and Means Committee's power.

POLITICAL PROCESS

In 1946, 18 years before federal action and ahead of many other Southern leaders, Mills suggested abolishing the poll tax. He accurately predicted an eventual federal mandate (finally implemented in 1964).[49] Mills also predicted the mounting strength of organized labor in Arkansas elections, and advised unions to back industrialization in Arkansas. While Mills' national reputation was growing, his grassroots image was too, due to his relentless, effective casework, constituent relations, and project success. The challenge of rerouting Highway 67 through Searcy called for his diplomatic prowess. On September 1, 1943, Mills brought together in his Searcy office a federal Bureau of Public Roads engineer, a federal district engineer from Fort Worth, Texas, a representative of the Arkansas State Highway Department, and Searcy's business and professional leaders.[50] The result was a promise by the Federal Bureau of Public Roads—as its first postwar project—to let a contract for building a new rerouting bridge across Little Red River.[51]

By 1944, at age 34, Mills had risen to seventh in seniority out of 25 members of Ways and Means.

Looking ahead to the 1944 election, a delegation of Arkansas leaders convinced President Roosevelt to offer Senator Caraway a prominent federal position at her Senate pay or higher. She declined. She enjoyed Senate service and, in 1943, Caraway had become the first woman lawmaker to sponsor the Equal Rights Amendment. In the 1944 Senate election, Congressman Fulbright finished first, Adkins second, Col. Barton third, and Caraway fourth. Mills was not surprised.

This same year, Mills faced opposition in his re-election bid from Circuit Judge Marcus Bone of Batesville. Bone would be Mills' last opponent for the next 22 years, a period in which he rose steadily in power and prestige. Mills defeated Bone in a decided victory, almost three-to-one.[52] By 1945, Mills was sixth in seniority among Democrats on Ways and Means and began presiding over many committee meetings at Chairman Doughton's urging. During the 80th Congress (1947-1949), Mills was a member of the minority for the first time during his congressional career, and moved up in rank to fifth in committee seniority, working his way up a ladder with a tradition of little change at the top.

There was great speculation about his future ambitions. He eventually had to publicly announce he was *not* going to run for governor in 1948.

> My father never wanted me to run for office. He financed my campaigns but was never openly pleased with my political career. However, I had a brother-in-law, Did Billingsley, who looked like me and once Dad went up to him, put his hand on his shoulder and said, "Son, I am proud of you." He walked off and Did never corrected him.[53]

In 1947, Mills introduced newly elected Republican Congressman Richard Nixon of California to Speaker Rayburn:

> About the second day Nixon was in the House he came over and sat down with me and said, "I understand Batesville, Arkansas, is in your district." I said, "It is." He told me he had a good friend there who had been his roommate at Duke Law School. I knew the fellow, of course, an outstanding young lawyer. Anyway, two or three days later I was sitting with Mr. Rayburn on the sofa just off the House floor, where he sat when he wasn't in the chair. Dick passed and I stopped him and said, "Have you met the Speaker?" Dick talked to him about five minutes and walked off. The Speaker's comment: "I wouldn't get too close to him if I were you." Dick couldn't look you in the eye. He'd either look at your brow, your teeth, your nose, or something. He never had the ability to look you in the eye. Mr. Rayburn was uneasy about that.[54]

Wilbur Mills stands aside after introducing president Harry Truman on the rear platform of a rail car, c. 1948.

CHAPTER 5

CHAIRMAN-TO-BE
1949-1957

Mills was becoming an increasingly important voice and studious understudy. "I worked hard at it day and night. I tried to know as much about legislation as was humanly possible. I had it drilled into me that I needed to prepare myself to be chairman . . . I did put in long hours at home and in the office."[1] He read the Internal Revenue Code. He read the Social Security regulations. He read trade legislation. He asked the Library of Congress for copies of all major bills that had passed Ways and Means since its creation in 1789. "I wanted to get myself where I could explain a complicated tax bill on the House floor without having notes in front of me, I wanted to know it all."[2]

House Speaker Sam Rayburn convinced him that his success with legislation would depend on how much his colleagues trusted his knowledge. Mills often said, "You have to demonstrate that you know more about it than they do." Mills cultivated relationships with members who knew how to win tough votes.

Democrats returned to the majority for the 81st Congress (1949-1951) and Mills moved up in committee rank to fourth, behind Chairman Robert L. Doughton of North Carolina, Jere Cooper of Tennessee, and John D. Dingell, Sr., of Michigan. Chairman Doughton, 87, was known for his strong will. His nickname: "Muley."

Mills learned early on to get along famously with Republicans as well as Democrats. At one point an old friend back in Arkansas was upset when Mills, as a favor to Republican Senator Robert Taft, told Republicans back home he thought they should support Taft. Reminded of the event years later, Mills recalled with a smile:

> I had a little fellow named Elmer Webb, in my district, a
> Republican who was going to be a delegate. He came storming
> into my office–I had an office in the post office building in Searcy,
> just one great big room and I was in the back, with my secretary,
> Avinell Stevens, always right in front. Elmer never even paid any
> attention to her; he just charged right by her and came back to me

pointing his finger and said, "Wilbur Mills, what are you doing messing with Republican politics? You're a Democrat! You got no right to be telling us who to nominate."

I said, "Calm down, Elmer, and tell me what's the matter." Well, he'd been to Little Rock and talked to this lawyer down there who was Mr. Republican in Arkansas, always a great friend of mine. Webb said, "He tells me that you're advocating Taft. You're saying Taft is the brainiest man in the party." He then said, "You know he's not."

I said, "You're not for him?" "No." "Who are you going to be for?" "I'm going to be for Stassen." So I said, "Well, you go on and be for Stassen." And, he voted for Stassen. Of course, they later went to Eisenhower. But I always thought it was unfair to Taft for him not to get it. He was Mr. Republican, you know. Everybody referred to him as Mr. Republican." [3]

Democrats lost majority status for the 83rd Congress (1953-1955). Mills urged Rayburn to become minority leader and reorganize Ways and Means. When Chairman Doughton did not run for a 22nd term in 1954, Mills automatically moved up a slot to third in seniority and became the official committee spokesman. Mills became chairman of the House Democratic caucus.[4] Washington journalist Robert K. Walsh recalled years later, "Wilbur was a big shot even then."[5]

When Democrats regained majority in the next Congress (1955-1957), Jere Cooper became chairman. Dingell died in 1955, elevating Mills at age 46 to second in seniority behind the 62-year-old Cooper. Already a seasoned legislative negotiator, Mills was now in the thick of it. With Democratic victories in the 1954 elections, senior Congressman Percy Priest of Nashville, Tennessee, moved up to chair the House Committee on Interstate and Foreign Commerce, after serving four years as Democratic whip. Priest did not think he could be both party whip and committee chair, so he chose the latter. Washington was abuzz with rumors on who Democrats might name as whip. Talk focused on Mills, Hale Boggs of Louisiana, and Carl Albert of Oklahoma. Mills was not interested because he ranked second behind the new chairman of Ways and Means, and was chairman of both the Subcommittee on Internal Revenue Taxation and the Joint Economic Committee's Subcommittee on Fiscal and Monetary Policy. Rayburn consequentially, chose Albert.

On the anniversary of Roosevelt's death every year, President Truman returned to the "Board of Education" to see his old friends. On one such occasion, Mills was seated at his side.

[Truman] said he felt that there were millions of people in the
United States who were better qualified to be president than he
was, and, of course, a great pause fell over the group. Nobody
said anything and finally I said, "Yes, Mr. President, but all those
millions can't get elected." He laughed big and said, "I was waiting
for somebody to say that. That's the key to the whole thing."[6]

Mills was always conscientious in meeting roll calls and in casting votes. In
1950, for example, there were 154 key roll-call votes, and he was one of four
Democrats and seven Republicans recorded on every one.

In March 1949, Mills and two other conservative congressmen sponsored
a bill to legalize the "reserve clause" in professional baseball contracts. And in
1951, he proposed legislation exempting all professional sports from federal
antitrust laws. The Supreme Court upheld the controversial "reserve clause" in
1953, reaffirming the game is a sport, not a business, and therefore outside the
scope of laws restricting monopolies.

David Halberstam, author of *The Fifties*, considered that time to be a languid
decade, when nothing much happened. This was a period when Americans
worried about communism and kids. In Congress, Mills worked to invest in an
interstate highway system and a space program.

FLOOD CONTROL PROJECTS

In 1949, Mills secured authorization from the House Public Works
Committee to have the Army Corps of Engineers survey the White River in
the vicinity of Des Arc for flood control purposes. A recent flood had been
especially damaging.[7] In 1952, Truman came to Arkansas to dedicate Lake
Norfork, a project Mills had vigorously supported for 13 years. Mills came with
Truman, as did Rayburn, Oklahoma's Mike Monrony, and Les Biffel, secretary
of the Senate. Mills introduced Truman at Mountain Home. Truman, still
experiencing the public's anger over having fired Gen. Douglas MacArthur in
1951, was afraid he would hurt Mills politically, so he told the crowd, "I think
the world of your congressman. I just wish he'd vote with me sometime." Mills
appreciated the protection, though he had no opposition for 22 years.

In fact, Mills often told how Truman tried to talk him out of the invitation
to Arkansas: "If you are seen with me, they'll defeat you," Truman argued. Mills
laughed and explained, "Mr. President, I don't have any opposition." Truman
agreed to come, but cautioned, "Well, they will defeat you next time!" Mills
arranged train transportation in Arkansas for Truman. They stopped at several
towns, including Newport where thousands gathered. Truman and Mills rode
in a convertible together there in a parade.

Mills made frequent appeals to the House Appropriations Committee on behalf of construction funds for Greers Ferry Dam. He also supported the Arkansas Game and Fish Commission's request to obtain 80,000 acres of federally-owned lands for recreational purposes–hunting and fishing. Mills requested and received the transfer of lands from the U.S. Forest Service in Ouachita, Washington, Benton, St. Francis, Lee, and Phillips counties.

LEADERSHIP

By 1950, Mills was a regular participant, appointed by Chairman Doughton, in all conference committees related to tax, trade, and Social Security. His prominence in these sessions often resulted in his leading, or heavily influencing, the outcomes. Former Congressman Walter Judd explains how and why other members of Congress relied so heavily on Mills:

> If I did my job in foreign affairs, which was one of my two or three primary responsibilities, what time could I give to taxes? So what I did was to pick out members who seemed to know most about other issues and pretty much follow their lead. If a key Democratic member of a committee and a key Republican member agreed in their field; that carried enormous weight with me. On the Ways and Means Committee, the chairman was Wilbur Mills of Arkansas, who was extraordinarily competent before he had some difficulty with alcohol–and the ranking Republican was John Byrnes of Wisconsin, who also always knew exactly what was in the complicated bill and why. If the key Democrat and key Republican agreed on a bill from that committee, frankly I didn't even examine in any detail the several hundred pages in their bill. I voted as they recommended.[8]

One Mills friend from Izard County, a distant cousin of Mills' wife, remembers Mills spending a lot of time in that county. He once teased Mills, saying, "Wilbur, every person in this county knows you and even the birds know you." Mills agreed about people but was puzzled about the birds. His friend's punch line was: "Those birds are not calling out, 'Whippoorwill, whippoorwill.' They are calling out 'Wilbur Mills, Wilbur Mills.'" Both men dissolved into gales of laughter.[9]

Mills served as acting chairman of Ways and Means for the first time on July 3, 1952, a day he had envisioned for years.

TAXATION

President Truman told a 1949 press conference that he was impressed with a tax proposal by Mills (an unusual vote of confidence for a young congressman), and had asked the Treasury Department to consider it as a means to avoid a deficit in 1950. Mills' bill would have required corporations to pay all their 1949 taxes six months earlier than usual, a "painless" way of balancing the budget. The president had proposed $4 billion in new taxes; Republicans proposed a 5 to 10 percent across-the-board cut in government spending. Mills tried finding a middle ground to secure a bipartisan, balanced budget at no additional cost to taxpayers.[10]

As a fiscal conservative, Mills often said: "If we are to have economy in government, we cannot expect to have it in California and Wyoming unless we are willing to have it in Arkansas." In 1950, the House passed a bill to repeal most of the onerous excise tax measures leftover from World War II. The Senate was about to follow suit when the Korean War broke out. Suddenly, the government needed big sums of revenue, once again. The excise taxes were left in effect, at Mills' behest.

Early on, Mills was concerned for those taxpayers who could not afford to take their cases to court in grievances against the Internal Revenue Service. He proposed and passed a "Taxpayers Bill of Rights" to set up a Tax Settlement Board, with an independent agenda. The board would travel around the country to hear and settle small complaints. His proposal provided for 25 members, appointed for five years, paid $12,500, and directed to hold "speedy, informal and inexpensive" hearings close to taxpayers' homes.11 Taxpayers could represent themselves. The IRS would present its decision that led to the disagreement. The board would then work out a settlement to be signed by the two parties. If not, the taxpayer could then go to court. Mills contended that courts are only for the big taxpayer and that, since the IRS could only check 3 percent of 52 million tax returns, it relied on confidence from small taxpayers.

Mills secured a special exemption for Rural Electric Administration cooperatives on grounds that they didn't pay dividends.12 REA was a shot in the arm to Arkansans, serving communities not served by larger power companies.

Journalist Doug Smith, who covered Ways and Means for Scripps Howard newspapers, remembers Mills, at this time, as:

1. Amazing with figures;
2. A pleasure to watch him discuss legislation in committee or on the floor; and
3. The most charming member with the press, always agreeable and approachable.[13]

Mills supported increased taxes on corporations and excess profits taxes on profiteering by war contractors:

The people are more willing to make sacrifices when they know that profiteering has been taken out of war. The combination of an excess profits tax with defense contract negotiations will go a long way toward giving these assurances. [14]

In 1950, Mills supported increasing the federal income tax rate on larger corporations from 38 percent to 41 percent, while cutting the rate on small corporations earning under $167,000 per year, a proposal projected to produce $433 million in new revenue. At the same time, Congress cut the excise tax, reducing revenues by $1 billion and increasing equity in the tax system, Mills' career-long goal. Mills' vote on this proposal showed his independence by voting differently than Ways and Means Chairman Doughton. Doughton contended the legislation went too far. In an unusual move, the committee voted with Mills, against the chairman. President Truman also saw the wisdom of Mills' argument.[15]

In the summer of 1953, Ways and Means held hearings on the excess profits tax. To fund World War II, Congress had passed four excess profits statutes between 1940 and 1943, with rates ranging initially from 25 to 50 percent and then from 35 to 60 percent. In 1942 a flat rate of 90 percent was adopted, with a postwar refund of 10 percent; in 1943 the rate was increased to 95 percent, with a 10 percent refund. The Korean War induced Congress to re-impose an excess profits tax, effective from July 1, 1950, to December 31, 1953. The tax rate was 30 percent of excess profits with the top corporate tax rate rising from 45 percent to 47 percent, a 70 percent ceiling for the combined corporation and excess profits taxes.

President Eisenhower suggested that the 30 percent levy of profits found to be excessive, compared with past profits, and on top of the regulatory corporation tax rate of 52 percent, making a total levy of 82 percent on excess profits.[16] The committee decided to extend the tax through the end of 1953.

In early 1954, Mills advocated exempting $100 per month of retired persons' income, breaking from his theory on tax breaks that tax burdens should be relieved by cutting the rate, rather than new exemptions, believing one exemption leads to others, complicating tax forms and reducing equity. He made an exception, saying, "I favor treating all retired persons the same, and Social Security payments and railroad annuities are not taxed."[17]

Mills asked for a congressional investigation in 1955 into possible "windfall" profits by businesses from previous year's Republican revision of tax laws. Mills cited private tax attorneys who estimated the government might be losing as much as $1 billion. Treasury Secretary Humphrey contended he knew nothing about it. Other Treasury officials insisted that the attorneys' projections were "extreme and unrealistic," as well as "inaccurate."[18]

The provision allowed business firms to deduct funds placed in reserve for estimated future expenses, not for past expenses covered by this reserve. Subsequently, Secretary Humphrey was called to testify before Ways and Means, at Mills' urging. The secretary, by then, asked that the provision's "loophole" be closed, admitting that Mills had been right about it all along. Mills, not one to say "I told you so," did say later, "Secretary Humphrey had to eat crow—without any salt."[19]

Mills also spied another loophole in that 1954 tax law, one he said cost over a billion dollars a year, providing that for income tax purposes: "No gain or loss shall be recognized to a corporation on receipt of money or other property in exchange for stock including treasury stock of such corporation." The term "treasury stock," in this context, referred to a corporation's own stock held in its own treasury. Mills pointed to the common practice of the nation's corporations buying some of their own stock on the open market and retaining it for a time in the company's treasury. For that reason, he saw the new provision as an "open invitation for corporations to speculate and invest in their own stock."[20]

His analysis was that corporation officials, knowing their firm's plans, could well buy their own stock at low prices before taking some action that would tend to increase stock prices, and then sell it for tremendous profit, without being taxed. Under the old law, Treasury tried to collect taxes on all profits from a corporation's dealings in its own stocks. Sometimes courts declined to uphold the tax where the stock transaction was considered a regular part of business operations. However, Mills pointed out, "The courts always have held that such profits are taxable, if the stock transaction's main purpose was to make a profit."[21]

In January 1955, Mills was selected to serve on the prestigious Joint Economic Committee, as chairman of the Subcommittee on Fiscal Policy, a training ground for the future chairman of Ways and Means. Mills also served on the Joint Committee on Internal Revenue Taxation, staffed by Larry Woodworth, on whom Mills relied heavily. The panel reviewed all tax legislation, both for the Joint Committee and for Ways and Means. His presence there extended Mills' influence more directly to the Senate than any other House committee chairman.

When Congress received President Eisenhower's Economic Report in 1955, the Joint Economic Committee held three weeks of hearings. Seven Democratic members found the president's report "less forthright and emphatic than the statistics in reporting unevenness of the rise and numerous soft spots in the economy."[22] Mills went on to criticize the administration as "being used to promote interests of the lending and investing classes and a handful of giant corporations at the expense of the farmer, small businessman, and employees."[23]

In 1956, when the federal surplus was $1.8 billion, Mills stood firm on paying the deficit and balancing the budget, rather than cutting taxes. Some leaders, notably Senator Robert Kerr of Oklahoma and Majority Leader John McCormack of Massachusetts, entertained thoughts of reducing taxes, but Mills cautioned of possible inflationary dangers in a tax cut, and favored applying the surplus to payment on the national debt.[24]

In early 1957, Mills called for help for small business and proposed a detailed study to see how to help not just small corporations, but all small businesses. He wanted to cut their rate from 30 percent to 22 percent on the first $25,000 of income. The existing tax was 30 percent on the first $25,000 and 22 percent on excess. Mills wanted to help all small businesses, not just those that had incorporated, pointing out that only about one out of every 16 small businesses actually was incorporated. He felt that help should not be limited just to small corporations, merely aiding small-town banks and similar concerns, and ignoring the small merchant or factory operator.

In late 1957, as prognosticators and politicians began making their annual fiscal predictions, some looked for a tax cut. Mills again warned it would be better to see what happened with the national debt and deficit than to commit to a tax cut.[25] Eisenhower projected a $500 million budget surplus. All economists predicted "no depression." Mills called hearings of his Joint Economic Committee, because he felt the nation was going into an economic downturn.

He often remembered, "I just got a feeling about it. I would do that from time to time." His "feeling" was based on reading and research. There was a $12 billion deficit. Mills said he had the benefit of a weekly consumer survey conducted by a professor at Swarthmore College in Pennsylvania. *The Kiplinger Letter* predicted a downturn in consumer spending. Mills talked regularly to businessmen in his district, including his father and brother, and they all noticed a slackening in demand. Sure enough, the economy slowed. Government spending, rather than declining, was in the middle of an upswing when the Russians launched Sputnik, creating pressure to escalate defense, space, and missile research. While the country and Ways and Means listened closely, Mill said, "Prospects for any federal income tax cut next year are pretty dim–in fact, almost nonexistent."[26]

His motion to extend Social Security coverage for the first time to veterinarians, chiropractors, naturopaths, and osteopaths was adopted on July 6, 1955, and his motion to establish the first Subcommittee on Narcotics was adopted on July 29, 1955.[27] As these bills came out of committee, they quickly cleared the House and Senate.

Mills was an early advocate for providing working parents with a childcare deduction. Fifty-five percent of working women were married, 29 percent were single, and 16 percent were widows. His proposal was defeated in committee 7-14, largely a partisan vote.[28] Mills continued to seek universal coverage for all Americans under Social Security. His amendment to include student nurses under Social Security passed on May 19, 1954, and, on the same day, his motion to extend coverage to police and firefighters was adopted.[29] In an interview in early 1957, Mills said that Social Security benefits would not be increased if actuarial studies showed that increased benefits would require increased taxes to pay for them.[30]

In 1955, Mills, as chairman of the Fiscal and Monetary Policy Subcommittee of the Joint Economic Committee, led a study on economic effects of various taxes. Members of his subcommittee were Senators Paul Douglas of Illinois, one of the most liberal Democrats, Joseph C. O'Mahoney of Wyoming, Barry Goldwater of Arizona, one of the most conservative Republicans, and Representative Tom Curtis of Missouri. Mills said, "Curtis was argumentative and I was too, but we could always come to an agreement on major economic policy positions every year because, when important matters of public affairs were at stake, serious members always rose above partisan differences."[31] Goldwater emphasized stimulating investment; Curtis supported Republican tax policies; Douglas and O'Mahoney wanted personal income taxes cut, subscribing to consumption-first tax philosophy.[32]

The committee was successful, working out study methods, covering subjects it chose, and brought in the best thinkers in business, labor, and universities for background papers. These papers were published, along with staff documents. The authors wrote in a scholarly vein, scrupulously maintained by Mills. Economists exchanged views freely as in university seminars or think tanks, and produced landmark studies on credit (conducted by Senator Paul Douglas); an inquiry into general credit control and debt management (conducted by Representative Wright Patman); and a sweeping study of economic factors in tax policy (conducted by Mills).[33]

DISASTER ASSISTANCE

In 1952, a tragic tornado struck Judsonia and Bald Knob in White County, as well as Lonoke County, killing 120 people, injuring hundreds more and causing millions in structural damage. Mills immediately flew to the area in an Air Force plane, accompanied by Senators Fulbright and McClellan and Congressmen Norrell and Tackett. Mills comforted his constituents and assured them that the federal government would furnish 100 percent loans through the Reconstruction Finance Corporation to aid commercial enterprises and the Federal Housing Administration to help restore private homes.[34] Upon his return to Washington, he introduced a revolutionary bill in disaster legal history, providing federal help to rebuild school buildings damaged or destroyed by recent tornadoes. It would authorize up to $500,000 in federal disaster assistance for replacing other public buildings in disaster areas. The law, up to that point, had provided only for repair, not replacement.[35] Mills' bill was the forerunner of the current FEMA Public Assistance Program.

INTERNATIONAL RELATIONS

Mills viewed his duty to his district and to his committee in an international context. Speaking to the American Association of University Women in Searcy in 1949 on international relations, Mills predicted that America would soon be faced with deciding whether to increase benefits for people on the home front or to "keep spending in the international field for continued peace and prosperity."[36] He strongly supported the United Nations, saying, "The United Nations is a power for peace and prosperity. Even if it takes 60 years to achieve permanent peace, the United Nations will have accomplished more than has been done in 6,000 years.[37]

On January 31, 1951, Mills took the House floor to speak for a three-year extension of the reciprocal trade program:

> That an expanding world economy is an indispensable factor
> in maintenance of political stability of the countries of the free
> world, that a high and expanding level of international trade is
> of vital importance in increasing world production and world
> living standards, and that the trade agreements program is a
> real assurance that the United States will exert its influence,
> commensurate with its importance and world leadership in
> expanding international trade.[38]

Eisenhower had a struggle to pass an extension of the reciprocal trade act that was scheduled to expire in 1953. Secretary of State John Foster Dulles testified before Ways and Means that the president needed this power to negotiate lower tariffs for foreign goods in exchange for trade concessions to the United States, that defeat would be "psychologically bad" for the free world defense alliance. Allies regard open trade as symbolic of America's good faith in the world. Mills saw dissent for treaty extension in some longtime members of Ways and Means, and he fretted that Eisenhower's leadership might take a beating if extension did not pass.[39] Mills was a stalwart in support of extension, a strong trade advocate and one determined to help America move forward economically. Mills' theory was that the United States was a creditor nation and could not follow protectionist policies suitable for a debtor nation.

Mills, as a member of the conference committee in 1955 charged with ironing out differences in tariff legislation, spoke out nationally against Senator Donald Millikin's (R-Colorado) effort to revise the "escape clause" (designed to protect domestic industry from harm by foreign imports). Mills opposed Millikin's proposal as favoring protectionist tariff forces. Mills favored a higher rate of imports of manufactured products at the end of the Marshall Plan for European recovery: "That's the only way those foreign countries can get American dollars with which to buy American cotton."[40] He foresaw a tremendous surplus of American cotton if we could not find a way to maintain our export volume.

Mills was always concerned about America's drug problem and started fighting it early in his career. He sponsored legislation to prevent smuggling of opium and other narcotics into the United States.[41]

NATIONAL RECOGNITION

In late 1954, he spoke to the Searcy Kiwanis Club, predicting a friendly attitude toward business, no change to the Taft-Hartley law, an increase in the minimum wage, changes in the cotton allotment, and no revision in taxes–absent a security threat from Russia.[42]

Mills' honors grew both at home and through national organizations. Motion picture theater owners in New York in 1956 praised Mills as a friend of small business. Robert W. Coyne, special counsel of the Council of Motion Picture Organizations, thanked Mills for his help in securing passage of the King Bill, exempting amusement admissions of 90 cents and under from the federal excise tax. [43]

In 1951, Leslie Carpenter, Texas journalist and husband of Liz Carpenter, Lady Bird Johnson's press secretary, covered Congress for a national newspaper syndicate, including the *Arkansas Gazette*. "Mills," he said, "had already been an important lieutenant of Rayburn for many years and had been receiving training for speakership."[44]

Carpenter observed that Rayburn, calling Mills "one of the best parliamentarians in the House," had relied heavily on Mills to preside while important legislation was being considered. He had first called on Mills in the early 1940s, and every year after to preside when the State Department's appropriations bill was considered. Carpenter pointed to Mills' immediate work–two weeks presiding over consideration of bills to which 70 amendments were offered. He also presided over extensive Committee of the Whole sessions on the Interior Department's appropriations bill,[45] with battles over reclamation–an issue of utmost importance to the Southwest Power Administration, an agency of vital concern to Arkansas, Oklahoma, Missouri, and Texas. At one point, Carpenter said, Mills even ruled out of order three amendments to weaken the agency by Arkansas Congressman Boyd Tackett of Texarkana as not germane.[46]

WAR/PEACE

Mills continued his strong advocacy for the United Nations, telling constituents that, although it was not a perfect organization, it would be a key structure for achieving world peace over time, "Let us continue to support the United Nations for it appears to offer the only hope we have of ultimately establishing peace in the world."[47] He hailed the U.N.'s success in eliminating tedious troubles among nations since World War II, and in exercising the strongest power in eliminating possible future differences among the "Big Five" Powers. Speaking to the White County Council of Home Demonstration Clubs, he pointed out women's important role in maintaining world peace and in supporting the U.N.[48]

Mills often centered his speeches on the nation's satellite and missile programs, as to the Searcy Kiwanis Club at the Mayfair Hotel, regarding failure in 1957 to get an earth satellite sooner than the Soviet Union. He pointed to the satellite and missile programs' positive effect upon business and the economy, foreseeing a greater push for money from Congress to finance these programs. He pointed out that, although there was a military importance to the rocket that propelled the satellite, America had suffered loss of prestige, not a military defeat, through losing the satellite race with the Russians.[49]

FARMERS

Mills and Representative Clare Booth Luce keynoted the American Farm Bureau Convention in Chicago in 1957. Mills called for a new direction in farm programs, to be worked out by farmers. He saw existing farm programs (price supports, acreage controls, soil banks, surplus exports) as not working to solve farm ills.[50] On June 10, 1957, Mills introduced a bill to allow placing land with excessive rainfall or flooding under the Soil Bank Plan's acreage reserve. If farmers didn't get crops planted due to weather, they would put their land in the soil bank and receive payment. He held hearings on June 29, and it passed almost immediately.[51]

Mills composed a telegram to Agricultural Secretary Ezra Taft Benson in 1957–signed by Arkansas and Oklahoma congressional delegations–urging speedy action to aid farmers hard hit by floods.[52] Soon thereafter, a special House Public Works Subcommittee inspected flood-damaged areas of Arkansas, Oklahoma, Texas, and Kansas. The group requested a speed-up of flood control and water conservation in the southwestern states, completion of already authorized projects, an appropriation of a quarter million dollars above Budget Bureau requests for the Army Corps of Engineers to conduct new surveys, and expediting upstream projects to retard water runoff.[53]

Mills urged all farmers and businessmen to begin thinking about federal financing of the European Recovery Program ending in 1952, and what they wanted to do about importing European goods, painting a clear picture of the international context in which this legislation should be viewed and designed.[54]

Observing a drop in farm income, Mills tried to stop further acreage reductions in cotton and rice. He said United States' exports had declined greatly, due to the State Department's encouraging foreign trade among other nations to boost their economies. For example, Mills said Indonesia wanted to buy about 60 million pounds of rice from America, which had too much rice in storehouses; but Indonesia, denied the ability to buy rice here, was told to buy it from Burma to boost the Burmese economy. He rested his case by saying that new State Department policies would increase American farm prices.[55]

In 1956, when Eisenhower announced his farm program, several members of Arkansas' congressional delegation were not enthusiastic, especially Mills, who diplomatically said only: "First, I want to give considerable study to the president's suggestions."[56] Mills decided his best strategy would be to protect farmers as much as he could and add them to Social Security coverage, one of the best things ever for Arkansas farmers. Mills knew Eisenhower's program would cause a serious decline in the agricultural economy.

BUSINESS ENVIRONMENT

Mills sought to build confidence in the national economy, to encourage savings and investments, and to build a financial environment for long-run business profitability. Mills believed that government should create an environment of confidence, committing itself to policies of sustained expansion, making investments attractive causing encouraging investment. Businesses would borrow, he knew, expanding capital, and constructing new plants to enhance employment.

INFRASTRUCTURE

President Eisenhower proposed to pay for a new interstate highway system with a bond issue. Mills opposed that method, advocating "pay as you go" with a gasoline tax, earmarked for that specific purpose, creating a highway trust fund. The House Public Works Committee, authorizing the entity, feared the stigma of a tax increase. Speaker Rayburn came to Mills frustrated, afraid they wouldn't get the highway program out of committee. Mills asked him for permission to talk to the committee. Rayburn was delighted. Mills met with Public Works Congresswoman Gracie Bowers Pfost of Idaho, Congressman Jim Wright of Texas, and Jack Sullivan of their staffs. After listening to them, Mills was convinced they would refuse to move, so he tried one last strategy. "Well, if you aren't going to report this bill, I'm going to introduce a highway bill with a tax in it. If it has a tax in it, you know where it'll go. It'll be assigned to Ways and Means, and we'll report it and pass it through Congress. From then on, highway authorizations will be under Ways and Means. You aren't going to stop this. We are going to have us a road program!"[57] Afterward, Mills reported happily to Rayburn that they had it worked out. Pfost and the committee had agreed to put a tax in their bill. Rayburn was surprised and impressed, as well as amused at Mills' modicum of trickery, Mills recalled years later, "Of course, I was bluffing, but they didn't know it. Anyway they finally got around to where they'd go ahead and authorize that gasoline tax if I'd defend it on the floor. I did and the tax was passed."[58]

The highway trust fund and national defense interstate highway legislation, passed by Congress in 1956, included 40,000 miles of new interstate roads as well as rebuilding and repairing of primary and farm-to-market roads.[59]

In connection with this, Mills planned to bring Highway 67 from Little Rock through St. Louis to the standard of an interstate highway. He was convinced every county would benefit from the improved road. He hoped that federal spending would boost national spending and create jobs, especially for Arkansas. The small state of Arkansas had not felt a full economic effect from earlier such programs because "in the past, federal spending has been concentrated in a few industrialized areas."[60] Eventually, this enormous project was recognized as "the greatest construction project in human history," larger than Roman aqueducts, pyramids, and the Great Wall of China.[61] It totaled $129 billion. Mills' friend, Henry Correia of New Bedford, Massachusetts, in Arkansas for Mills' funeral in 1992, observed, "You folks in Arkansas have better highways than we do in Massachusetts. Too bad we didn't have a Wilbur Mills in our state." Professor Lester Thurow observed, "The interstate highway system contributed as much to productivity in America in the 1960s as did anything else because it allowed business to build warehouses further away from each other."[62] Under Mills, by 1960, 20 percent of the national budget was spent on infrastructure, compared to 7 percent by 1990.

CIVIL RIGHTS/EQUAL RIGHTS

Mills, often ahead of the times, in 1951 sponsored a House Joint Resolution proposing the Equal Rights Amendment.[63] Again, in 1955, Mills sponsored a House Joint Resolution for Equal Rights.[64] Congresswoman Martha Griffiths of Michigan, member of Ways and Means, enlisted his help with the same proposal two decades later. Mills got the amendment dislodged from the House Rules Committee, so that it could be voted upon by the whole House. It passed the House, but died in the Senate.[65]

In 1956, the proposed civil rights bill finally came to a vote after years of maneuvers, delays, and frustrations. In April, the House Judiciary Committee voted it out favorably under Congressman Emanuel Cellar's (NY) leadership and reported it on May 21. Knowing the vote would be close, Mills told Sam Rayburn, who pushed for passage in keeping with the Democratic Party platform, that he would vote for HR 627 "because it is the right thing to do."[66]

Rayburn warned, "Have you thought about what would happen to you if there was a big explosion in one of your school districts? Wilbur, this is not good for you. You should stay with your people and vote against it."[67] So, Mills voted with the majority of Southern congressmen against it and signed a resolution against it. Only two Southerners voted for it–Republicans Howard Baker, Sr., and Brazilla Carroll Reese.[68] The Senate killed the bill with both Arkansas Senators Fulbright and McClellan opposing it. In 1957, a civil rights bill to ensure fairness in jury trials (HR 6127) was again opposed by Mills, along with all Southern congressmen, except Reese.[69] Fulbright and McClellan opposed it in the Senate, although it passed 72-18.

POLITICS

As noted earlier, when Mills first entered Congress, the salary was $10,000 per year. He was not only conservative with taxpayers' funds, but also with his own, managing to save $5,000 a year.[70] The pay grew to $12,500 in 1947. Then, in 1955, Congress' largest pay raise, an 80 percent increase, came in those boom times and raised no ascertainable public outcry. Mills' salary was then $22,500, where it remained for 10 years. In 1965, it was raised to $42,500, the level at his retirement. Mills was faithful to his political party, always advocating party loyalty. In a 1954 speech to the White County Democratic Committee, he said, "The Democratic Party is the party of the people. I don't mean this little group or that little group ... but the party of all people. It represents the vast majority of thinking of the people of Arkansas.[71] Of course, there's bound to be some shadow boxing on some things. There always is between two parties when government responsibility is divided. But on important matters affecting the common good, Democrats will work with the president along the lines which all of us can accept."[72]

Mills and Senator John L. McClellan were fond of then-Senator John F. Kennedy, a member of McClellan's Senate Committee on Government Operations. The pair urged Kennedy in 1956 to seek the Democratic nomination for vice president. As Arkansas delegates to the Democratic National Convention, they worked hard for Kennedy's nomination. In the midst of their single-minded ardor, each of them received a transatlantic phone call from Joseph P. Kennedy, who said, "What in hell are you trying to do to my son, ruin him?" Kennedy wanted his son to become president, nothing less. They retorted that their efforts were helpful to his goals for his son.[73]

THE NEW CHAIRMAN

Ways and Means Chairman Jere Cooper died on December 18, 1957.

Cooper had been a "great influence" on Mills, as all previous chairmen, including Doughton, Reid, and Knutson. When Mills, who became chairman on January 3, 1958, was interviewed at this time by *Congressional Quarterly*, he explained their influence:

> I always tried to observe what they were doing. If what they did
> succeeded, I tried to emulate it and make it my own method
> of procedure. If they failed, I didn't want to try it. So, what
> I had done over the years was to follow actions of chairmen
> that preceded me, as much as really studying legislation and
> jurisdiction of committees. It worked out all right.[74]

Gordon Brown of the Associated Press' Washington Bureau characterized Mills as "a conservative with liberal leanings."[75] The late James Roosevelt, son of FDR and a House member from 1955 to 1965, said in 1991 that Mills was the "nicest and ablest" member of Congress with whom he served.[76] "He had no personal agenda of specific policies, just a commitment to peace and security and to an environment for productivity and capital growth."

Louis Cassels in *Nation's Business* observed, "Mr. Mills' mastery of his subject is enhanced by the fact that he is a good speaker and a superb legislative technician. When the House takes up some bill of interest to the Ways and Means Committee, he remains on or near the floor from the time the opening gavel falls until the chamber adjourns. His speeches, particularly those outlining proposed tax measures, are always lucid and sometimes eloquent; his answers to members' questions are direct and to the point."[77]

Randall Ripley in his book *Party Leaders in the House of Representatives*, observed that: "... it is behind the closed doors of a committee room that his legislative skill shows best. Compromise may be a nasty word in some lexicons, but it is the indispensable art in getting bills through Congress. Mr. Mills is one of its most accomplished practitioners, both in the Ways and Means Committee and in joint conference committees which are appointed to iron out differences between Senate and House versions of legislation.78

His technique is to maintain friendly personal relations with members of both parties, avoid taking any extreme positions of his own, listen quietly while others take their stands, and then try to offer a solution that will satisfy the majority without driving the minority into irreconcilable, bitter-end opposition.79

The *New York Times* called him "an urbane lawyer from rural Arkansas, an economic statesman, with a keen legal mind, a persuasive baritone voice and a reputation for knowing his subject."80

The *Wall Street Journal* observed, "Democrats and Republicans consider him to be an expert on tax policy, tariffs, Social Security, farm policy, labor legislation and–in fact–on legislation in general. In addition, he is an expert on parliamentary maneuvering, political compromise–two important congressional arts."[81]

The *Washington Evening Star* noted "the range and variety of his activities and information sometimes astonish his colleagues."[82]

The *Congressional Quarterly* examined his record, along with many others, on issues that came before his committee and outlined a forecast of his leadership, basically predicting he would be a just friend to business and taxpayers and would concentrate on balancing the federal budget and paying off the national debt.

His philosophy on taxing income, "I think the first and foremost principle we should adopt is that the tax we levy–the income tax–shall be applied neutrally upon those who are subject to payment of the tax. By neutrality, I mean simply this: that the amount of tax an individual pays should not depend on the source of his income but only on the amount of his income–that the tax law should not offer any advantage in getting your income one way rather than another."[83]

Mills was strongly supportive of progressive tax rates on personal income and equally opposed to progressive rates on corporate income, "I have always thought that a tax based on ability to pay is the fairest–that is, as far as human beings can make a tax fair–and is perhaps the best way for the federal government to derive the largest proportion of its overall revenue needs."[84]

Then, on progressive corporate tax rates, "I have always opposed graduated corporate tax rates. For one thing, a fully graduated tax would penalize relatively risky businesses with fluctuating incomes as compared with less venturesome businesses with the same total income over a period of years. In addition, a graduated corporation income tax would encourage corporate split ups which, while not affecting real control over the various aspects of a business' operations, would nevertheless provide tax savings to some really big companies ... Finally, a graduated corporation income tax would aggravate a number of really serious equity problems, which stem from the fact that individual and corporation income taxes are not adequately integrated."[85]

Mills enjoys a quiet moment with Polly and their girls.

CHAPTER 6

EARLY YEARS IN THE CHAIR
1958-1962

Mills was widely recognized as a giant in councils of government and as "master of consensus." Ways and Means became known as "The Third House of Congress."

Mills at age 48, the youngest person to chair Ways and Means, was the subject of a *Business Week* cover story in early 1958:

> Someone recently asked House Speaker Sam Rayburn if Wilbur Mills has a promising future. "When you're chairman of Ways and Means you've already arrived," snapped Rayburn.[1] The article characterized chairmanship of Ways and Means as "third most powerful position" in the legislative branch, trailing only speaker of the House and Senate majority leader.[2] Mills, the article continued, is a "man who works hard, knows his subject, keeps his eye on where he's going—and gets there.[3]

Wilbur Cohen, a social scientist who helped form FDR's New Deal and Lyndon Johnson's Great Society, noted that Mills, although enormously sophisticated and brilliant, never escaped the influence of his birthplace, ". . . he could turn off and on a Southern 'cracker' voice like running water. During a conversation in which he was speaking as a knowledgeable Harvard-trained leader of Washington, he might answer a call from Little Rock as if he had never left Arkansas; then he would replace the receiver and resume his national accent and demeanor unperplexed."[4]

The press had a close relationship with Mills. Columnist Robert Novak relied heavily on him for inside information. NBC newsman Sander Vanocur remembers him as "one of my key news sources."[5]

When Mills had become chairman, the committee had three subcommittees—Internal Revenue Taxation, Excise Taxes, and Foreign Trade Policy. The following Congress had Administration of Internal Revenue Laws, Administration of

Foreign Trade Laws and Policy, and Administration of Social Security Laws. Mills dispensed with subcommittees in 1961, dealing with all matters at full committee level.

The committee staff was much smaller than those of other standing committees. Mills was extremely careful and conservative with committee funds, urging members to work hard on issues themselves, and assuming much work and research responsibility himself.

Since the committee did not employ investigative staff or use subcommittees, committee staff worked under the chairman's control, instructed to be nonpartisan. The Library of Congress Legislative Research Service (LRS) supplemented the small committee staff. The committee's professional staff numbered only 11, eight serving the majority and three the minority. They tended to be policy experts who had experience with programs within the committee's jurisdiction. Eight of 11 professional staff members had previously worked in the executive branch, either the Internal Revenue Service, Department of Health, Education, and Welfare (now Department of Health and Human Services), Social Security Administration, or a White House task force.[6]

In early 1959, *Time* ran a cover story and picture of the House's five top leaders—Speaker Sam Rayburn, Majority Leader John McCormack, Rules Chairman Howard Smith, Appropriations Chairman Clarence Cannon, and Mills. The picture's caption highlighted their ages—67, 75, 77, 79, and 49, with Mills being youngest by far. The story indicated they could all say: "I love this House. It is my life."[7]

Although Mills preferred to work quietly behind the scenes, Kennedy raised his profile by courting him, conferring with him regularly at the White House, often on a daily basis, working collegially on legislation. In 1961 and 1962, Mills was the first Democratic leader with whom Kennedy conferred.[8] Mills held the fate of Kennedy's legislative program most tightly—with ability to secure a tax bill, a trade bill, and a Social Security bill.[9]

Meanwhile, tragedy befell Mills' mentor. In 1961 Speaker Rayburn, diagnosed with extensive cancer, headed home to Texas for hospitalization and rest, probably not to return. Others began speculating on succession. Mills was strictly concerned for his friend's welfare. He deeply missed their daily association. "It is a great shock to me. He was like a father to me."[10] Mills exchanged final, very personal goodbye letters with his mentor.

Close scrutiny followed Mills after Rayburn's demise, for many viewed him as heir apparent and future speaker. Mills enjoyed high regard among his fellow committee members, congressional colleagues, academic economists, business leaders, and interest group representatives for his extensive knowledge and thorough command of complicated financial questions. He was widely admired for his ability to explain most technical and complicated provisions clearly and simply in House debate, speaking without notes or oratorical flourishes and with a resonant baritone voice, commanding members' quiet attention and then their votes for his legislation.

Although his courtly manner in personal relations with his colleagues and newsmen was outgoing and cordial, he rarely shared confidences with anyone, and on occasion could be purposefully distant.

Mills never confided extensively about his personal thoughts, policy directions, or political strategies. "Wilbur has become more and more of a loner since he became committee chairman in 1958. Now, it's impossible to tell whether he likes you or hates you, and you never can tell how he stands on a given issue until he votes. He'll talk as if he's for an amendment or compromise, for example, and wind up voting against," said a fellow Ways and Means member.[11]

Mills, who was regarded by his committee as a fair, impartial chairman, was quoted as saying, "Never ride roughshod over any minority, because if you offend too many minorities, they'll one day add up to a majority." And, "Never try to trick a fellow member of the House; even if you succeed, you'll pay more in the long run than you gain in the short run."[12] The Democratic committeemen seldom caucused because Mills usually consulted them individually on committee bills. He also worked closely with the Republican leadership on most legislation where party lines were not too tightly drawn. One Republican committee member stated, "The chairman frequently begins [a question] at the lower end of the seniority scale and works backward. In the entire time I have been on the committee I have never seen anybody who wanted to ask questions fail to have adequate opportunity to do so."[13] He believed he "must guard a reputation for invincibility if his handiwork is not to be torn apart by the competing pressures."[14]

> I tried to settle our dirty linen in committee and get everybody into the act as much as I could where I always had a one-sided vote in committee. If you can't satisfy the committee, you can't satisfy the membership of House.[15]

Mills even refused to report a bill in 1959, although it was favored by a majority of the committee, because only five of his fellow Democrats supported it.[16] To stay in close touch with capitol circles, he held court daily in Room H208, sitting behind a long, green-felt table, a cigarette holder tilted jauntily between his teeth–FDR-style. Cabinet officers found him there, as did ambassadors, White House emissaries, presidents of giant corporations, and Congress members. Treasury Secretary Robert Anderson showed up one day late in 1958. "President Eisenhower wants you to know he has to veto the Social Security bill you just passed," Anderson announced.

"Will you take word back to the White House, Mr. Secretary?" said Mills. "Certainly."

"Tell the President the Ways and Means Committee will report out the same bill again on January 3 and the House will pass it January 4." Anderson reflected a moment. "You know," he said at last, "it is rather useless for him to veto that bill."[17]

HOUSE POLITICS

After less than three years as chairman, Mills was one of two or three individuals considered for House speaker in 1961 when "Mr. Sam" became ill and died at age 80.[18] Mills did not pursue the post and, in fact, was in Kensett when Rayburn died. He went down to Bonham, Texas, for the funeral.

As Leslie Carpenter observed, "A number of Capitol Hill columnists and political writers complained it is a shame that politics of the time made it out of the question for the man most suited to succeed Rayburn as speaker to be able to do so. Representative Wilbur Mills of Kensett, they agreed, was best fit for the post."[19]

Carpenter also described Kennedy's attitude toward Mills as a potential Rayburn successor, "President Kennedy is known to have considerable respect for Mills' mind and political judgment. It is no secret that the president has sought Mills' advice on a number of important matters."[20] Carpenter wrote later in 1961 that, after McCormack was elected speaker, Mills was urged to seek the majority leader post.[21] Texas members were strongly in Mills' corner because of close political and personal ties, and because of their concern that Missouri's Richard Bolling might make a strong race for it. When Carpenter contacted Mills, he refused to comment.

Carpenter indicated it would be difficult for Mills, coming from a small state, to ever become Speaker without first being majority leader.[22]

Many press people thought that two other political factors caused Mills' ascent to plateau: the widening Northern-Southern Democratic chasm, resulting from the U.S. Supreme Court's 1954 Brown vs. Board of Education of Topeka, Kansas, school desegregation decision and its dramatic aftermath at Little Rock Central High's integration; and Arkansas' declining population, forcing the state to lose two congressional districts.[23] Also, Mills, along with the Arkansas delegation, signed the Southern Manifesto in 1956.

His personal reason was indecision about when to run for a leadership position, and perhaps fatal reluctance to fight necessary battles against McCormack, Bolling, Albert, and Boggs along the way. Unless he personally took action to prevent it, Mills was to be nominated for House majority leader when congressional Democrats caucused on January 9, 1962, to select new leadership.[24] An active Mills-for-majority-leader campaign among his House friends was under way. Participants claimed Mills did nothing to encourage or discourage the maneuver; he said he'd think it over.[25]

Promised significant support, Mills was urged to announce his candidacy to be next in line to House speaker. However, Mills finally declined.[26] John W. McCormack of Massachusetts, second in the House Democratic leadership for 21 years, was assured of elevation to speaker from majority leader. Representatives Richard Bolling and Carl Albert then announced their candidacies for majority leader.[27]

KENNEDY

Mills often said, after retiring from Congress years after Kennedy's assassination: "I respected him as a president and I loved him as a man." In fact, Mills was Kennedy's most effective and best congressional ally. Kennedy's electoral victory had been slim and Congress' attitude was reserved.

As Lawrence F. O'Brien, Kennedy's congressional liaison, wrote in his memoir, *No Final Victories*:

> The reality Kennedy faced as he looked toward Capitol Hill was
> that he had, at best, a slender Democratic majority there. Our
> party had lost 21 congressional seats in the 1960 election. Kennedy
> had no sweeping mandate from voters, and he had few, if any,
> representatives or senators who owed their election to his political
> coattails. Our honeymoon with Congress was over before it began.[28]

However, with Mills and Rayburn's help, Kennedy was able to build a strong record, originating in Ways and Means during his "one thousand days." Mills recalled being introduced for a speech by only one president, during his congressional career. When Kennedy and Mills began their efforts toward the Trade Expansion Act of 1962, the president introduced Mills to a group of businessmen meeting at Washington's Shoreham Hotel. Mills said:

> He thought this crowd would receive me better than they would
> him. Just that they might view him with suspicion or something
> coming from the viewpoint that he had on these things. In other
> words, he thought I could sell them maybe better than he could.
> That's why he asked me to do it. I was all for the program anyway.
> But this was the only time I was ever introduced by President
> Kennedy, or any president, to speak, you know.[29]

Another time, Mills related:

> Kennedy talked to me one time about me giving him my

evaluation of [Arthur] Goldberg, who was secretary of labor, and Abraham Ribicoff, who was secretary of health, education and welfare. And I told him that I thought Goldberg made a better appearance before our committee. And I noticed a few days later Goldberg was appointed to the Supreme Court.

Later on, Mills told Kennedy: "Well, if I'd known you were talking about the Supreme Court, I'd have recommended Ribicoff, because I thought he was a better lawyer."[30]

ECONOMY

Mills relentlessly and successfully sought public works and defense projects for his district. On June 22, 1960, it was announced that 18 Titan missiles, called "birds of war," would be located in his district. State and local leaders lauded news of the $80 million project as an economic boon and assuring permanence of the Little Rock Air Force Base.[31]

He sought increased waterways development to attract new industry, such as chemicals and electronics, which "will become a giant industry in the years that lie ahead."[32]

FARMERS

Mills wired Agriculture Secretary Orville Freeman in 1961 requesting a 20 percent increase in rice acreage allotments for the next year, contending that information presented earlier by representatives of rice producers and cooperative groups from Arkansas, Louisiana, Texas, California, and Mississippi fully substantiated their need for increased acreage allotments.[33]

As for cotton, he indicated that, under the Agricultural Act of 1958, each farmer had to decide whether to accept his assigned allotment and a price support of 60 percent of parity, or take a 40 percent increase in acreage along with a price support at 65 percent of parity.[34]

Mills requested location of an agricultural research station in the rice belt,[35] as well as increased funds to improve and expand Mammoth Springs' Arkansas Fish Hatchery, saying that it would serve to preserve natural resources and stimulate the state's tourist industry.[36] Senator McClellan joined Mills in these efforts.

In 1959, Mills contacted Brigadier General William F. Cassidy, assistant chief of engineers for civil works, regarding modification of Greers Ferry Dam to protect fishing in the Little Red River and part of the White River.[37] Cassidy responded by letter that modification would cost at least $1 million and delay dam construction for a year, increase claims against the government, raise costs by up to another $2 million, and decrease benefits of more than $3 million.[38] Cassidy did not tell Mills that modifications would not be made; he just required a strong justification and in-depth study. Mills would not accept excuses. The project was completed within three years.

INTERNATIONAL RELATIONS

Mills reassured Perrin Jones, Jr., publisher of the Searcy *Daily Citizen*, "I believe firmly that Russia will listen only to force or a show of strength," emphasizing that America's defenses must include retaliatory power sufficient to overcome any threat.[39]

Economically, Mills gave much credit to the late Cordell Hull of Tennessee, Secretary of State under FDR, and a leader Mills admired greatly for originating the Reciprocal Trade Agreement, which increased both export and import trade.[40] Further, he reassured his constituents that Russia would have to go a long way to catch up with U.S. productivity, saying we should confidently welcome an economic war with Russia because "history will write the final chapter in favor of capitalism over communism."[41]

UNEMPLOYMENT COMPENSATION

Shortly after taking office, President Kennedy proposed one of his key emergency anti-recession measures. Embodied in a Mills bill (HR 4884), it made families of unemployed workers with dependent children temporarily eligible for federal public assistance payments. The bill had two major aims: reduce personal hardships for children of unemployed Americans, and pump buying power back into the economy. When HR 4884 was enacted, several amendments had been adopted, adding other public assistance and anti-recession programs.[42] President Kennedy also sent draft legislation to Congress on February 6, 1961, to temporarily extend aid to dependent children and children of the unemployed "pending completion of a study of a permanent program" of public assistance. Mills introduced it the day it arrived.[43]

SOCIAL SECURITY/MEDICAL CARE

Mills saw a milestone legislative year in 1960 with Social Security, setting the stage for perhaps his crowning achievement as chairman–Medicare. The 1960 Social Security amendments bill (HR 12580) covered subjects ranging from retirement age to unemployment compensation. Only one caused major controversy: Medical care for the aged, the top domestic issue of Congress' 1960 session, as well as the 1960 presidential and congressional campaigns.

On December 5, 1959, Mills had advised caution on any proposed Social Security changes that would raise tax rates. Many medical insurance proposals were in this category. Mills listed several examples of improvements that probably could be financed without new taxes, including repealing the age limit of 50 for disability insurance benefits eligibility, and allowing monthly benefits to wives and widows who are permanently and totally disabled. All were subsequently enacted.[44]

In May, after nearly a year of study, the Eisenhower administration offered a counter plan calling for federal Treasury grants to states and localities to help the aged with their medical bills. The plan included subsidies for purchasing private medical insurance policies.

The new administration plan was, in its turn, criticized by backers of Social Security, saying it was inadequate because state participation was optional. Many states would probably choose not to come in since the plan involved a dollar windfall to private medical insurance firms, and it would depend on annual appropriations by Congress, and therefore would be less soundly financed than a plan that operated through automatic Social Security payroll tax deductions.[45]

GOP presidential nominee Richard M. Nixon supported a revised version of Eisenhower's plan, while Democratic nominee John F. Kennedy strongly backed the Social Security approach. The stage was set for a dramatic confrontation in Congress' post-convention session in August 1960.[46]

Speaker Sam Rayburn, Senate Majority Leader Lyndon Johnson, and UAW Chief Walter Reuther asked Mills to urge Social Security-type legislation for a limited, contributory health plan, covering the minimum of hospital and nursing home care for Social Security recipients. In hearings, Mills introduced his own proposal, which quickly passed Ways and Means, then passed the House, under closed rule, then went to the Senate. Senator Robert Kerr, chairman of the Senate Finance Committee, was of the same mind as Mills, not wanting to expand Social Security to pay for it. Thus, Kerr-Mills, Medicare's forerunner, was born. Both the Nixon and Kennedy-backed plans were rejected on the Senate floor. Kerr-Mills was adopted. The Democratic platform endorsed the Social Security approach, so medical care was certain to retain major attention in 1961.[47]

The 1960 election was the sixth straight election year in which Mills and Congress had improved benefits under the Social Security Act.[48] Mills, recalling extensive press on Kerr-Mills' passage, laughingly and frequently told of a woman in Kensett, who, on mishearing the bill's title, felt insulted for him. She told him she did not appreciate the press referring to him as "cur Mills," since he was such a nice gentleman and not a dog at all.

A 1961 Kennedy task force on health and Social Security, headed by Wilbur J. Cohen, University of Michigan professor and later assistant secretary of HEW under Kennedy, and secretary of HEW under Johnson, on January 10, issued a report recommending hospitalization and health services for the aged, financed by Social Security.[49] Mills called Ways and Means hearings on Kennedy's proposal to finance health care for the aged through Social Security, which remarkably resembled Mills' own 1960 proposal.[50] Abraham A. Ribicoff, secretary of HEW, recommended a change in the administration's original proposal: The earnings base on which Social Security taxes for the program would be levied, should be increased from $4,800 to $5,000. Ribicoff said he favored increasing the earnings base to $5,200 due to a recent re-evaluation of cost estimates, resulting in a "substantial increase" in estimates of the number of persons who would use nursing home and home health care services, as Mills had predicted. He said the increase was "the prudent and advisable course" to provide necessary financing.[51]

Ribicoff said about 95 percent of those working would be covered when

President Kennedy signs Aid to Dependent Children Act in the White House Oval Office, May 8, 1961. Standing (l.-r.) areSenator Robert Kerr, HEW Secretary Abraham Ribicoff, Senator Harry Byrd, and Congressman Wilbur Mills. Photo courtesy Carl Albert Center Congressional Archives, University of Oklahoma.

they reached age 65, with those unprotected largely federal employees, self-employed physicians and certain state and local government employees. Among those already retired, he said, 80 percent would be protected immediately, and 95 percent or more would be protected in the long run. Mills, at one point, asked Ribicoff, "What is the connection between Social Security and medical care?" Ribicoff's response was that each was a part of the minimum protection for everyone. Mills thanked him. "That's the best explanation I've heard."[52]

Republican committee members criticized the proposal. Rep. Bruce Alger (R-Texas) said the program was not financially sound and would "crash of its own weight."[53] Ways and Means took no action and Congress adjourned.

Meanwhile, Kerr-Mills had gone into effect, expanding federal matching payments to states for persons 65 and over receiving old-age assistance (OAA). It also established a wholly new program of federal matching payments to help meet day-to-day living expenses of older citizens whose resources were insufficient to meet medical costs (MAA). The Kerr-Mills program went into operation in October 1960. The Department of Health, Education and Welfare on March 15, 1962, issued the first annual report on Kerr-Mills, saying that from October 1960 to October 1961, 41 states or territories (out of a total of 54) expanded their medical care provisions for needy persons. It also declared that it was "obvious [that] states have relatively restricted programs of medical assistance for the aged. That is, states are not extending benefits of their programs to a very large segment of elderly who are above the level of the old-age assistance program," reflecting a wide range among states adopting medical assistance. Numbers ranged from fewer than 50 in Arkansas, Utah, and the Virgin Islands to 27,920 in New York. Per-person expenditures varied from under $100 in Kentucky, Maryland, Tennessee, and West Virginia to over $300 in Washington. The average MAA payment was $207.14.[54]

Early in 1962, liberals began pushing for Senate action, hoping passage would force the House to vote on the measure. Even if the House voted it down or sent it back to Ways and Means a roll call could have important election-year consequences. Senator Anderson, author of S 909, the administration's Medicare bill, encouraged the Senate to act, but it eventually tabled his bill. President Kennedy called the action "a most serious defeat for every American family."[55]

Mills was very close to Robert Ball, the Social Security commissioner, who shared his concern for keeping Social Security actuarially sound. Both wanted to be certain that any benefits increases were paid for immediately with increases in payroll taxes going to the Social Security Trust Fund. At Mills' invitation, Ball once came to Searcy to dedicate a new Social Security office building.

TAXATION

Mills said, "We must re-examine our tax structure and concepts on which it is based. To speed up growth, the nation has to encourage investment." To do that, "we must review rates of progression in our income tax brackets." Mills always came down on the side of investment, rather than demand, in securing economic prosperity and stability. If one accepts that premise, he said, burdensome taxes become a brake on, not an accelerator of, economic growth. Mills undertook a monumental study of the federal income tax, hoping to reduce rates without sacrificing revenues required for responsible government financing.

His goals:

1. To create a tax climate promoting economic growth;

2. To provide a tax, whereby people with the same income pay the same tax;

3. To design a tax that would not interfere with operation of the market;

4. To assure fair tax burdens;

5. To inject tax-law components that respond promptly and vigorously to changing economic conditions; and

6. To ease taxpayer compliance and government enforcement.[56]

Mills was sensitive to taxation's impact on people: "Of course, we pass taxes primarily for revenue and always will. But let's not fool ourselves–you can't tax people as heavily as we do now without having a powerful effect on their lives and on the economy." He sought to broaden the base and lower rates. "More personal and business income should be put back under income tax laws" and "high rates bring requests for relief."[57]

Mills tried to balance sound tax theory with politics. He said, "Only by spreading the tax load as widely and fairly as possible can we obtain necessary revenue without seriously undermining incentives."[58] Striving for fairness, Mills frequently called existing tax laws "a house of horrors":

> Can you believe that two more or less average American men could earn the same amount of actual income, live side by side in identical houses on an identical standard of living–but that one of them must pay five times as much federal income tax as the other?[59]

He counted on Americans to understand his efforts:

> If we have a tax system riddled with preferential benefits and falling on only a part of our economy, the heavy tax burden on

those who must carry more than their share will limit our whole national program. As I see it, a fair and equitable tax system is not only desirable for itself but may well be an element in our national survival.

Naturally the job Ways and Means Committee is now tackling is a tremendously complex and difficult one, and it will probably force us to step on a few toes. I hope we can rally a majority of our citizens to support us, because everybody will be better off in the long run—and our nation more secure—if we can improve our tax system.[60]

On June 8, 1959, in debate on the House floor, Mills admonished, "We should not reduce taxes at the expense of further deficit financing or creation of more public debt. Tax reductions should come when there has been an accumulation of surpluses by reducing federal expenses.[61] He added, "The federal tax on transportation of property is least defensible of all existing excise taxes."[62] At the same time, he sought to extend the safety net and to encourage all workers. Mills supported President Kennedy's proposal to increase the minimum wage.[63]

Perhaps Mills' most compelling concern was the federal deficit, a burden on future generations. In early 1958, Mills said, "It is not so important that we avoid an unbalanced budget in any single year, but it is decidedly important that we do not, over a cycle of say 10 years, accumulate a deficit to pass on to coming generations for government services we have demanded.[64] Also in 1958, Mills held a joint press conference with Speaker Sam Rayburn to announce full accord with Eisenhower's recommendation that Congress prevent substantial tax reductions.[65]

Existing corporate and excise tax rates were set to decrease automatically on July 1, unless Congress acted. Eisenhower requested an extension to prevent a $3 billion drop in revenues. Mills and Rayburn backed his recommendation. Many members of Congress had indicated plans to seek reductions in excise taxes on automobiles because sales had been lagging, viewing a cut as an anti-recession measure.[66]

On the House floor in June 1958, Mills spent 45 minutes explaining his bill to continue war-time corporation income and excise taxes. He predicted a deficit of $3.9 billion if expenditures reached $73 billion. The next year's deficit was estimated above $11 billion, with at least $3 billion more resulting from proposed tax reductions.[67]

Mills sought a tax policy that would respond automatically to economic conditions, a self-adjusting policy that would not require tinkering for cyclical variations. "The tax law itself has a counter-cyclical impact. Revenues drop as conditions drop, so that you do not need to reduce tax rates or that you do not need to reduce over-all impact of tax law upon the economy. The economy itself takes care of that."[68]

In 1962, President Kennedy sent Congress a tax revision package, promising a "comprehensive tax reform program." The key proposal: tax credits for new investment designed to stimulate new spending for plants and equipment. Business leaders opposed the investment credit proposal, preferring instead liberalized depreciation rules. Mills believed additional depreciation incentives would cost the Treasury twice as much as the investment credit proposal, and he could not support that. Kennedy went on to seek a tax cut by 1963. But Mills responded casually: "You have not heard me advocating tax reduction this year or next year. I have not committed myself to that course of action. I have not said I would be for a reduction in our total revenues while we are spending more than we are taking in."[69]

However, once Kennedy promised to tighten controls on federal spending, Mills agreed with the tax cut. He became the House's chief force promoting the bill, cooperating closely with John McCormack, Carl Albert, and Hale Boggs in planning a winning strategy.[70]

Republican opposition to the bill seemed assured; consequently, Mills opted for a largely partisan effort, assuming a bipartisan vote because some Republicans would listen to business groups. Thus, Mills and the administration expected a recommittal motion attaching an amendment, tying the tax cut to a cut in federal spending. The most conservative Democratic members of Ways and Means spoke to fiscally conservative Democrats who met regularly on policy matters, a group the press dubbed the Boll Weevils, and asked them to oppose the Republican motion.[71] In a dramatic move, McCormack, Albert, Boggs, and Mills signed a letter on the speaker's stationery to all Democrats a little less than two weeks before the final vote, attaching the bill's chief provisions.

Mills had the highest regard for Kennedy's Treasury secretary, C. Douglas Dillon, calling him "a wonderful choice, although he had not been a student of taxes." When Dillon was preparing to present Kennedy and Mills' tax proposals to Ways and Means in 1962, Mills advised, "You impress the committee with a display of knowledge." Mills did not want him having to defer constantly to his staff to answer questions, "like Morganthal." Mills advised Dillon to consult Professor Stan Surrey of Boston for six to eight weeks to become thoroughly familiar with existing tax law and proposed reforms. Mills saw Dillon make an "impressive and masterful" presentation.[72] As Mills led Congress in securing consensus, passing 1962's major tax revision, he rose to legendary status, executing the first omnibus tax revision bill since 1954.

Mills helped write Kennedy's speech to the prestigious Economic Club of New York, delivered on December 14, 1961. It outlined in great detail the tax cut they had developed.[73] Kennedy quoted Mills as pointing out that the federal deficit is to be "regarded with concern, and tax reduction must be accompanied by increased control of rises in expenditures." Kennedy then indicated that Mills had persuaded him to pursue that particular path to stimulate the economy, balance the budget, improve balance of payments, all without causing inflation. The bill's key provision, and the section estimated to cost government the most revenue, was an investment tax credit for business and industry–designed to help modernize and expand production facilities and capacity by investing in new assets. The bill required taxing earnings of non-manufacturing foreign subsidiaries of U.S. corporations that set up "tax havens" in other nations to avoid all taxes. The bill, reported by Ways and Means on March 16, 1962, passed the House by 219-196 on March 29, and the Senate by 59-24 on September 6. The conference report passed the House and Senate on October 2. The president signed the bill on October16, saying the new law "makes a good start on bringing our tax structure up to date and provides a favorable context for the overall tax reform program I intend to propose to the next Congress."[74]

Kennedy praised Mills' efforts midway through the process, before the bill reached the House floor, saying the tax reform legislation "truly serves the national interest."[75]

The committee's Democrats had accepted decisions, arrived at jointly by Mills and Secretary Dillon. Mills knew what would be acceptable to the House, and Dillon knew what Kennedy would accept. A dissenting member would make his case in executive session or personally with Mills, never courting the chairman's displeasure by carrying it to the House floor.

After shepherding a tax bill through his committee, Mills next had to persuade a majority of the House Committee on Rules to report the bill to the floor. The key man on Rules was Chairman Howard Smith of Virginia. Mills asked the House to pass a bill that increased taxes in 19 of its 21 sections and stiffened tax collections in still another section. It was March, only eight months from the November elections, a difficult time to persuade representatives to vote for tax increases. Mills stood in the House well and explained the bill in detail. Then he answered hostile questions. Through it all, Mills did not consult a note, a performance of remarkable deftness and mastery of the complex legislation which quickly became a part of congressional legend. "No other member of Congress," said Republican Congressman Tom Curtis, at a centennial celebration of the Ways and Means Committee, "would have dared to do that."[76]

Noah Mason of Illinois, one of the bill's leading opponents, felt compelled to take the floor when Mills was through. He complimented Mills as the "most capable" chairman of Ways and Means he had known in his 25 years in the House. Mills' performance played a major role in persuading the House to pass the bill.[77]

For a clear view of the tax bill's uphill battle, Benjamin Bradlee, *Newsweek* Washington bureau chief and later editor of the *Washington Post*, visited with President Kennedy following the bill's passage. Kennedy told him about talking to Larry O'Brien and his legislative liaison colleagues at a conference the night before in the White House private living quarters:

> Charlie Halleck had votes to recommit the bill and that would have killed it. Recommittal would have meant defeat on the first of the New Frontier's three big bills, and would dim the future of the other two. He described the problems as "tremendous," and the first problem was the GOP discipline. "We didn't get one single Republican vote on motion to recommit, and only one on the final vote itself. Second, there was nothing in this bill for anybody. Nobody was lobbying for the tax bill … We turned the tide by calling in every chit we had. Twisting, promising, cajoling. I made a few calls, but the leadership really did it: Hale Boggs, Carl Albert, Wilbur Mills" and, as a muted afterthought, "John McCormack."[78]

Kenny O'Donnell remembered an instance when President Kennedy did not take Robert Kennedy's advice regarding taxation, with Mills as the primary reason. During the Berlin crisis, the younger Kennedy suggested at a cabinet meeting that income taxes be raised to heighten people's awareness of the international crisis. Reportedly, HEW Secretary Abraham Ribicoff called O'Donnell immediately, and asked him to warn the president that such a tax bill would never get out of Ways and Means. Economic Council Adviser Walter Heller argued against it with Robert Kennedy. The president heard them out and publicly decided against it. Robert cornered O'Donnell and charged him with never being for it. O'Donnell confessed to being influenced by Mills and said: "That's an understatement, Bobby, that tax bill would have been stuck in the House of Representatives for the next 25 years."[79]

In 1962, several members of Congress threatened to write into tax law that the president must cut back on government expenditures before any new revenue would be authorized. Mills, vigorously opposed, said their plan was unnecessary and an affront to Kennedy,[80] quite a contrast to the battle to come with President Johnson over an income-tax surcharge in 1967-1968, when Mills was chief advocate of a similar provision. President Kennedy promised in 1963 to reduce the 1964 federal budget by $98 billion.

TRADE LEGISLATION

In 1962, Mills returned from Arkansas for a meeting with President Kennedy, who wanted a trade bill. Undersecretary of State George Ball had told Kennedy the bill couldn't pass Congress. Mills remembered, "I told [the president] that George had misevaluated the situation. At least the House would pass it. He outlined what he wanted and said, 'You mean you think you could pass that?' I said, 'Sure I can!' It passed by the biggest vote ever on a trade bill."[81]

According to the *Bicentennial History of the Ways and Means Committee*, when President Kennedy signed the Trade Expansion Act of 1962, he acknowledged Mills' consensus-building leadership and ideas, fashioning this trade agreement. Considered a key legislative victory for Kennedy, the act provided the president with a five-year authority to negotiate tariff reductions of up to 50 percent, especially with the European Common Market. Kennedy signed the bill on October 11, 1962, referring to it as "the most important international piece of legislation affecting economics since passage of the Marshall plan."

In a May 17, 1962, address before the Conference on Trade Policy, Kennedy paid tribute to Mills: "I want to express my great appreciation to Wilbur Mills who has seen and taken advantage of a unique opportunity to serve his state and country and the whole free world by his untiring efforts that he is now applying, with the greatest possible skill, courage, and diligence, securing passage of an effective trade bill. If he can't do it, no one else could."[82]

Author William S. White wrote in 1965:

> In the 87th Congress the one man most truly responsible, apart from President Kennedy himself, for a national turn toward free world trade which had had no real parallel in the life of the republic was a great member of the House named Wilbur Mills from Arkansas. Mills, as chairman of the House Ways and Means Committee, first broke all the way through the ancient ice jam of protectionist sentiment, of "Buy America" and so on, which for a century and a half had forbidden the executive power of this country to deal with any fully flexible authority with the matter of tariffs.[83]

The Trade Expansion Act of 1962 provided legislative authorization for the Kennedy round of tariff reduction negotiations under the General Agreement on Tariffs and Trade (GATT) of 1947. The United States agreed to lower import duties an average of 35 percent on nearly 6,000 items over a five-year period (1968-1973) in return for reduced tariffs on American goods. Kennedy's admiration for Mills' skill in parliamentary management of the trade bill was summed up in one word: "magnificent."[84] Kennedy suggested:

> Those who preach the doctrine of inevitability of class struggle and of Communist success should realize that in the last few years, the great effort which has been made to unify economically

the countries of the Free World offers far greater promise than sterile and broken promises of the Communist system ... That is why passage of the Trade Expansion Act is so important and that is why I salute men such as Chairman Wilbur Mills of Arkansas.[85]

Kennedy was just like Sam Rayburn in respect to those who differed with him, according to Mills:

> He didn't get mad at you. I know when he asked for authority to increase taxes by 10 percent, the press interviewed me and I indicated I was opposed, so he called me when I was having breakfast the next morning and said, "Could you stop by the White House this morning? I want to visit with you." I said, "Sure." I got there and he said ..."You wouldn't be opposed to me having authority to reduce taxes by 10 percent, would you? I wouldn't have to have a hearing." I said, "Yes, I would." He said, "Why?" I said, "That's the only thing that Congress has got complete control of, is taxes. The only thing left that we're given under the Constitution, responsibility that we've preserved, and I'm not going to give it up." He said, "Well." He never again pressed me anymore on it.[86]

ARKANSAS POLITICS

In 1958, when reaching his peak in national power, Mills was already a legend in White County. His father had passed away that April. Wesley Morris, a local man, was run over along a roadway. Both bodies were at Roller-Daniel funeral home. The families of each had requested the same time for a service. As Mills entered the funeral home, he heard the staff discussing the conflict. Mills quickly suggested the Morris family be given the time they had requested. The Mills family could wait until later. As Ernest Everett remembers, "Wesley Morris was a friend of Wilbur's, but his sons didn't know Wilbur. But, I guarantee you, they do now!"[87]

Mills worked hard for Kennedy's good showing in Arkansas in 1960, and hosted Robert F. Kennedy in his visit on his brother's behalf. Mills suggested his state manager be Pat Mehaffey of Little Rock, later appointed as federal judge.

Mills demonstrated his legislative acumen when lining up support for the proposed Beaver Dam and Lake in Arkansas' Third Congressional District. Mills advised Congressman Jim Trimble not to talk to the House Public Works Committee chairman, Clifford Davis of Memphis, when Davis was drinking. Trimble waited for weeks on end, then finally tried his luck. Just as Mills expected, Davis balled out Trimble and threw him out of his office. Then, Mills and Trimble went to Representative Bob Jones of Alabama, also on Public

Works, and secured his assistance with Davis. Jones went to bat for Beaver Dam. Mills and Trimble always credited Jones with their success.[88]

Mills' own drinking habits were gradually changing. He'd usually have cocktails before dinner to whet his appetite and relax. Then he began having two to three drinks to perk him up so he could work longer on legislation at night, usually until midnight. Drinking began taking over his evenings. He would usually get home around 7 p.m., take his first of several drinks, and put off dinner, sometimes never getting around to it.

In earlier years, he would have drinks with Rayburn, Truman, Johnson, and others at Rayburn's "Board of Education," but he would eat dinner when he arrived home. Now, he had less companionship on Capitol Hill and more liquor at home. Mills stopped answering his home phone, unplugging it at night, not wanting anyone to know he was drinking or hold him on the phone for long periods, when he needed time to prepare for the next day's business. In 1958, when their father died, Mills' brother Roger had to call Mills' friend, shoe manufacturer lobbyist Pat Matthews, to knock on Mills' apartment door to tell Wilbur of his dad's passing.[89]

Congressmen Beerman (NE), Olsen (MT), Burke (MA), President John F. Kennedy, Congressmdn Wilbur D. Mills (AR), Harrison (VA), and Shriver (KS), May 18, 1961.
Photo courtesy the White House.

In 1962, Mills was completing his 12th Congressional term and Orval E. Faubus was completing his fourth term as governor. J. William Fulbright was thought to be as vulnerable in 1962 as Brooks Hayes was in 1958. Arkansas congressional redistricting put Congressman Dale Alford in the same district with Mills and added six new counties to the district, four of them counties from Alford's old district, including the populous and challenging Pulaski County. Faubus was giving some thought to running against Fulbright, opening the governorship for Mills, and leaving Alford in the Congressional seat. A large gathering of Arkansas political "movers and shakers" met at Witt Stephens' invitation to discuss this plan. Stephens and his friends would raise money for Mills to run for governor and dry up money for all other candidates. Mills, however, wanted to stay in the House. He discouraged Faubus from running against Fulbright, saying "as governor here in Arkansas, you are a big duck in a little pond; in Washington, you would be a little bitty frog in a great big pond!"[90] Faubus eventually decided to seek a fifth term. Alford, knowing he could not defeat Mills[91] and feeling obligated and loyal to Mills because Mills secured him a committee assignment, decided to oppose Faubus' re-election.

Mills came home when Congress adjourned, and left his district only three times–once to meet with President Kennedy in Washington, once to join Treasury Secretary Dillon on a mission to Oklahoma, and once to attend the funeral of his old friend, Senator Robert S. Kerr in Oklahoma City. Mills was re-elected without opposition; Faubus won an unprecedented fifth term, defeating Alford, as well as former Governor Sid McMath; and Fulbright defeated Winston Chandler.

Congressman Mills receives an engraved plaque from officers of the Better Government Foundation.

CHAPTER 7

MR. CHAIRMAN
1963-1966

After receiving the House's overwhelming vote of confidence in passing the Trade Expansion Act in 1962, dubbed by the press "the Mills bill," Mills became national lead expert on tax and trade, with accolades[1]: "shrewdest of politicians," "man who matters most," "leading legislative psychologist,"[2] "congressman's congressman," "de Gaulle of the Ozarks," "most powerful man in Washington," "King of the Hill," "top lawmaker," "a living legend," "fourth branch of government,"[3] and "Mr. Chairman."

During 1962, Mills had not only given Kennedy the trade bill, but also a tax bill and a Social Security bill. Mills remained modest: "It is almost physically impossible to do those three things in one year, but we did. It shows again Congress can move when Congress wants to move. Nothing is impossible until you try it."[4]

One of Washington's longtime observers said in 1993, "Of all of the people who have been here in Washington during our memory, I believe those who wielded the most power and made the biggest difference were Franklin D. Roosevelt and Wilbur D. Mills."[5] Ways and Means and Wilbur D. Mills were made for each other. Two secrets of Mills' increasing power were his ability to anticipate committee members, and to gauge the whole House's mood. He responded to each with grace. No authoritarian, Mills was "as smooth as silk, but people knew he was not to be trifled with."[6] Mills would say, "I don't think I had power, but, from time to time, I was persuasive."[7]

His introductory speeches were written by staff, but he didn't just read them mechanically. Instead, he revised them considerably, so that he could often speak without notes for more than an hour. In floor debate, Mills was at the top of his game, answering questions and justifying proposed legislation. He was one of few members who could change others' minds on the day of a vote.

In January 1963, in recognition of Mills' influence, both *Newsweek*[8] and *Time*[9] magazines featured in-depth profiles of Mills, with his picture on their covers. *Newsweek's* article described contrasts in Mills' personal style, wearing a dark gray Homburg hat, driving a 1962 blue Chevrolet Impala, knowing all his constituents' names, and finding "the endlessly complicated and laborious task of writing tax laws infinitely satisfying."[10]

Later that year, rumor spread that Mills was Kennedy's first choice to succeed Justice William O. Douglas on the Supreme Court. When questioned by the Associated Press, the administration indicated there was no vacancy and discussion was, therefore, "premature."[11] Mills said simply, "No one has talked to me about it."[12] Kennedy told many associates: "Wilbur Mills knows he was chairman of Ways and Means before I got here and that he'll still be chairman after I've gone–and he knows I know it. I don't have any hold on him."

> Kennedy gave me many projects, including a lot of missile sites. I asked him for them. He said, "Why do you want those?" "I want the labor, the jobs." It cost about $53 million dollars for every one of those 18 sites. A lot of labor involved, and my people always appreciated it, and I never had any reaction to a bomb being there. Put them all over my state, you know, most of them in my district. I just asked him for it.[13]

As noted earlier, Kennedy came to Arkansas in October 1963 at Mills' invitation to dedicate Greers Ferry Dam at Heber Springs, to visit Little Rock Air Force Base, and the Arkansas State Fair in Little Rock. To emphasize his respect for and responsiveness to Mills, Kennedy observed that the *New York Times* had speculated that Kennedy would do anything to please Mills, even sing "Down by the Old Mills (sic) Stream." Kennedy confirmed at Greers Ferry, "And, Mr. Chairman, I'd be happy to!"[14] Mills laughed and shook his head self-consciously.

Mills' mother made the 1963 trip to see the president and to give him a kiss, as the token of respect and admiration she and her entire family had for him personally. Mills would say, "I loved him as a man and respected him as the president."[15]

A month after Kennedy spoke at Greers Ferry, he was assassinated in Dallas. Mills was meeting with his committee when he got word of the assassination:

> Senator Howard Baker's father was on the committee, from Tennessee, a Republican. He and I were there on health care/Medicare. A girl came in and said that the president had been shot, that she'd heard it on the radio. Baker and I broke out in tears. Here's a Republican crying about Kennedy being shot. And I adjourned the committee then. It wasn't long until the same girl came into my office and told me that he was dead. It was quite a shock. John Connally had been shot, too, you know. I stayed at the Capitol for a long period of unbelief. I did, yes. I had some work in the office to do, and stayed on in the Capitol, sad for his family

and for the country. I went on home and listened to television; that's all that was on television. That's all you heard all night and all weekend. I had no thought about any initial fear that it was a conspiracy.[16]

Mills always viewed Johnson as "the most effective leader the Senate ever had, at least in my years":

> In the House, he was not as prominent as he later became in the Senate. He was a little reticent about being out in front. I don't know why, but he had that Naval Affairs Committee completely under his control, chairman and all. Carl Vinson wouldn't do anything without him. He came there a year ahead of me, in the House. But he was something. He didn't like to take a strong policy position. Maybe just because he hadn't been there long, like I hadn't. But for some reason, I didn't see him take positions like he did in the Senate later on.
>
> My wife and I had dinner with him and his wife the second day after he was sworn in [as president]. It was very pleasant. I always thought so much of Lady Bird. We ate right upstairs there in the private dining room in the White House. But my wife thought that Lyndon's table manners were not too good. She's always fussing at mine. She said, "He's as bad as you are."
>
> Nothing was on his mind apparently, just friendly. We didn't discuss anything private beyond what we had discussed in front of our wives. They were very close at that time; they were very friendly. I had a daughter that was very close to Lynda Bird Johnson Robb. But I often wondered why he had me there. He was talking to me about what he had to do and all, and that he wanted to carry out Kennedy's program."[17]

In 1964, Mills was dubbed the most effective representative by both his fellow members and the Washington press.[18]

DEBT CEILING

Mills missed Kennedy. He began opposing presidents more openly and directly than ever. Mills' public statements, private conversations, and traditional handling of debt-limit legislation reflected his continuing commitment to sound fiscal management, balanced budgets, and extreme care with taxpayer dollars. In fiscal 1965, the debt was $318 billion and was expected to rise to $326 billion during fiscal 1966.

Ways and Means reported HR 8464 in the form ultimately enacted.[19] Although Treasury Secretary Henry H. Fowler had requested a $329 billion ceiling, the limit instead was set at $328 billion, at Mills' suggestion. Then, once again, Congress extended the temporary national debt limit in 1966 and raised it to $330 billion, effective through fiscal year 1967. At that time, the limit would return to its permanent level of $285 billion unless increased or extended again.[20] On June 30, the end of fiscal 1966, actual debt subject to limitation was $320.1 billion, reflecting Mills' hard work to reduce federal expenditures.[21]

The administration had requested a $4 billion increase. Ways and Means reduced it to $2 billion. A staff report by the Joint Committee on Internal Revenue Taxation predicted a possible budget surplus of $3.4 billion in fiscal 1967, even though President Johnson's January budget message had estimated a $1.8 billion deficit in fiscal 1967.[22]

The Treasury Department estimated it would need a debt limitation of more than $330 billion at three points in fiscal 1967, with a peak of $331.7 billion on March 15, 1967, including a $3 billion allowance for contingencies. As signed into law, HR 15202 increased the temporary statutory debt limit from $328 to $330 billion through June 30, 1967.[23] Mills believed the debt limit tended to hold down federal spending. The best way for Congress to curb spending, he felt, was by smaller authorizations and appropriations.[24]

He provided the framework for debt ceiling legislation, "There are four factors that we have to take into consideration in figuring the ceiling on the debt under procedures that we have followed for a number of years. One is seasonal variation, the second one is the deficit in revenue and expenditures, and then the third and fourth are these matters of maintenance of a cash balance and some leeway for emergencies for contingencies."[25]

TAXATION

Mills said, "The function of taxation is to raise revenue . . . I do not go along with economists who think of taxation as an instrument for . . . manipulating the economy."[26]

> One of the things that I had found over the years is the desire to use the tax structure, not for just economic purposes but for so many social purposes. We have so many provisions in the law today that tend to complicate the law a great deal, not for purposes of raising or reducing revenue but, for purposes of social policy.

It's a social matter really, to encourage people to own homes, so
we provide for the deduction of interest from income tax in the
payment of a home. Many, many things like that, we've written in
that have more to do with a social desire than with the economy,
or with raising revenues. All of these things have happened and
they've resulted in a material complication alone.[27]

Mills had the committee staff investigate whether tax regulations or
tightening record-keeping requirements for business expense accounts were
burdensome. Mills urged them not to touch on which business expenses should
be deductible, just whether businesses' required record keeping had become
burdensome.[28]

Mills explained, "I've always been impressed with the fact that tax law is so
complicated and I've never tried to mislead anybody that tax reform would be
easy. The pressures against change are very strong."[29] However, he called the tax
system a "house of horrors."[30]

The Revenue Act of 1964 resulted from long discussions, held early in
Kennedy's administration with Treasury Secretary C. Douglas Dillon, regarding
the nation's faltering economy.[31] When Mills looked back to the Tax Reform
Act of 1964, he said:

There's no question but that the tax cut worked, set the economy
on fire. Of course, compared to GNP, our cuts were big. But
we made the president commit to holding the budget to $98
billion in fiscal 1964–think of that, a $98 billion budget–to keep
inflation down. Even then we had to call it tax "reform" instead of
"reduction" so European bankers wouldn't get all worried, start a
run on our gold or something. And it was only Vietnam that kept
us from a balanced budget before 1969.[32]

The U.S. Treasury and the automobile industry each got a part of what they
wanted. Mills, thus, solved the legislative and political stalemate, as Professor
John Manley observed in his book, *The Politics of Finance: The House Ways and
Means Committee:* "After passage, Mills and Johnson jawboned business to pass
along savings to the customer, stimulating the economy enough to prevent an
actual revenue loss, providing states more flexibility in their tax systems."

Mills sought simplification of tax forms[33] and several reforms to make
tax regulations easier to understand. Such as: speeding up processing of tax
returns; raising the ceiling on the standard deduction so taxpayers with higher
incomes could use it instead of calculating their deductions; eliminating the
standard deduction; cutting income tax rates by 10 percent, foregoing itemizing
deductions; dropping the standard deduction; permitting deductions only above

a certain level; providing an option of paying taxes at a substantially lower rate if one gives up all deductions and exemptions; and other techniques for reducing the tax load.[34]

When inflation and interest rates rose in 1966, Mills took action. He had Ways and Means accelerate tax collections, enlarge income tax withholdings, and raise Social Security rates. These tweaks took $10 billion out of circulation and reduced inflationary pressures.

There was always escalating pressure for spending. Mills confronted President Johnson frequently about the difficulty of having both "guns and butter":

> I talked to him about it, but it didn't appear to make a lot of difference to him. Lyndon Johnson was always a spender, in a sense, different from Kennedy. He thought that you could always stimulate the economy better, I think, through public spending than you could through private spending. That's the old Roosevelt doctrine, you remember, and he grew up in that environment, under that influence.[35]

HEALTH CARE

On October 24, 1963, Kennedy signed the Maternal and Child Health and Mental Retardation Planning Act into law, initiating a new program of comprehensive maternity and infant care designed to prevent mental retardation, and arouse local communities to problems of mental retardation. The law authorized planning grants. Kennedy said, "Children may be victims of fate, but they will not be victims of our neglect."[36]

Meanwhile, the most significant change during the 1963 hearings on elderly health care was in Mills' attitude. Mills was not quarreling, at this point, with the basic philosophy behind Medicare. His concern was that, if the program were enacted, it should be funded at a tax rate–making it actuarially sound. He disliked forwarding debt to future Congresses. Mills believed the proposal presumed a static economy, and did not allow enough flexibility for increased costs.

The committee had rejected a similar health care program in 1960 by a vote of 17-8, with all 10 Republicans and seven Democrats, including Mills, with the other six Southern Democrats, in opposition. Over the next five years, Mills replaced every Democrat who left the committee, including three who were opposed to Medicare, with a Medicare supporter. With the Democratic landslide in the 1964 elections, in which two Republican committee members were defeated, the panel's ratio changed from 15 Democrats and 10 Republicans to 17 Democrats and 8 Republicans. Therefore, Mills transformed a 17-8 majority against Medicare[37] into a tenuous 13-12 majority in favor of the

Medicare program.[38] Mills, who voted against Medicare in 1960, maneuvered its passage later, because he was able to broaden its reach and to keep it separate from Social Security.

Mills also said, "I have always ... since this matter has been up, been more concerned about taking care of the medical problems of those who are in need than anybody else."[39]

"Wilbur," said Kennedy, "we could not have passed the tax bill without you. You were magnificent. If you could only see your way on the medical bill ..."

"Mr. President," Mills said, "I am not as enthusiastic as you about that one."

"The House will follow you."

"Mr. President, the only way you can be defeated in 1964 is to pass that bill—if you pass that bill and people find out how little they are getting."[39] In 1965, 86 percent of the population over 65 had adequate private health insurance. Subsequently, the cost per patient a day escalated. Hospital personnel per occupied bed had multiplied geometrically.

Mills worked on developing Medicare legislation, despite his private concern.[40] Mills' early opposition to Medicare-type proposals also was based on his personal commitment never to endorse a bill that lacked majority support in Congress and in the nation, as well as his concern for Social Security's financial soundness.[41] Mills did not hold hearings on the bill, considering them unnecessary for consensus, since extensive hearings had already been held.

Throughout proceedings, Mills was deliberate and attentive. In private, he detailed his major reservations about the administration-backed King-Anderson bill to Wilbur Cohen and Larry O'Brien, including his concerns about commercial insurance companies serving as fiscal intermediaries, and inequities resulting with everyone over 65 receiving Medicare benefits, although many could not qualify for Social Security if they were still working. Mills thought that some kind of retirement test should apply to Medicare. He was deeply worried that hospital costs were rising faster than wages and a large discrepancy existed between HEW's $1.6 billion estimate of Medicare cost and private insurance companies' estimate of $2.7 billion. "Mills was not willing to jeopardize the entire Social Security fund by guessing which figures were more accurate."[42]

Mills was dubious about financing Medicare through general revenues rather than payroll taxes. The next year, he designed a bill, often referred to as a "three-layer cake," incorporating aspects of the administration's proposals, Byrnes' alternative, and a plan submitted by the American Medical Association. Under terms of Mills' final bill, hospital insurance, financed through payroll taxes, with added medical care benefits, would be financed through combining general revenues and participant contributions.[43]

More specifically:

Chairman Mills in the Ways and Means Committee Hearing Room, c. 1965.

Basic health plan: Benefits for 19 million aged, up to 90 days of hospital care, 100 days of nursing-home care and 100 home health-care visits and outpatient diagnostic services, with some deductions required.[44]

Supplementary health plan: Benefits for 16.9 million aged; 80 percent of cost of a variety of health services, including doctors' services, after a $50 annual deduction.[45]

Kerr-Mills: Medical assistance to the needy aged was extended to needy persons under all public assistance programs. Federal funds for the programs increased to benefit 8 million people.

Child health care: Federal funds increased for existing programs, and new programs were added.92

Social Security: Cash benefits for about 20 million people increased by 7 percent and regulations were liberalized to provide further benefits. Coverage extended to self-employed doctors and tips.

Financing: Increased Social Security benefits and most of the basic health program were financed by payroll taxes. The supplementary health plan was financed by contributions from participants and general revenue. The bill's other benefits were financed by general revenue. The first full year projected cost of operation (1967): basic health plan $2.5 billion; supplementary health plan $1.2 billion; Kerr-Mills $200 million; Social Security benefits $2.3 billion; child health and public assistance $339 million; grand total $6.5 billion. Payroll taxes would provide $4.5 billion; $1.4 billion would come from general revenue; and $600 million from individuals' contributions.[46] The joint conferees were about to end their deliberations and simply quit. Mike Mansfield held a private meeting with Mike Manatos and Senators George Smathers, Russell Long, Mike Monroney, John Pastore, Alan Bible, and legislative assistant Frank Valeo. Manatos suggested a recess for the Conference Committee, until after the November election.

Mills had other plans. He wanted finished business, a completed record, and a trouble-free election for his colleagues. On the meeting's final day, he told conferees to return for one more morning. No one knew why. The next morning he asked for a final vote on the record. Senate conferees were 4-2 for the Senate version and House conferees were 3-2 against it. The conference could not report out a bill.[48]

Mills came back the next year with his surprise "three-layer cake." Meanwhile, the president and the press blamed Mills for refusing to pass Medicare. The *New York Times* wrote, "The chief reason the country does not now have a Medicare program is a one-man blockade exercised for four years by Chairman Wilbur Mills."[49] The *Times* saw Democrats as deciding to risk losing the rest of the Social Security amendments. No legislative tactics, the newspaper proclaimed, were morally justified that forced old people to live "through another winter on the edge of penury."[50]

Speaking in Arkansas, Mills explained his primary concern for the system's financial soundness. He said the taxable wage base would have to be increased annually just to keep up to costs–up to $7,200 by 1976. Mills had another reason for not letting HR 11865, with the Gore Amendment, get to the House floor. Many House members had privately beseeched him not to force a public vote before the election. They did not want to get caught between the medical profession and business community on one side and seniors and organized labor on the other. Mills saved these friends from political embarrassment and took the blame. Ultimately, each colleague so spared, owed a great debt to Mills.[51]

Then, in 1965, Mills moved forcefully. Wilbur J. Cohen, assistant secretary of HEW, described Mills' final committee markup on Medicare:

> . . . All the time he had me up there testifying, dragging me
> back and forth over all the alternatives, he was searching for a
> formula that would take some of what the administration wanted
> yet would be neither what the administration wanted nor what
> the opposition wanted. It would be a Mills bill ... At the time
> it happened, I thought he was playing cat and mouse. Wilbur
> usually takes three steps forward and two steps backward, one step
> sideward to the right and two steps sideward to the left before he
> does anything. But, when he turned to me suddenly and asked if
> I could weave the two proposals together, electric lights lit up and
> began to flash in my mind. Then, I knew what he had been doing.
> I said, "yes, sir" . . .[52]

In those few words, Mills launched a historic departure in Social Security laws.

Ranking member John Byrnes described the same magic moment:

> All three major proposals–the administration-backed King-Anderson
> bill, Eldercare, and the Byrnes package–had been presented, analyzed,
> and discussed. I had just finished my defense of the Republican
> proposal, when Mills leaned across the table to Cohen. "Would it
> be possible, Mr. Cohen," asked Mills, "to have both these elements
> together in this?" The question seemed to come out of the blue, but
> committee members–Republicans and Democrats alike–instantly
> grasped the political possibilities. "Yes, sir," replied Cohen; and the
> three-layer Mills plan was born. I was surprised.[53]

Mills had provided virtually all committee members and Congress with some reason for satisfaction, creating a program more far-reaching than anyone ever believed could come out of Ways and Means, much less Congress.[54] As Alton Frye observed, Mills' pivotal role and genius lay "in deriving workable and constructive accommodations from the welter of claims and pressures."[55] He would "compromise, bargain, cajole, swap, bend, plead, amend, coax, and unite until as much controversy as possible is drained from a bill."[56]

Only one significant area of disagreement arose between Cohen and Mills. Cohen met privately with Mills, Carl Albert, and Hale Boggs discussing whether to include hospital specialists, pathologists, radiologists, anesthesiologists, and psychiatrists under Medicare reimbursements. Mills was adamantly opposed; HEW and the AFL-CIO supported inclusion. They yielded to Mills' wishes, keeping all doctors including hospital specialists out of the bill's Medicare portion.

Finally, the bill was ready. Ways and Means approved it 17-8 in a straight party vote. Mills' bill was dubbed Elder-Medi-Better-Care. Mills simply called it "Social Security Amendments of 1965."

In its first section, the bill included a basic plan of hospital, nursing home, and home-health coverage, under the Social Security program with separate payroll tax financing and a separate trust fund. In its second section, a voluntary plan covered doctor's fees financed by a $3 a month premium deducted from Social Security benefits and matched by general revenue funds. The third part expanded the Kerr-Mills program for medical care for recipients of welfare, outside of the Social Security system, as well as the medically needy, eventually called Medicaid. In addition, the bill provided a 7 percent increase in Social Security payments.

Mills spent 39 minutes explaining the bill's provisions to his House colleagues, mostly without notes. "Let us be sure that the design of benefits is not defined by whatever it takes to get a bill passed—with the feeling that details can be solved later." Medicare passed the House on April 8, 1965, 263-53.

President Lyndon Johnson was pleased:

> Cohen called the [Mills] plan "ingenious." It was almost certain, he said, that a majority would not dare to vote against the bill on the floor of the House. According to the plan, the government would subsidize a substantial portion of the cost of the voluntary, supplemental program out of general revenues. I asked how much that would cost. "About $500 million a year," Wilbur answered. Then he put the essential question to me: "What do you want to do about it, Mr. President?" . . . I approved the proposal at once. I thought that $500 million would be cheap if we could pass the bill into law. I sent Cohen away with instructions to "call them and raise them if necessary, but get this bill now."

Congressman Mills in the halls of the Capitol Building, Washington, D.C.

The Ways and Means Committee reported out this broadened bill late in March. Chairman Wilbur Mills, so long the villain of the act, was now a hero to the old folks. A delegation of senior citizens threw a victory celebration lunch in the Ways and Means Committee room, rewarding Mills with two standing ovations. "We've seen the promised land," the delegation chairman said.[59]

Johnson had become frustrated with Mills' cautious, careful consideration, meticulous crafting. Later, Johnson confided to Doris Kearns Goodwin, his biographer, in 1969, "WDM is so interested in saving face that he almost loses his ass." Seeing his words in her rough draft, Johnson reacted, "Oh, I can't be quoted saying that, he may be speaker or president someday."[60]

Later, in 1992, Mills reasoned on Medicare/Medicaid:

> I do not believe these programs are perfect. They can and will
> be expanded and improved as we gain more experience in
> implementing them. But I believe they are here to stay. They are
> now part of the American way of life.[61]

> I have always thought there was great appeal in the argument
> that wage earners, during their working lifetime, should make
> payments into a fund to guard against risk of financial disaster,
> due to heavy medical cost. One of the difficulties that impeded
> the reaching of a sound solution is the insistence by proponents of
> medical care on proceeding toward a solution through the existing
> OASDI system, not a sound approach to this matter.[62]

One of the least-noticed aspects of the Mills bill was what it did for the private health-insurance industry. Besides providing a role for private carriers in administering the program, it relieved them of providing coverage for the highest-risk part of the population, those least able to afford health insurance. Potentially even more important for private carriers and the taxpaying public generally was a tax incentive for those under age 65.[63]

The House considered HR 6675, under a closed rule on April 8, 1965, passing the bill 313-115. "After all these years," Mills observed, the committee and administration had developed a bill "that I could wholeheartedly and conscientiously ... support ... I believe we have finally worked out a satisfactory and reasonable solution of an entire problem, not just a partial solution."[64]

President Johnson praised Mills "for his statesmanlike leadership in working out, on a sound and practical basis, a solution to one of the most important problems which has been pending before the Congress."[65]

Johnson signed Medicare into law on July 30, 1965, at Mills' suggestion,[66] in Independence, Missouri, in the presence of the first president to propose a national health insurance program, Harry S. Truman.[67]

Both before and after the bill's passage, Mills was concerned about Medicare's escalating expenses due to rising hospital costs. He feared the trend was irreversible, with nothing he could do about it. He said in the early '90s, "We provided for various procedures that we thought within the law and regulations of the department would tend to hold down these costs, but despite all of our effort to hold them down, they've still gone up. Medical costs have risen faster than anything else in the consumer budget. They have gone up faster, about twice as fast, as have incomes."[68]

POLITICAL PROCESS

Meanwhile, at home in April 1964, Mills, along with Representative Oren Harris, filed for re-election. In announcing, Mills endorsed emergency relief for damage from the Alaskan earthquake, and a single system of voting, time to end poll taxes once and for all.[69]

Speaking before the Arkansas Association for the Crippled, Inc., Mills lauded President Johnson's proposed anti-poverty bill, emphasizing the assistance it would provide the handicapped. Mills campaigned across Arkansas and the nation for Johnson's re-election, and tended his own race daily. At one time Nelson Cruikshank, an advocate for labor retirees, hinted that unions had been considering support for somebody to oppose Mills, citing three reasons why they didn't do it:

1. They didn't have the money;

2. Word came down from the White House to lay off; and

Chairman Mills with vice president Gerald R. Ford, March, 1974.

3. They didn't really want to because they thought too much of Mills.

Mills' response, upon hearing they were going to support him:

They didn't find anybody. For a lot of money they could have bought somebody. Among lawyers there was a relationship that existed that was ideal. I had developed a relationship with lawyers generally in the district that made them want to be for me. And it was hard to find somebody, really, during that 22 years from 1944 to 1966 to run against me.

I lost practically all my district [in 1965 through reapportionment]. I ended up with only three counties of the original 12 that I had had. It was all gone, you see. And I could have had, if I had any substantial opponent in '66, some trouble probably. I would have had to work. I don't think they would have defeated me, because I was pretty well known. The state papers had always been rather favorable to me and very seldom did they ever write anything critical. I was about as well known over the state as I was in my own district. I spoke a lot over the state; I was always very active in presidential campaigns and things like that, and I had been chairman of the State Democratic Convention for years in a row, and I knew the leadership over the state.

I had a phone in my congressional office—one phone—that was direct to Arkansas.

I did get an awful lot of calls there after prosperity came to us.

I campaigned whether I had an opponent or not. I campaigned in even years harder than I did in odd number years. Russell Long also did that and he said he got it from me, but he got it from his daddy, Huey. Anybody who was successful in politics did that. I was doing what the old timers in the House were telling me to do.[70]

In early August 1965, an explosion and fire in a Titan II missile complex killed 53 civilians near Damascus in Mills' district. Mills was deeply shaken by the worst tragedy in a U.S. missile system. He brought Secretary of the Air Force Eugene M. Zuckert and Senators McClellan and Fulbright to view the scene.[71] Workmen, modifying the silo's physical plant at the time of the explosion, were injured or killed. Mills moved quickly to get the Air Force and Social Security Administration to aid the victims' families.[72]

The 1960s' biggest issue was the war in Vietnam. Mills had a predictable, practical view: "We should never send our soldiers anywhere without providing them adequate support, equipment, training, and funding to win. Once we send them, we should support them."[73]

In 1966, Arthur Mills, a 56-year-old Little Rock insurance man, and Jack Eardley, a 35-year-old staff psychiatrist at the State Hospital, filed for Congress, saying Mills was a "status symbol that Arkansas could no longer afford."[74]

Eardley had been part of Faubus' faction of Young Democrats when they, including the governor's son, Farrell Faubus, John Browning, Bill Carter, and Sheffield Nelson, lost their battle to keep control of the YDs. The victors back then had been Mills' former administrative assistants Sam Boyce of Newport, Jack Files of Hunter; Tom Johnson of Tuckerman, and Roy Lee Height of Little Rock.[75] Mills won re-election by overwhelming majorities in each county of the district.

Following Democratic gubernatorial nominee (and avowed segregationist) Jim Johnson's defeat by Winthrop Rockefeller in 1966, the Arkansas Democratic Party saw increasing division among stalwarts. Mills, widely sought as best positioned to unify the party, was chosen unanimously as permanent chairman of the State Democratic Convention. He used the podium to stress the importance of building a better future for Arkansas.

Chairman Mills addresses a political rally, 1971.

CHAPTER 8

MAGNIFICENT YEARS
1967-1970

When the words "Mr. Chairman" were spoken, everyone from the president to the newest elevator operator knew the reference meant Wilbur Mills. He had a "personal network of influence" in the House, somewhat like Pat McCarran and Lyndon Johnson in the Senate, "not seen in Congress since."[1]

When *Vogue* magazine ran Mills' large picture, it called him "an agreeable enigma whose choleric face fails to hide the most powerful man ..." The writer warned, "No one can make Wilbur Mills move until he is fully ready," and "for some arcane reason of his own, Congressman Mills shows to the public a sour puss, reserving for his friends a jolly ease and a round charm."[2]

The *Boston Evening Globe* called him "the suave and savvy sphinx from Arkansas."[3] *Fortune* called him "a kind of de Gaulle of the Ozarks."[4]

Edmond Le Breton with the Associated Press in Washington described Mills as "given to a quiet life, dark suits, white shirts, conservative views and the deft exercise of political power," and quoted a liberal colleague of Mills as saying, "I never vote against God, motherhood, or Wilbur Mills."[5]

After noting Mills' native and acquired intellect and powerful position, former Speaker Carl Albert observed, "The final element of Wilbur Mills' power was that he was Wilbur Mills–no one in the House, no one in the Senate, no one in the Treasury Department–knew more about the incredibly complex tax code than this Democrat from tiny Kensett, Arkansas. So thorough was his knowledge and so complete his preparation, members would often give him a standing ovation when he presented a bill."[6]

In Mills' own modest words, "Well, I try to get a consensus of the committee, then a consensus of the House."[7] Mastery of rules can be a formidable resource in the legislative process; Mills was the consummate master of rules. Catherine Rudder, executive director of the American Political Science Association, called Mills "knowledgeable, respected, and consensus-building," and Ways and Means as "restrained in partisanship, responsible in legislating, and given to apprenticeship."[8]

I. M. Destler saw Mills as the model of a unifying chairman–a "screener and broker for the whole House on issues within a broad jurisdiction."[9]

Steven Smith and Christopher Deering described Mills as "a renowned expert on tax policy, who operated the committee with a strong hand, closed markups, appointed no subcommittees, and was committed to the apprenticeship-seniority norm."[10] However, while many were intrigued with Mills, few, if any, were confident they truly knew him. John Manley wrote books and articles on Ways and Means and the House, many of which emphasized Mills' leadership, personality, power, and influence. He readily admitted his emphasis was on Mills' relationship to the committee rather than on Mills personally, calling Mills "the inscrutable personality who intrigues and frustrates those in Washington whose view is restricted to him as a particular kind of individual."[11] Manley even quoted a reporter close to Mills, who had studied him for 10 years, "I know Wilbur Mills better than anyone in this town, and I don't know him at all."[12]

The *New York Times Magazine* in a 1968 article by Julius Duscha, later head of the Washington Journalism Center, illustrated Mills' common touch:

> His office door is always open, too. No matter how insignificant
> a lobbyist may seem to be, he can generally get to see Mills . . .
> Not only will Mills talk with the lobbyist; he will readily pose for
> pictures with him, even though he knows the pictures are being
> used by the lobbyist to prove to his clients how important he is in
> the halls of Congress. Mills is generally an accommodating man.[13]

George H. W. Bush was elected to Congress from Houston in 1966, in a class of 40 new Republican freshmen. A first-term lawmaker's appointment to the prestigious Ways and Means was an unlikely possibility. Bush's father, Prescott S. Bush, former U.S. senator from Connecticut (1953-1963), was a longtime friend of Mills, having served on the Senate Finance Committee and often in conference committees with Mills.

[Prescott Bush] short-circuited the process for his son, calling Mills, saying "Mr. Chairman, I want George to serve on the Ways and Means Committee because I want him to serve under your tutelage." Mills thanked him, but indicated that Republican Committee appointments were made by the minority conference, specifically Minority Leader Gerald Ford, rather than by Mills as the Democratic Committee on Committees chairman. Bush said, "I know Jerry would appoint George if you would call him." Mills' response, "Well, I'll be glad to give him a call, Prescott," made senior Bush very happy. Mills put Bush on hold and called Ford. Ford's reaction: "Well, Mr. Chairman, if you'd like him on the committee, I'll put him there."[14]

Thus, George H. W. Bush became the committee's first and only freshman selected to the committee under Mills. Bush characterized Mills as an extremely even-handed and democratic chairman, making certain that all committee members had ample opportunity to question witnesses, make points, have press time, and have input on legislation.[15]

In a biography, George H. W. Bush is described as thinking Mills "was a model of what a congressional leader should be."[16] Mills won Bush's loyalty in many ways. One was in forcing star witness Walter Reuther, president of the United Automobile Workers, to remain until after 5 p.m. at a committee hearing for interrogation by all Ways and Means members, including freshman George H. W. Bush. Mills thus made it possible for Bush to receive radio and television coverage back home early in his congressional career.[17]

In 1989, Mills and his wife Polly were planning to attend the Ways and Means Committee bicentennial. A call from the White House informed them that President Bush and First Lady Barbara Bush would like to pick them up, so they could go together. Their personal friendship and working relationship remained strong until Mills' death, when President and Mrs. Bush were the first friends to call Polly Mills to offer sympathy.

Mills also shared the vision and plans he and Daniel H. Garner, Jr., had for a global breakthrough in educational telecommunications, through direct satellite broadcast to schools globally. Mills chaired the Foundation for Educational Advancement Today, backing Garner, an entrepreneur of Little Rock, to provide resources to the proposed Your Educational Services Networks (YES). Mills also served as chairman of Advanced Communications Corporation, which planned to develop direct broadcast satellites, a digital telecommunications system, designed to serve educational purposes. Mills' untimely death, in 1992, left Garner and his gifted associates without his sage advice, insight, and influence.
[18, 19]

SOCIAL SECURITY

In 1967, President Johnson requested Congress to enact a 15 percent across-the-board increase in monthly Social Security benefits and expand Medicare to cover 1.5 million disabled Americans under age 65. Mills held extensive hearings on the administration's proposal–numerous public hearings, as well as more than 60 executive sessions.

Ways and Means, under Mills' leadership, initially feared that the additional costs of extending Medicare would threaten Social Security's financial security. The committee initially agreed to a 12 percent increase in Social Security benefits–eventually agreeing to 13 percent in the final conference committee report. This raised the taxable wage base from $6,600 to $7,800, increased the payroll tax rate from 4.4 percent on employers and employees to 4.8 percent in 1969, raised the minimum benefit from $44 to $55 per month, and liberalized the retirement test. A provision to require mandatory work-training for all able-bodied AFDC recipients proved controversial. Aid to Families with Dependent

Children (AFDC) included federal support to send preschool children to day-care centers while their mothers received job training as a condition to remain eligible for AFDC payments. Mills, seeing the value of making "taxpayers out of tax-eaters," defended the work-training program on the House floor: "What in the world is wrong with requiring people to submit themselves, if they are to draw public funds, to a test of their ability to learn a job? Is it not the way we should go? Is that not the thing we should do?" Mills won 416-3. Later, he won 390-3 for the conference report.[20]

Mills said Congress faced a taxpayers' revolt, if mounting welfare costs were not reduced: "We on the committee felt the time had come when taxpayers want us to be rough, and do not have any doubts in your mind about it, we intend to be rough in a constructive manner, but we are not inhumane about it. We intend that anyone capable of working be made to work where possible."[21]

Reflecting the administration's position, several Democrats criticized the bill's welfare provision. When Johnson signed the bill on January 2, 1968, he also appointed a commission to recommend changes in the "outmoded" welfare system. Discussions began in 1968, and by 1972, the Social Security Act amendments introduced the new concept of indexing—that is, linking benefit increases to cost-of-living rises. Mills questioned this and cautioned members that they would never again be able to claim any credit for increasing benefits:[22] "I have a very fixed view about that ... I have thought that Congress itself has done a pretty good job of enacting Social Security increases to take care of cost-of-living increases. ... The American people can rely on Congress to continue this practice without us having to enact automatic adjusters."[23]

Although each of the 1960s' four major Social Security bills originated from administration proposals, Mills revised them all in a conservative direction. The committee did not act on a compulsory national health insurance proposal in 1960, but substituted the Kerr-Mills plan for federal and state assistance. President Kennedy's request for increased benefits in 1961 was substantially reduced by the committee. Mills added a supplementary voluntary insurance plan, favored by the American Medical Association, to Medicare. Thus, Mills always displayed independence on Social Security legislation, as with other areas, reflecting practical application and fiscal concern, serving as the congressional watchdog on Social Security: "I always believed that we should take in as much in Social Security trust funds each year as we spent. Since we had the power to tax we didn't have to have this big buildup of reserve that was initially considered necessary. I always felt like, so long as we took in a dollar more each year than we spent, that we were on sound grounds. I still believe that. I did always want that to happen and to that extent it was fiscally sound if that approach was fiscally sound. We did protect that."[24]

Then, on December 15, 1969, by a 399-0 roll-call vote, the House passed

HR 15095, a bill to increase Social Security benefits by 15 percent, effective January 1, 1970.[25] Mills called it "extraordinary Social Security legislation" since it was "unique to present a bill increasing benefits while withholding action on other needed improvements" and "necessary" in light of a 9.1 percent increase in cost of living since the last benefit increase went into effect in February 1968.[26] Mills, assuring the House that HR 15095 was not Ways and Means' final recommendation for changes in the Social Security or welfare systems, declared his firm intention to report a comprehensive Social Security bill by March 1970.[27]

Mills hoped other House conferees would accept the Senate amendment, identical to HR 15095, to avoid sending the bill to the Senate floor. Referring to Senate action that many said had turned the bill into a "Christmas tree," Mills said Senate floor action on HR 15095 should be avoided because "the holiday season of the year might well affect the number of amendments that would be offered to it."[28] His suggestion was accepted and his bill became law.

INTERNATIONAL TRADE

On December 30, 1967, President Johnson met at the Cedar Guest House, a bungalow near his main Texas house, with Mills, Charles Schultz, Walter Rostow, Senator Russell B. Long, William McChesney Martin, Speaker John McCormack, and Representatives Carl Albert, Hale Boggs, and George Mahon. They agreed to the essentials of a complex balance-of-payments program.[29]

TAXATION

Mills' own personal tax situation revealed his dedication to propriety. He avoided outside financial holdings, and always took the standard deduction, all of which cost him dearly. "I never wanted anyone to be able to say I took advantage of some provision I put into the tax code."[30]

In 1967, Mills supported a bailout of American Motors Corporation in the form of $22 million in tax relief. His persuasive fiscal justification secured congressional support: "The loss in competition, if we let this company go down, and the ultimate loss in revenue, resulting from such an event, were considered by conferees to be most important."[31]

By summer, 1967, foreseeing a budget deficit, Mills included a warning in a speech in Rochester, New York, for Representative Barber Conable. "The president called me up and said, 'Wilbur, come down here, I want to talk to you.' I got down there, and he started giving me fits for making a speech that Republicans could use. And that wasn't true. I said, 'Well, hold on just a minute. You have got a tremendous buildup in projected corporate profits, and therefore corporate taxes which will not develop.' So he picks up the telephone and gets

Gardner Ackley on the squawk box. He said, 'Chairman Mills is here, and he says we've got corporate profits overestimated.' 'Yes, Mr. President, we do.' 'Why?' 'Because you cannot as president of the United States predict a downturn in business.' 'How much will it be?' 'Well, considerably less than we have in the budget.' 'Is he right then that we are going to get a lot less corporate taxes?' 'Oh, yes, he's right.' He shut up; never said another word about it."[32] Mills worked closely and well with President Johnson, but felt Johnson's interest in economics was secondary. "I don't think, he ever did quite understand the economic impact of some of the things that he set out to do, and, therefore, he was not in a position to guard against the consequences of a single act by connecting it with some other act."[33]

Mills often baffled many capital observers and he enjoyed doing so. In a single week he was described by various publications as "an enigma," "icily aloof at times," and "universally respected." However, Mills' attitude was quite simple: "If you can get a majority of the committee for a bill, you can be pretty sure you have a comparable majority in the House. The committee is a cross section of the House, and the House is a cross section of the country."[34]

Mills opposed the Vietnam War from its inception.[35] His growing economic concerns and questioning of the war centered on the seeming unwillingness to fight to win, the war's doubtful purposes, and the resulting economic inflation. Mills became especially concerned when expenditures spiked precipitously, beginning in late 1965. Although Mills was never perceived as an opponent of the Vietnam War, he saw Johnson as too optimistic about the war's size, cost and economic impact. LBJ, in Mills opinion, feared that harsh facts and required sacrifices would shatter public support. Mills said, "Not even the United States is rich enough to fight a war, police the world's trouble spots, land a man on the moon, and cure the social problems at home, all at the same time."[36] Mills told *U.S. News and World Report* in 1967, "I'm convinced that had we known in 1965 what we know now about acceleration of the war in Vietnam, there would have been fewer of these new programs passed. We were not advised anywhere along the line that we could expect acceleration of the war, with all that additional cost. The combination of new federal programs plus Vietnam spending pushed up federal expenditures from $96.5 billion in fiscal year 1965 to an estimated level of more than $140 billion for fiscal year 1968."[37]

Later, he analyzed the war: "Well, there was no danger to us from that area, and we had no interest, really. And France had been there for years trying to win and couldn't win. But Johnson is not to be blamed for it. Actually, Eisenhower is the one that started it. We didn't sign the agreement, but Eisenhower said we would act under terms of the agreement, as though we were a party to it, that is, the separation of two countries, you remember, the arrangement they'd worked out at Geneva. And then Kennedy sent some observers over there. It wasn't long [until] you had to send somebody to defend your observers. And we never could get him to see the danger of what he was pursuing, just that holding action, not winning but just holding. The American people don't support that kind of a war; they just won't do it. And Dick [Richard B. Russell, U.S. senator from Georgia] and I knew that, but he wouldn't listen and finally just quit having us down there. Russell's advice was basically along the same lines. He also was afraid that war might even be escalated, that China might enter it."[38]

Ways and Means on October 3, 1967, by a 20-5 vote, adopted a motion to lay aside the president's surcharge proposal. Immediately after the vote, Mills told reporters, "We have to have a degree of expenditure control before the bill could be passed by the House. I don't know if it can pass the House even then, and I don't know if I'd be for it . . . but I do know that in the existing situation there is no chance of getting a bill through."[51]

In a long statement issued on October 6, Mills called the panel's action "an expression of anxiety which many Members of Congress feel–fortified by the uneasiness they found in their constituencies over the recent Labor Day recess–about the recent sharp rise in federal outlays and proliferation of federal government activity. A change in spending programs is essential . . . The surcharge proposal is dead unless the president makes some basic long-range changes in federal spending policies. Even if this were done, I don't know if the bill can be resurrected."[40] [41]

During this strained period of heated dialogue, Mills enjoyed relating how President Johnson invited him to the White House. Upon arrival, he discovered all the other House committee chairmen were there. Many were Texans, including George Mahan of Appropriations, Wright Patman of Banking and Currency, and Bill Poague of Agriculture. Johnson went around the room asking, "How do you feel about this tax increase?" Each dutifully said, "I'm with you, Mr. President." Johnson then looked at Mills. "Now, see where you are on this? You are alone." Mills quickly replied, "Yes, Mr. President, I see where I am, I am in the wrong place!" And he abruptly left the White House, returning to his office, shocking Johnson and his congressional colleagues. Mills adamantly insisted on a sizeable reduction in federal spending as a qualifying condition for reporting out President Johnson's bill for a 10 percent income tax surcharge: "I just do not believe our economy can tolerate expansion of nonessential expenditure programs at the same time that we must spend to support our troops in Southeast Asia. This is what has been done, however, and we are today suffering the economic consequences of such unwise action."[42]

Johnson publicly countered Mills' opposition: "LBJ went public with a series of press conferences–I guess that were really aimed at me. They were; of course, they were. I knew what he was up to; it didn't bother me, didn't embarrass me in any way. That was just one of his ways of putting pressure on you. He thought he'd get some support from the public, really, that they'd start writing me, I'm sure. But it didn't work that way. But he did everything in the world to twist my arm, I know that. And I admire him for it. He wanted to get the job done."[43]

Johnson had the Defense Department announce a federal freeze on projects, already appropriated, including Corps of Engineers projects such as flood-control dams, dikes, and harbor improvements.[44] Mills' reaction was direct, strong and simple: "Unless there is substantial cutting in spending programs, I don't see how we can justify a tax increase."[45] Secretary of State Dean Rusk joined Treasury Secretary Henry Fowler on a discreet mission, meeting Mills at the Coachman's Inn in Little Rock, spending two intense hours and ten minutes to enlist Mills' support for the president's tax bill. Mills was courteous, unimpressed, and unmoved.

Johnson lined up his whole cabinet, the Federal Reserve Board and battalions of bankers, businessmen, and economists behind the tax bill. Meanwhile, Mills was called "Wilbur Willful, an immovable sea wall."[46] John Byrnes: "This is a lot of malarkey about Mills' holding up this bill. It isn't the committee or Congress. It's the people."[47] Mills urged, "Let's get back to the old-fashioned concept that taxes are levied to meet the government's revenue needs" and argued that no one is smart enough to use the tax system "to fine tune the economy."[48] Byrnes said, "The president apparently hasn't gotten the message. The committee and the House sent a very clear message that spending must be cut. We want a new schedule of spending priorities, and he'd better send us one soon."[49] Johnson countercharged that this failure would ultimately cost taxpayers far more than higher taxes, including increased interest rates on short-term Treasury bills, high home mortgage and personal loan interest rates.[50]

Noting President Johnson's increasing criticism, Mills said he would be saddened if his firm opposition cost him LBJ's personal friendship of 29 years.[51] Throughout his public career and based on his experience in banking, the general store, and farming, Mills employed a rational economic test to spending proposals. He said, "My philosophy is that government is not entitled to all of the increment that comes from a tax system when the economy is booming. In periods of normal growth, we generate $4 billion to $5 billion in additional tax revenue each year. Some people think that belongs to the government for new programs, and the president's economic advisers seem to feel that way. But instead, I think there should be periodic tax reductions of these increments, and they should go back to the private sector and the people. Why? Simply because I believe it generates more and better economic activity than government can."[52]

Johnson sent his 1968 budget to Congress without proposing a cut in spending. Mills, patient and persistent, urged him, once again, to cut spending. Budget projections hit $186 billion with an $8 billion deficit–$21 billion without a tax hike.[53] Mills put aside the tax bill pending more spending cuts.

He adjourned the committee until February, and set hearings on balance of payments at that time, delaying the next tax consideration to March or later. His schedule pressured the president, who now would not get a tax bill before April 1.

The AFL-CIO joined Johnson in his efforts to win a surcharge on income taxes.[54] Labor was concerned about defense-industry jobs, and welfare and housing programs. Mills argued, "The administration thinks that if I'm for a tax bill, then everybody on the committee will be for it, except a few Republicans. That's not true."[55] However, Mills' prestige among his colleagues meant his opposition would undoubtedly cost the tax bill crucial votes, not the reverse.[56]

Then, Johnson took himself out of the presidential race in 1968. Mills was surprised, watching the March 31 speech on TV at his Connecticut Avenue apartment: "I have never talked to the president, either at the time or since, as to what motivated him. I think what he was trying to do was get himself into the posture of exercising a degree of influence on world thinking all for the good of us as a non-candidate, which he could not have as a candidate. I don't think for one minute that he made the decision on the basis of any estimate of whether he could be re-elected or not. I have always thought that he could have been."[57]

Mills surprised everyone by winning Ways and Means' approval of an income surtax on May 6, based on a spending cut of at least $4 billion. Then, on May 8, he pulled off another surprise by arranging House-Senate conference approval of the surtax, requiring a $6 billion reduction in expenditures, basically saying to the president, if you want a tax increase, here it is, take it or leave it.[58] The *Washington Star* described the months of debate as "the Battle of the Titans" and Mills as the man "with the last word."[59] The president predicted that a $6 billion reduction would cause "chaos" and accused Mills of attempting "blackmail."[60]

Mills was frustrated, but he charged forward successfully: "I was hoping to get an agreement from him. Finally I just gave up on it and went ahead. But I couldn't get anything out of him. This whole matter pointed up the need for reform in the budgetary process. I was struggling when Arthur Burns suggested we establish this joint budget committee, House and Senate. I was struggling for something to give Congress a better perspective of where it was going, and just the fact that they were appropriating money [and] they had no idea when it was going to be spent or anything else. They'd get a report back that the Treasury had paid so many bills. That's about the only way we could tell where we were going financially."[61]

Ultimately, Johnson secured a historic federal surplus. He called up Mills and said, "You sorry son of a bitch, I have outdone you." "Well, what have you done, Mr. President?" "I reduced spending by $8.5 billion."[62] Mills was proud of Johnson, affectionately known as "the big spender": ". . . when newspapers thought President Johnson and I were at dagger points, my relationship with him was very good and very close. All I was ever trying to do was to describe circumstances that would have to be brought to bear in order to get the 10 percent tax increased passed. The president knew what I was doing. He couldn't buy it."[63]

Johnson saw Mills as powerful and principled: "As chairman of the Ways and Means Committee, Representative Wilbur Mills had a different constituency than I. His leadership would be judged by his Arkansas electorate and his colleagues in the House. In building his reputation, Chairman Mills followed a basic principle. He wanted to report a bill to the floor when he felt there was a good chance of passing it. Over the years he developed great skill in estimating votes in the committee and the House. When votes were lacking, he preferred to wait rather than risk the reputation of his committee and the image of his leadership. In the tax fight Mills was particularly sensitive about his reputation. ... He was determined to proceed with maximum caution. By contrast, I felt the need for maximum speed. When the economy shows signs of faltering, prompt countermoves are absolutely essential. The conflict between Chairman Mills and the president provided headlines. The press enjoys a fight between the White House and Capitol Hill. With each newspaper report, our disagreements escalated. In all this, no mention was made either of the many long White House sessions in which Mills participated in the initial drafting of the tax message or of dozens of hours the secretary and under secretary of the Treasury spent with him throughout the entire legislative struggle. Actually, Mills was an extremely skillful congressman and a man of integrity. I like him, and I enjoyed a close working relationship with him. Yet a myth repeated often enough soon becomes the accepted truth. Before long, in some strange way the dignity of our offices became involved, making natural compromise more difficult."[64 65]

NEW ADMINISTRATION

After the 1968 election, President-elect Nixon invited Mills to meet for legislative and transition purposes at the Pierre Hotel on Fifth Avenue, on the west side of Central Park in New York City. Mills took his wife Polly and their younger daughter. Mills was in town to make a speech, and came by Nixon's hotel to look over his proposed budget. Charles Morrissey interviewed Mills 10 years later. Mills read the Nixon budget document thoroughly: "You have cut back on Johnson's last budget by only $100 million! This is not enough." "No, Mr. Chairman, I have cut back by an additional $4 billion." "You have just put that $4 billion off until the next fiscal year, so it is still in the spending stream and won't do a thing to cut back on inflation." Nixon countered, "I am not going to try to control inflation with the budget. I am going to do that by creating a modicum of unemployment." Mills' face blanched and he retorted,

"You can't control unemployment once you create it. It doesn't matter whether unemployment is created by government action or economic downturn. It has a ripple effect. There is no such thing as having a little unemployment, just like there is no such thing as being a little pregnant." Nixon replied, "Well, I am sorry you feel that way about it because it is going to be the policy of my administration." Mills said, "Well, there is nothing I can say about it."

Mills was thoroughly disappointed. Vietnam contributed to inflation and kept Mills from balancing the budget. Mills saw Nixon as focused on government programs, more than on the economy, saying "Nixon could've stopped it dead if he'd listened. All he did up in New York [when he was working with the law firm after being defeated for governor of California and running for president] was sign bond papers."[66]

Accepting the Arthur V. Watkins Distinguished Congressional Service Award at the University of Utah, while speaking at a fundraiser for Congressman Gunn McKay in early 1969, Mills summarized his goals for the nation's fiscal health, hoping Nixon would listen: "The deficit for fiscal 1968 was a regrettably large $25.2 billion, but the present estimate is that we will end this year–that is the year ending this June 30–with a small but welcome $2.4-billion surplus. A surplus is also presently estimated for fiscal year 1970 in the amount of some $3.4 billion based on a one year's extension of the tax surcharge proposed in the Budget Message. However, let me say that if we do attain a surplus as presently estimated this year, it will be the first time that we will have done so in nine years. It will be only the second time in over 11 years that I have been chairman of the Committee on Ways and Means that we will have enough revenues to cover federal expenditures."[67]

McGeorge Bundy observed: "If there is a congressman of higher general ability and character, I do not know him."[68] Milton Viorst predicted in 1969, "Mills will not only be in the news, but ... he will come through as a serious man, an expert, with greater power over legislation than the president himself." Further, Viorst observed the unintended effects of Nixon's new economic policy "may turn out to be the nomination of Arkansas' Wilbur Mills on the Democratic presidential ticket."[69]

TAXATION

The Johnson administration had held its original proposals for major tax reform requested by Mills until after the close of the 1968 election. Just before Nixon's inauguration in January 1969, Treasury released its proposals. Mills introduced them, and held extensive February hearings considering:

- the most extensive changes in the tax code's history to that time
- a six-month extension of the 10 percent tax surcharge to offset

general reductions in rate schedules

• increases in personal tax exemptions

• new tax benefits for pollution control equipment, railroad improvements, and renovations on rental properties

• increased taxes on capital gains

• repeal of the 7 percent investment tax credit

• decreased the sacrosanct oil depletion allowance

• eliminated tax-exempt status of interest on state and municipal bonds, although this latter provision was not included in the Senate or conference-committee versions.[70]

In an interview with *U.S. News and World Report*, Mills was asked, "What in your mind is the No. 1 goal of tax reform?" He replied, "The true aim of tax reform should be to adjust your rates downward and simplify the whole tax system. That's your prime goal. 'Tax reform,' as we've been discussing it here, is reform in one sense. But the kind of reform that I have talked about over the years, that I would like to see happen, is more far-ranging, more basic. What we're doing now is to try to eliminate some of the preferences that exist within the law." Preparation of Mills' 368-page bill took six months with 14 pounds of testimony transcriptions, and resulted in what some dubbed "The Lawyers' and Accountants' Relief Act of 1969."[71] The bill affected 27 broad areas of tax law, hundreds of Federal Code sections, 3 million Americans filing individual income tax returns, most businesses, all universities, churches, museums, and private foundations.[72]

Mills called a special committee meeting to correct an inadvertent omission, adding tax relief of $2.5 billion for the poor. Granted a closed rule, the bill passed 395-30.[73] A committee member said, "Mills is very careful about this. He checks with all major groups in the House, to make sure nobody important is offended."[74]

Mills had tax reform on the march, especially going after estate and gift taxation, and potential pyramiding of tax benefits for the wealthy.[75] The Senate made greater tax reductions, resulting in a Nixon veto threat. Projections of eventual revenue gains of $5.7 billion in fiscal year 1970 won his signature. Mills led the conference committee with determination and urgency. "If we don't start making progress, there's no use sitting around."[76] As finalized, the Tax Reform Act of 1969 instituted progressive tax changes, reducing tax liabilities more for lower income groups, and increasing taxes by 7.2 percent on incomes over $100,000.[77] It increased Social Security benefits by 15 percent as of January 1, 1970. At least 75 preferences of prior law were erased: undue tax advantages from accelerated depreciation for commercial and industrial real estate, misapplications of the alternative tax to large capital gains, and the unlimited charitable contributions deduction used to wipe out tax liability on large incomes.

With the 1971 Revenue Act, it provided substantial tax relief to people with modest incomes. To prevent hardship for low-income people, the personal exemption was raised to $750 from $600, and a low-income allowance of $1,300. About 12 million individuals owing small tax amounts were taken off the federal tax rolls. Mills won concessions because of his precise knowledge of just how far House conferees would go with him. He ran the conference with a firm hand, allowing only coffee, soft drinks (they were allowed to send out for hamburgers only during a night session, ending at 3 a.m.). Mills kept conferees at it for stretches of 10 hours or more, often into the next day. "After 10 hours things kind of bog down," Mills said.[78]

The next-to-last "Mills marathon" session, where major decisions were made, broke the rule. "I feel like I'm in training to be an astronaut," said beleaguered Assistant Treasury Secretary Edwin Cohen, as he headed for a rare break. "I've been in the same chair for the last 18 hours. But I'll be back, this time with some peanut butter crackers."[79]

By keeping conferees busy and postponing key votes, Mills insulated the conference against pressures of lobbyists who clustered outside the committee room waiting for word of how their interests were faring. Little leaked out, mainly because conferees themselves were uncertain how the big issues would settle. This ingenious technique was familiar to Ways and Means members: "He just doesn't like to have the committee vote point by point through a bill– especially when he suspects he won't win his way on some of the points. He will just sit there and let everybody talk themselves out, and then he will move on to the next issue. One time, I interrupted him when he did that and asked him whether we shouldn't vote to get the committee's sentiment on this one point before we moved on. The chairman just smiled at me and said he didn't think it was necessary. We could bring it back up later when we reviewed work and, of course, we didn't."[80]

Mills liked to have the press in attendance. Closed sessions lead to varying answers to inquiring journalists because "members did not know that much about what had transpired sometimes." Also, Mills recalled how he and Senator Bob Kerr of Oklahoma often retired to Capitol Room H208 to settle matters before a conference. "He knew what I had to have and I knew what he had to have, so it didn't take us long to make decisions."

DEBT CEILING

After one day of hearings on March 5, 1969, Ways and Means, in closed session, recommended a bill raising the permanent debt limit to $365 billion, providing a temporary limit (until June 30, 1970) of $377 billion, rejecting a change in debt calculation, marking the Nixon administration's first legislative defeat. Mills and Byrnes introduced HR 8508 on March 10.[82]

Several members questioned the effectiveness of the ceiling as a curb on federal spending. When Mills said the only effective way to slow growth in spending every year was to set limits in each appropriations bill, he acknowledged that the ceiling of the Revenue and Expenditure Control Act of 1968 (PL 90-364) had not been effective. Mills called the proposed change a "tight ceiling–in fact we may have drawn it too tight."[83]

The Treasury Department reported that the debt on March 14 rose to within $282 million of the old ceiling, a spread insufficient to cover even one day's bills.[84]

Mills with former president Lyndon B. Johnson at the Johnson Ranch, c. 1971.

Minority Leader Ford also agreed with Mills.[87]

Nixon's revised fiscal 1970 budget proposals frustrated Mills, congressional fiscal conservatives and liberals. Conservatives said proposed cuts were not enough to end inflation. Liberals objected to cuts in some domestic programs, and the modest $1.1 billion cut in the $80 billion defense budget. Mills supported cutting another $5 billion. He argued that Nixon's proposed $4 billion reductions were insufficient to offset inflation. Mills predicted Nixon's budget would bring a $5.9 billion deficit in fiscal 1970, not the $5.8 billion surplus predicted by the administration. The surplus forecast by the president was based on a new unified budget concept that counted accumulated government trust funds as assets. Mills viewed these as sacrosanct commitments to designated programs and future generations.

HOUSE POLITICS

During 1969-70, approximately 3,450 bills were referred to Mills' committee. They ranged from federal taxation and Social Security programs to tariffs and trade, and constituted 15 percent of all public bills introduced in the House. Mills conducted public hearings for 96 days, involving 1,200 witnesses, and recording 47 bound volumes of testimony, plus 221 executive sessions for a total of 246 days of hearings.[88]

In addition to the Tax Reform Act of 1969, the most comprehensive reform of the Internal Revenue Code since the income tax's enactment in 1913, Mills secured historic, and important legislation:

> • the Employment Security Amendments of 1970, the most significant amendments to unemployment compensation law since Congress approved the law establishing federal-state unemployment compensation in 1935;
>
> • Social Security Amendments of 1970, involving extensive substantive changes in the Old-Age, Survivors' and Disability Insurance Program (including benefit increases) and in the Medicare and Medicaid programs;
>
> • "Family Assistance" Bill of 1970, HR 16311, intended to provide comprehensive reforms in the nation's public welfare programs;
>
> • Airport and Airway Revenue Act of 1970, establishing an Airport and Airways Trust Fund for long-range improvement of the   nation's airports and airways;
>
> • highway revenue amendments, extending the Highway Trust Fund to provide monies to complete the national system of interstate and defense highways;

• Title III of the Comprehensive Drug Abuse Prevention and Control Act of 1970, described by the Attorney General as the most comprehensive and important improvement in the country's drug control statutes in many decades;

• two bills raising the public debt limit;

• Excise, Estate, and Gift Tax Adjustment Act of 1970, providing over $4 billion of additional revenues;

• act to extend the income tax surcharge for a one-year period as an anti-inflationary measure;

• Interest Equalization Tax Extension Act of 1969;

• Social Security Amendments of 1969, providing a 15 percent benefit increase; and

• the Trade Act of 1970, involving exceedingly significant proposed changes in U.S. trade and tariff laws.[89]

With these legislative triumphs, Mills was considered a strong candidate to succeed John McCormack as speaker or Carl Albert as majority leader.

Mills was surprised when McCormack told him he wouldn't seek re-election as speaker. Soon thereafter, Mills told Carl Albert that he looked forward to nominating him for speaker. Albert replied, "Oh, I'm not going to run against John!" Mills quickly ended the conversation since obviously McCormack had confided in him and not in Albert, perhaps reflecting McCormack's long-held preference for Mills to succeed him.[90]

However, Mills' boyhood dream was already achieved with his Ways and Means chairmanship.

Democratic members of the Ways and Means Committee spent great effort at the outset of each Congressional session making committee assignments for incoming members and incumbents seeking new assignments. New member Shirley Chisholm was initially assigned to the House Agriculture Committee, even though she had preferred the Education and Labor panel, Banking and Currency Committee, Post Office and Civil Service Committee, or Government Operations Committee.[91] She was further disgruntled to be assigned to Agriculture's Subcommittees on Rural Development and Forestry. She called Speaker John McCormack to complain–going over Mills' head– causing many members to predict her immediate demise in Congress. However, when McCormack told Mills, Mills suggested they visit with William R. "Bill" Poage of Texas, chairman of Agriculture, to request an improved subcommittee spot, such as food stamp and surplus food programs or migrant labor. Poage "really blew his stack."[92]

Chisholm then decided to approach the full Democratic caucus, with Mills presiding. The senior member standing was always recognized first by tradition, so after six or seven attempts, she walked down to the House well. Mills asked, "For what purpose is the gentlewoman from New York standing in the well?"[93]

She explained that she wanted to reject her committee assignment and gave a speech to explain reasons; she offered a resolution removing herself from the Agriculture Committee and requested a new assignment. Doing so, she created a parliamentary problem. Mills asked her to withdraw her motion, promising to recognize her later. Later, she remembered fondly, "He did, and he was as good as his word. He recognized me and it passed."[94]

Subsequently, Mills and Chisholm became great friends and strong allies in many common causes, including the Democratic National Convention at Miami, Florida, in 1972, where both had significant support for presidential and/or vice presidential slots. They joined forces as a strategists' working group seeking input into the final nomination, not wanting to lose a second time to Nixon.

The Legislative Reorganization Act of 1970, the first since 1946, had snubbed the seniority system, the House Rules Committee's power, and the two-thirds rule for cutting off Senate debate. It also included many important provisions designed to provide more transparency in government finances, to guarantee minority party rights, and to maintain a continuing review of legislative needs, through a Joint Committee on Congressional Operations.[95] The 1970 act required all committees to maintain written rules, a check on arbitrary power of committee chairmen, and to record roll-call votes in closed committee sessions, a step toward holding members accountable for their committee work.[96]

The House chose Carl Albert, majority leader since 1962, as speaker. In 24 years in the House, Oklahoma's Albert made few enemies and was acceptable to all Democratic Party factions.[97][98]

Hale Boggs of Louisiana overcame strong reform opposition, advancing from Democratic whip to majority leader. Boggs rankled liberals by making no commitment to reform procedures or a new distribution of power. After Boggs died in an Alaskan airplane crash, Democrats chose "Tip" O'Neill of Massachusetts for majority leader in January 1973. Although he represented the traditional system of promotion (majority whip under Boggs), O'Neill sided sometimes with reformers. When he called Mills for his support, Mills teased him, saying he might run himself, O'Neill gasped in shock. Mills laughed and responded by reassuring him, offering to nominate him.[99]

In 1969 Mills began to question oil depletion allowances. For years, he and the great majority of Congress, especially his mentor Sam Rayburn, fended off attempts to take this tax benefit away from oil companies. However, Mills observed "things have changed on oil depletion." Mills pointed to an outside research study ordered by the Treasury in 1968: "They [oil companies] sold this thing on the fact that it would build up our reserves. Now, this study has some pretty convincing arguments that say depletion allowances don't really build up reserves. The oil industry told us it would and we believed them. Now, we're not so sure."[100]

POLITICS

In 1968, unopposed for re-election for the 12th time, Mills campaigned enthusiastically for Senator J. William Fulbright, who faced Justice Jim Johnson in the primary and Charles Barnard of Earle, State Republican Party chairman, in the general election. Mills also worked for the Hubert Humphrey-Edmund Muskie Democratic ticket. Mills brought Fulbright to White County and escorted him around the square and throughout Searcy, introducing him to a large courthouse crowd. He brought Humphrey and Muskie to Arkansas, introducing them privately to contributors and publicly to large crowds.

In 1970, Mills worked for Dale Bumpers for governor. Bumpers defeated former Governor Orval E. Faubus in the primary, and then Winthrop Rockefeller, Arkansas' second-term governor.

In 1970, Arkansas' four congressional districts' share of federal outlays showed Mills' influence, even during the Nixon administration.

- The first district $363,359,029.
- The second (Mills') district $567,316,226.
- The third district $348,701,099.
- The fourth district $295,749,075.101

Mills' support of President Nixon's legislation in 1970 was 57 percent and his direct opposition was 28 percent.

When Mills visited Lyndon Johnson on his ranch in 1971, he became worried about his old friend, telling his Administrative Assistant Gene Goss, "He is wearing out, rusting out. I think it is a shame for a man to ... He ought to be back in politics somewhere. I suggested that he ought to run for the Senate. I think he could win it, just staying at the ranch. All factions within Texas, he could solidify."

CHAPTER 9

PRESIDENTIAL POLITICS
1971

Whenever serious speculation rose regarding Mills' future, commentators joked that becoming speaker of the House would be "a step down" and becoming president would be "merely a lateral move." Representative Sam Gibbons of Florida asked, "Why would Wilbur want to become president and lose his grip on the world?" Many in Washington became professional "Wilbur Watchers." No one, including his family, staff, and closest friends, ever knew for sure what Mills would do next professionally, politically, or personally.

Representative Al Ullman (D-Oregon), ranking member on Ways and Means, said, "He can be tough. He can be lenient. He can change his mind. He's a master at keeping people guessing."[1] The *Washington Star* called him "undisputed King of the Hill" and the *New York Times* opined, "By almost any standard these days, Representative Mills is the single most powerful man in Congress and second most powerful in Washington, and there are days when President Nixon might take issue with the second judgment."[2]

Business Week called him "the formidable chairman" and "Mills the omnipotent."[3] It also observed that the most frequently asked question in Washington had been for several years, "What will Wilbur do?" A *Reader's Digest* article on him was entitled "The Most Powerful Man in Congress."[4]

Hugh Sidey's famous column, "The Republic of Wilbur Mills," observed, "If the White House were to rate the independent powers of this world with which it must deal according to their formidability, Arkansas Congressman Wilbur Mills probably ranks just below Germany and above France."[5]

Charles Zuver, director of governmental affairs for the Credit Unions' National Association, former staffer for President Lyndon Johnson, and husband of one of Mills' secretaries, recalls watching Mills dictate a seven-page letter to the Internal Revenue Service commissioner on a new law's legislative intent. When it was typed, he read it for editing, but changed only one or two typos.[6]

Marshall Frady wrote in *Life* magazine that Mills had "become the single most conspicuous and consequential figure in Congress."[7] Frady wrote:

> Despite his staggering clout, he has remained a resolutely unassertive figure, possessed by an implacable shyness. To expect from such an eminently unpresumptuous creature that most towering presumption of all—to run for president of the United States—could not have seemed more unlikely.
>
> Occasionally, if importunings of a colleague or lobbyist grow somewhat blustery and dogmatic, Mills would slump slightly lower in his chair and studiously run a penknife under his fingernails while a small furious tremor briefly flutters in his right cheek. "Whenever I walk in his office," declared one of his aides, "and see that little jumping in his cheek, I start shuddering." But Mills allows himself no more release of passions than that.
>
> During testimony in committee hearings or appeals from petitioners in his office, Mills narrows his eyes and shakes his head sympathetically, maintaining a slightly squeezed and squinty expression of attentiveness and commiseration. He seems devoutly and amiably all-absorbent, responding to interminable recitals of woes and exhortations with nods, murmurings, "I understand you, yes . . . Yes, that's right, sure wouldn't," agreeable hums and grunts . . .
>
> In the view of some of the White House, "the man is almost Oriental." Actually, such a sense of his impulses arises out of the fact that Mills is probably Washington's most exhaustive assembler of consensus approaches since Lyndon Johnson departed the Senate. With an indefatigable deliberation, Mills gradually constructs the meticulous complexities of his consensus into a new legislative program. "Of course," says one of his committee members, "Wilbur is always very careful about who he reaches a consensus of. It tends to be who can influence, who can help the most."
>
> . . . But Mills does hold fierce personal persuasions on certain principles of fiscal policy. They comprise a synthesis of New Deal social-program financing and the orthodox frugalities of a puritan economic ethic. He answers to those nostalgic integrities of sound money, balanced budgets, actuarial stability of insurance programs like Social Security, while he is also given to certain populist instincts lingering from his Arkansas origins . . .

Mills has professed considerable exasperation with the White

House's assumption that inflation and unemployment can be remedied simultaneously. "You just can't use the same formula to reduce unemployment and inflation," the chairman asserts. "And between the two, I'd attend to all these people out of jobs first."[7]

According to *Newsweek:*

> Speaker Carl Albert is quoted as saying of Mills: "He is unquestionably one of the greatest members in the history of the House." Martha Griffiths, a veteran of Ways and Means, enthused, "He is probably the best informed economist the federal government has ever had, and that includes the Council of Economic Advisers." Such widespread admiration bordering on awe, shrouded Mills with a hint of mystery and mystique. Whenever Mills cropped up in the headlines, "the Mills enigma" rippled through Washington, reflecting that the introverted Mills was a loner–confiding in no one, participating in no political clique or cabal, and building his legislative strategy with meticulous care and multiple escape routes.[8]

"Mills was not a typical Southern chairman, generally regarded as adroit and fair . . . always trying to channel progress rather than block it."[9] Joseph Alsop said, "Few men that one can think of are better fitted for the presidency."[10] Occasionally, Mills said, "It is a job I wouldn't wish on my worst enemy." Edmond LeBreton quoted Mills as saying, "You don't need the title to run things in Washington."[10][11]

Meanwhile, Arkansas State Senator J. A. "Dooley" Womack of Camden sponsored an election law to permit a candidate for the U.S. House or U.S. Senate to be on the Arkansas ballot while being a candidate for president or vice president. This so-called "Mills bill" passed unanimously. The primary was moved to May from August to qualify delegates to the Democratic National Convention for the new "McGovern Rules."[12] When Mills was told of this political prediction and legislative action, he laughed, "I am not a candidate."[13]

On April 13, 1971, he spoke for 45 minutes to the African-American student body at Horace Mann High School in Little Rock. The students waved signs saying "Welcome Wilbur Mills," "Mills for President," "Wilbur's Our Man," "We Want an Arkansan in the White House."[14] Mills' easy rapport with young people was evident. "It's a great thrill for me to get to be with you this morning: It's always that way when I can get to be with a group who are about my own age." The students loved it. He was 61.[15]

Mills encouraged students to take advantage of all opportunities available to them for an education:

We live in an era . . . where it is not the color of one's skin that is of major importance anymore. There is no limit to what any young person can achieve if he/she has proper inspiration and drive and desire and has opportunities for education and training. Don't let anybody tell you any different. [16] I hope we can get out of Vietnam just as quickly and as it's humanely possible to do so, and bring out at the same time those who are prisoners of war in North Vietnam.[17]

I hope we've learned one lesson about it–that we'll never again send an American into any kind of conflict such as this just to fight and not to win. If we're not going to win, let's keep our people at home.[18]

Relations between Nixon and Mills degraded further with the increasing visibility of the Draft Mills Movement.[19] Mills respected Nixon's mind, comparing him to Senator Robert A. Taft in intellect, as "a person who knew what you were going to say before you said it."[20] Nixon's criticism of the Social Security benefit increase bill, supported by Mills, signaled trouble ahead for Nixon's so-called "New American Revolution" of proposed programs, focusing national attention on Mills' policy positions, not Nixon's.

Mills seldom consulted professional economists. Elliott Janeway and Raymond J. Saulnier, Council of Economic Advisers chairmen under Eisenhower, had ready access to him during their tenures in office and afterward. Kennedy-Johnson economists Gardner Ackley, Arthur Okun, and Walter Heller seldom saw Mills outside a hearing room.[21]

Mills frequently consulted former tax commissioner Sheldon S. Cohen on taxes and former Health, Education and Welfare Secretary Wilbur Cohen on Social Security, as well as Anthony Solomon on international trade. Mills had special regard for business leaders whom he met regularly through committee work, especially those from Arkansas and its Second Congressional District.

Mills relied most heavily on his own broadly trusted staffs on Ways and Means and on the Joint Committee on Internal Revenue Taxation to feed him news of opinions voiced by leading economists. The two staffs, while small, made up one of the Hill's ablest such teams. Laurence N. "Larry" Woodworth, on the joint committee's staff since 1944, was chief counsel, brilliant. Woodworth was valued by GOP members as well as Democrats for his integrity and neutrality. Another was John M. Martin, a lawyer and expert on government operations, with Ways and Means since 1956. Their approach to economic issues was pragmatic, shy of innovation, until a consensus for change began to emerge.[22] The economist who seemed most influential with Mills was Dr. Norman Ture with the Brookings Institution, a widely respected scholar on monetary policy.

"Taxes should not go up and down like hemlines," Mills said. Later, Mills was more receptive to anti-cyclical actions and his dramatic conversion to the idea that a tax cut could help eliminate budget deficits carried the day in Congress.[23] In 1962, he was firmly against it, according to Kennedy administration officials who tried to sell him on the notion. As business leaders began to accept and support the idea, Mills became willing to try it.[24]

Mills told George Herman on "Face the Nation" his view on tax reduction: "There'll be no tax reduction under any circumstances, in my opinion, without the administration supporting the idea. And in order to get me to go along, there must be this incomes policy established; there must be this willingness to reduce the spending side, and get the government out of the business of trying to buoy the economy, and get the private sector back. The private sector can do it; government may, but it takes too long and it's too expensive."[25]

The usually reserved and reticent Mills in 1971 scheduled at least 100 speeches around the country, including California, Wisconsin, Florida, and New Hampshire, important primary states. Some 100 House members were ready to endorse his candidacy for president.[26] Mills remembered 1968, when the Democratic Party lost its unity, as Senators Eugene J. McCarthy (D-Minnesota) and Robert F. Kennedy (D-New York) engaged in a highly charged campaign throughout the primaries. Since 1968, Mills had built a strong domestic program on which candidates could wage successful campaigns for the presidency and Congress. He thought people "want us to move—to see that those who are qualified and able to work and are on welfare go to work."[27]

Meanwhile in Congress, Russell Long (D-Louisiana), chairman of the Senate Finance Committee, asked the House to take quick action to raise Social Security benefits. The House did not respond. Long maneuvered to force Ways and Means and the House to act by offering a Social Security increase amendment to HR 4690, the bill to increase the debt ceiling.[28] Long's amendment proposed a 10 percent increase in Social Security payments, a $100 minimum benefit, and increases in earning limitations. It passed by a vote of 82-0 in the Senate.[29] The same day the Senate passed HR 4690, after approving these amendments by a vote of 80-0.[30] It did not go that fast in the House or in Ways and Means.

The House, on March 3, 1971, by a 228-162 roll-call vote had passed historic HR 4690 increasing to $430 billion the national debt ceiling past its existing $395 billion, the largest single increase since World War II. The bill's debt ceiling portion included a provision allowing the Treasury to sell up to $10 billion in long-term bonds, without regard to the existing 4.25 percent interest ceiling in effect for 53 years. An amendment, offered by Wright Patman (D-Texas), to delete the interest rate ceiling provision was defeated by a vote of 181-212, representing a great victory for Mills.

Mills, the bill's floor manager, led off debate on HR 4690:

> I don't relish the opportunity to be a proponent of an upward
> adjustment of the debt ceiling. However, an upward adjustment is
> necessary if the federal government is to pay its obligations. A vote
> against the bill is not an economy vote ... This is no time for regret.
> That time was when we were considering authorizations. I have
> the greatest concern about what would happen if the U.S. Treasury
> couldn't pay its bills. A real "money panic" could possibly occur.[32]

The American Bankers Association, U.S. Savings and Loan League, National
Association of Real Estate Board, and the Investment Bankers Association of
America agreed with Mills and supported repeal of the 4.25 percent interest
rate ceiling on government bonds. Groups opposing repeal included the United
Auto Workers, Rural Electric Cooperatives, Consumer Federation of America,
National Rural Housing Coalition, National Farmers Union and the National
Council of Senior Citizens.[33][34]

No change was made by conferees in debt ceiling provisions, with both
chambers' actions identical.

On the Social Security provisions, conferees under Mills' leadership accepted
the Senate's 10 percent benefit increase, but reduced the $100 minimum benefit
to $70.40 (a 10 percent increase over the previous $64 minimum) and made
several other modifications.

On March 16, 1971, the House adopted the conference report 360 to 34.
On March 16, 1971, the Senate adopted the report 76 to 0.[35] Mills would have
supported a big increase in the minimum benefit for those who had only Social
Security benefits, but, at that time, such a mechanism had not been designed.[36]

HEALTHCARE/WELFARE

Nixon proposed a national health care program. Mills promised to keep an
open mind on it; however, he didn't like people no longer being responsible for
making a contribution. At the time, participants were paying $5.30 per month
for insurance against doctor bills.

> Personally, I think it is really important that we retain this
> requirement that people make some payment, regardless of how
> small, with respect to their medical costs. Otherwise, we would
> lose any restraining influence upon growth of these programs.[37]

Nixon's proposal became HR 1, the Family Assistance Plan, which remained
in the Senate for more than a year because of controversy over welfare reform.
The Senate approved HR 1 and the conference dropped all family welfare

provisions. The final version of HR 1 contained provisions federalizing and consolidating adult public assistance programs for needy, aged, blind, and disabled persons in a new "Supplemental Security Income" (SSI) program.

Debate on HR 1 dealt mostly with welfare provisions, passing the House 288-132 on June 22, 1971,[38] and the Senate 68-5 finally on October 5, 1972.[39] On October 17, 1972, the House adopted the conference report 305-1[40] and the Senate adopted it 61-74.

ECONOMY [41]

With inflation heating up in 1971, Nixon asked Congress for wage and price controls, a 10 percent import surcharge, a 10 percent cut in foreign aid, and a tax cut favoring business to stimulate economic recovery, including re-instatement of an investment tax credit and added depreciation benefits. Mills opposed "trickle down" economics and he scaled down the administration's requested 10 percent investment tax credit to 7 percent, granted depreciation benefits, and doubled deductions for individuals. It was one of the largest tax cuts in history to that point. The final bill, almost identical to Mills' bill, reduced revenue an estimated $25.9 billion over a three-year period.

In early 1971, Mills proposed tax breaks for business and low-income individuals to stimulate the economy. He spoke to Utah Democrats, indicating Nixon's economic plan failed to cut unemployment or curb inflation. Thus, Mills proposed reviving the investment tax credit, allowing businesses to charge off, against their taxes, a part of their equipment investment, and increasing the minimum standard deduction, helping reduce the tax bill for low-income taxpayers.[42] When asked if this tax reduction for business would work politically, Mills' response was enormously positive: "Yes, it can be done. We did it in 1962. In any event, we have scheduled tax cuts for individuals occurring this year and 1972 and 1973."[43]

Mills justified capital gains relief, saying, "It's pretty hard to justify treating a capital gain differently from ordinary income. I've never felt there is anything more sacrosanct about profit from the sale of an asset than from the sweat of your brow."[44] To make these cuts possible, Mills suggested a spending ceiling and an "effective incomes policy" to hold down price and wage increases.[45] Mills suggested wage and price guidelines. Nixon had resisted up to that point, but yielded to Mills' advice after Mills cited how well the spending limit had worked during LBJ's administration, when it achieved a balanced budget.

On December 9, 1971, Congress passed an economic stimulus bill reducing business and individual taxes.[46] Final action came when the House, by 321-75, and Senate, 71-6, adopted a conference report,[47] delaying beyond the 1972 election the effective date of a controversial rider, added by the Senate, to create a public fund financing presidential election campaigns. The president had threatened to veto the bill unless the campaign funding amendment and Senate revenue-cutting amendments were dropped or made effective only after the 1972 election.[48] Ways and Means on September 29 reported HR 10947 (House Report 92-533), incorporating the president's tax proposals for implementing his new economic policy.

As reported, the bill reinstated the 7 percent investment tax credit, rather than setting the investment credit rate at 10 percent for the first year and 5 percent the second year, as requested in Nixon's August 15 message. The committee increased individual tax exemptions to $675 for 1971 and to $750 in 1972 and increased the low-income allowance for taxpayers to $1,300 for 1972. It repealed the 7 percent excise tax on automobiles and the 10-percent excise on light trucks.[49]

Mills' bill passed largely intact. It cost the Treasury $1.3 billion, compared to Nixon's, which would have cost $2.1 billion according to congressional projections.

INTERNATIONAL TRADE

Never enthusiastic about artificial quotas, Mills delayed protectionist legislation while he worked out his own textile agreement with the Japanese industry spokesmen, not the government:

> The textile people didn't support what I got from them, but I did finally get them to cut back on their shipment of textiles to us. I had a very cordial relationship with the Japanese manufacturers in those days, and they'd believe anything I told them. I just told them, "If you don't do something, I'm going to have to impose some limitations on it. I don't want to do that." And they agreed with me. I'll tell you, there's a fellow named Tony Solomon who was in the State Department at the time, who helped me on that. But then in Johnson's day, we worked out an agreement on stainless steel. I got an agreement on that, to limit importation of stainless steel to us. I never had any argument with him about that; I don't know that he was even trying to get it. But I know Nixon was mad as hell at me about this thing."[50]
>
> The fact that I could get an agreement that he couldn't. Only two times did I have differences with Nixon, and one was about the amount of money that he owed in taxes and then this situation.[51]

Nixon, joining the U.S. textile industry in criticism, promptly declined the Japanese offer. Mills challenged the administration to do better and continued his warm contacts with Japanese business toward his goal of reducing the international trade deficit.[52] In fact, he successfully waged a "one-man campaign to avert an international trade war."[53]

PRESIDENTIAL POLITICS

Nixon, doubting Mills' resolution to firmly discourage the mounting efforts to draft him as a Democratic presidential candidate, criticized Mills for pushing through a combination of Social Security and payroll tax increases, as overly generous, and called for an immediate tax increase to pay for them.

While Mills did not reply publicly to Nixon on Social Security, he knew the president was preparing to run against the Democratic Congress, denouncing its actions at every opportunity.

In 1971, Mills spoke to the Missouri Bar Association in Kansas City about congressional developments, and made a sentimental visit to Independence, Missouri, at Bess Truman's invitation. Mills arrived at 8 a.m. to find former President Truman "dressed and looking dapper." Mrs. Truman indicated he had lost interest in life, so Mills tried to rally his spirits by reminiscing and assuring Truman of his place in history.[54]

Mills described the visit as invigorating for Truman and inspiring for himself. Truman, Mills said, was "the president I most admired" because Truman always did what he thought was right, regardless of consequence. Mills foresaw that, though Truman's popularity was barely over 25 percent at the time he left office, history would treat him kindly. Truman always advised Mills, "Do what you think is right and you will never have any trouble justifying it. If you do what people want at a particular time, you won't be able to justify it."

Mills also visited former President Johnson on the LBJ Ranch in Johnson City, Texas:

> The president found out I was going to be down there speaking to a joint session of the legislature and asked me if I'd come out to the Ranch, said he'd fly me out there. And he did. The agreement was I was going to stay about 15 minutes, because I had a plane to go back. And I stayed an hour and a half. Couldn't get away. About the time I'd get up to leave, he'd say "Come on, I want to show you something else." He'd get in that danged convertible Lincoln, with the top down, take off at 70 miles an hour across a field, with no road or nothing, to show me something. Finally ended up he had to take me by and show me the graves of his mother and father where he'd placed them there. But he was waiting for photographers to come. He was the darndest guy in the world about pictures. I never saw anybody that loved pictures like he did."

Johnson and Mills discussed Nixon's welfare program.

> [Patrick] Moynihan, New York senator, was in the White House
> and developed the program. I was all for it and passed it through
> the House twice; couldn't get the Senate to take it. Along the lines
> now of what they're proposing to do: educate people to work,
> how to wake up in the morning, get ready to go to work ... to try
> to reduce the welfare load. It costs more money in the beginning,
> and that's why some people were against it then, including
> California Governor Ronald Reagan, incidentally.

> I called him from Miami because I wanted Hubert Humphrey to
> have a chance again, and I wanted Ted Kennedy to be his running
> mate ... This was the ticket I had worked out, and I had it worked
> out with everybody there, practically, that had any influence.
> Enough of the South would have supported that ticket. Sure they
> would. They loved Hubert, in spite of his liberalism. You couldn't
> help but like him, you know. He came to my state after he'd
> been vice president, after he went to Russia. He was very warmly
> received and widely loved.[55]

Rampant speculation about a possible Mills candidacy ran the gambit:

> That Mills permitted the prospect of his candidacy to get Nixon
> to work with him more closely on legislation.

- That Mills seriously intended to offer himself for nationwide
  office.
- That Mills was screening for someone else, perhaps Senators
  Hubert Humphrey, Henry "Scoop" Jackson, and others.
- That Mills wanted to keep the South in the Democratic
  Party, curbing influence of Governor George C. Wallace
  (D-Alabama).
- That Mills could strengthen his hand in the national party
  affairs, and dictate platform policies at the convention.
- That, with a sizable bloc of Mills-pledged delegates, he could
  barter to nominate a candidate of his choice or become a
  compromise candidate in case of a deadlock.
- That Mills could name the vice presidential candidate as price
  for throwing his support behind another candidate.

Speaking of efforts by Burke and other House members, Mills told the

Congressional Quarterly: "They are trying to put together a draft movement. I do not believe it has the remotest chance of succeeding, but in the event that the impossible should occur, I would naturally accept the nomination. I would not want it, but I would be the hardest-working candidate the party ever had. This party has been good to me, and I owe it a lot."[56] Meanwhile, he made a Southern speaking tour, extending political acquaintances in states, which, coincidentally, would hold presidential primaries in 1972.

In Nashville, Tennessee, he reminded newsmen, "I have said I do not want my name on the ballot." "However," he smiled, "I'm in the hands of my friends."[57]

Joseph Alsop explored Mills' possible candidacy, noting what had made him "a major power in Washington" was a combination of "immense knowledge, immensely hard work, genuine wisdom, and a very cold way of assessing hard facts."[58] Alsop believed Mills unlikely to receive the nomination because his civil rights record was "nearly identical" to that of Senator J. William Fulbright.[59]

In Arkansas, Mills went on statewide television to support Dale Bumpers, a progressive Democrat, for governor. Mills asked voters to turn away from the American Independent Party's candidate for Arkansas governor, in spite of their having given Alabama Governor George Wallace (the AIP nominee) a plurality in the 1968 Arkansas presidential vote. Mills quietly encouraged Democratic leaders in Arkansas, as well as other Southern states, to tighten their election laws, making it more difficult for Wallace's party to qualify for listing as Democrats on state ballots.[60] Meanwhile, Mills vigorously supported a new voter registration law, easing African-Americans access to the ballot.

Mills said he would consider an African-American running mate, if he decided to announce for the presidency in 1972. "I wouldn't care [about] the color of hair, eyes, skin. I would look, instead, for the very strongest candidate to run for vice president."[61] For a time, he and New York City Congresswoman Shirley Chisholm considered forming a joint ticket. On the vice presidency, Mills said: "I wouldn't [take the nomination] now. I wouldn't want to close the door. But I'd rather be chairman of the Ways and Means Committee."[62]

Mills was interviewed on NBC-TV's "Meet the Press," where he predicted that, if somehow he were nominated, he could defeat Nixon. Mills said Nixon had made "a number of mistakes," leaving him "caught on the horns of dilemma." With both unemployment and inflation running rampant, Mills said, Nixon had blundered so badly, that any Democrat nominated would unseat him.[63]

When Nixon sharply criticized Senator Edmund S. Muskie (D-Maine) for saying he did not think the American people were ready to accept an African-American on a presidential ticket,[64] Mills agreed with Nixon.

Mills kept Arkansas atop his agenda, securing $1 million from the Economic Development Administration for the proposed $2.6 million Joseph T. Robinson Convention Center in Little Rock. Then Mills secured more funds from the

Ozarks Regional Commission.[65] At the Little Rock Chamber of Commerce, Mills was introduced as "the next president of the United States," and bumper stickers circulated, proclaiming "Mills for President."[66]

On June 6, 1971, on "Meet the Press," Lawrence E. Spivak asked Mills about the presidency:

Spivak: Mr. Chairman, you say that you don't think there is much chance that you would be nominated, but there are many people who think you might be nominated. In the remote instance that you were nominated and you were elected, do you think, if you were chosen, that you could handle the job?

Mills: Mr. Spivak, I frankly wonder whether any one person anymore has the capacity mentally and physically to handle this most onerous job. I am not one to exaggerate my own virtues. I think I know something about the operation of government. I have been in it a long time. How good I could be, I wouldn't know, but I have no interest in it.[67]

ECONOMIC PHILOSOPHY

Mills' economic philosophy was widely analyzed by press and officialdom. In a speech at Ogden, Utah, Mills revealed his thinking in a five-point economic "game plan":[68]

1. Investment tax credit for business outlays in new plants and equipment: "An expansion in real investment in new plant and equipment would directly increase employment, reduce the number of labor-surplus areas and reduce the unemployment rate."[69]

2. Increase the minimum standard deduction for low-income families: Mills saw that low-income families spend all or most of their incomes, so giving them a tax break would increase consumer spending, even more than advancing the date for personal-exemption increases, already scheduled to take effect in 1972 and 1973.[70]

3. Mills opposed other tax relief, unless spending cuts and new inflation controls were part of the package.

4. Incomes policy to hold down wage and prices: "I completely disagree with [Treasury] Secretary Connally in his rejection of an effective incomes policy, which would really hold down rates of increase in prices and wages in the period ahead."[71]

5. Spending controls: Mills called it "imperative" that any tax reduction be linked with "appropriate limitations and cutbacks in federal spending increases. A ceiling on federal expenditures

at this time is in the best interest of the economy and would give the private sector an opportunity to do the expanding rather than having expansion occur through government expenditures.[72] Let me make it completely clear that I think economic policies of this administration are failing and that I agree neither with the conclusions reached by economic spokesmen of the administration nor the medicine which they are proposing. It seems clear to me that both the unemployment and inflation rates we face are unacceptable. Our economic policies are just not working."[73]

DRAFT MILLS GOES PUBLIC

With $200 in bumper stickers and a little help from friends, Congressman James Burke (D-Massachusetts), second only to Mills in seniority on Ways and Means, filed Mills for the 1972 Democratic presidential primary in Massachusetts. Eighty congressmen had endorsed Mills by June 1971, according to Burke, who admitted leaking endorsements piecemeal to boost campaign momentum.[74] Outside Washington, Burke said, he took an informal, admittedly unscientific, poll of 300 likely voters. Sixty-five percent chose Mills over Nixon.[75]

The *Chicago Tribune* endorsed Mills for president.[76] [77] [78]

Attorney General Joe Purcell, chairman of the Arkansas Democratic Party State Committee, announced a major statewide rally in Little Rock's Barton Coliseum on Thursday, August 26, 1971, to honor Mills. The gathering turned out to be the largest crowd for a political event in the state's history (11,000 inside and 5,000 outside)—until election night 1992, when Governor Bill Clinton was elected president. Governor Dale Bumpers, Senators J. William Fulbright and John L. McClellan, and Representatives David Pryor and Bill Alexander, as well as former Republican Governor Winthrop Rockefeller, praised Mills profusely. Congressional dignitaries and national labor union leaders heaped praise on Mills. Speaker of the House Carl Albert capped the evening: "Mills could hold with outstanding distinction any public office within the United States. His legislative contributions in the House are unsurpassed. Wilbur Mills, by any yardstick, is the greatest chairman of the Ways and Means Committee in my time if not in all history." Following the event, a reporter asked Mills, "Are you or are you not running for president?" Mills chuckled, "I am not."

Then, on "Face the Nation," Mills emphasized, "I have a great respect for President Nixon, and I have a degree of sympathy, certainly a great degree of sympathy for the predicament that he finds himself in. It isn't so much the president that I'm talking about, certainly not as a person, not as an individual, but the president's policies with respect to certain matters I find myself in disagreement with."[79]

In October 1971, the draft Mills campaign opened a headquarters in Suite 805 of the Madison Building at 1155 Fifteenth Street, NW, with a largely volunteer staff of 30. It was six blocks north of the White House. Charles Ward of Ward Bus Company of Conway and George Jernigan, Little Rock attorney, were in charge. The same month, a three-quarter page advertisement ran in the *Washington Post*, inviting contributions, volunteers, and orders for yard signs and bumper stickers.[80]

Hopping in and out of small planes as Mills' travel increased put pressure on his back, causing pain and accompanying stress. Mills self-medicated both ailments with increased doses of alcohol.

Mills never accepted honoraria, happily quipping, "I never charge $1,000 for a $100 speech."[81] He did accept transportation, especially during this national speaking tour. Sears, Roebuck and Company flew Mills to Chicago for a speech to the Illinois legislature and to Kensett afterward. Kerr-McGee Corporation, founded by the late Senator Robert Kerr, flew him to Oklahoma City to address the state legislature. John A. Cooper Company of Bella Vista provided a plane to Baton Rouge for a speech to the Louisiana legislature.[82]

Mills courted labor and wrote in their monthly publication, The *American Federalist*, "It has become commonplace to say that unemployment compensation is the nation's first line of defense against hazards of unemployment. Trite as that may sound, it is nevertheless an undeniable fact, as recent events have again proved. Welfare programs, on the other hand, are the final defense or last resort against unemployment, and rightly so."[83]

In Ames, Iowa, Mills spoke on Nixon's farm policy, "really to speak to Nixon," he said. On October 2, 1971, he was the featured speaker at an Iowa Cooperative Institute Month Rally, the first event held in James H. Hilton Coliseum on the Iowa State University's campus. He touched on the economy, inflation, and unemployment–with emphasis on farm policy.[84] Later, when the Watergate Committee investigated corporate contributions to Nixon's presidential campaign, it examined Democratic campaigns as well. Since Mills had become a candidate for a few months in 1972, his 1971 activities were examined. The Iowa Rally came six months after Congress had made corporate contributions illegal, so the committee studied whether the Associated Milk Producers, Inc., had followed its tradition of contributing directly to candidates or had changed its procedure when Congress changed the law. Court records showed that $29,132 of the rally's cost was provided by AMPI. Gerald Pepper, the sponsoring organization's executive director, contended the rally promoted a cooperative movement, not a particular candidate.[85] They found Mills did not solicit support for himself and the rally preceded his announced candidacy by four months. They found that the policy positions and the speech were Mills' historic positions on these issues.

Mills pointed to the first world trade imbalance since 1893 and the highest federal budget deficit in any two consecutive years since World War II.[86] Mills was also concerned on foreign policy direction and, when asked in a *Nation's Business* interview, "What changes would you make in foreign policy?" Mills replied, "We must make up our minds that we cannot continue, because of lack of resources, to stand as the world's only principal policeman and pay the cost in manpower and dollars. It is too much for the rest of the world to ask of us. In my opinion we don't have any more to lose than many countries which are not carrying their part of the load, or any part of the load. We need to be more cognizant, frankly, of economic consequences of foreign policy than we have been for the last 40 years . . . We have given up far more on the economic side than we ever received in return. We must return to the old doctrine of "Yankee trader."[87]

With Russia, he proposed a theory and a plan, "I think peaceful relations are more apt to follow peaceful trade relations than most any other event or occurrence. If we could work out some arrangement in the area of consumer goods which Russia is in need of and we have in super abundance, and receive from Russia the raw materials that we need and that we do not have here in the United States, then I think that such an arrangement would be advantageous to both countries."[88]

HEALTH INSURANCE

Mills opened hearings on a dozen or so legislative proposals to restructure the nation's health care system.[89] Mills believed that a health care bill–if ready for legislative action soon–would give Democrats a potent issue for the 1972 campaign. Opening the hearing, Mills said, "No one knows now what the final bill, which the committee develops, will look like." Health, Education and Welfare Secretary Elliot L. Richardson was leadoff witness.

A bill by Senator Edward M. Kennedy (D-Massachusetts) and the administration bill by Senator Wallace F. Bennett (R-Utah) raised key questions, according to Gene Goss:

• Would the government take over health insurance or would private insurers provide coverage under federal supervision?

• Could costs be cut and health care be improved by organizations providing prepaid, group-practice medicine?

• What was the most effective form of preventive health care, and how expensive would such a program be?

• What about coverage of related areas such as dental care,

psychiatric treatment, and prescription drugs?

• How much public accountability should be designed into a public health-care system?

• How much will it cost taxpayers and employers to reshuffle the country's health-delivery system?

The comprehensive, universal Kennedy plan, costliest of those proposed, used a Social Security-type system to provide medical services to every citizen, with half the financing coming from general tax revenues, and the balance from payroll taxes. The plan included a 3.5 percent employer payroll levy and a tax on individual earnings. Health manpower would be strengthened and private health insurance largely eliminated. Fixed annual federal health budgets would be relied on to maintain cost controls. HEW estimated that total health expenditures in 1974 would be almost $114 billion–$11 billion from individual out-of-pocket payments and the bulk from federal tax revenue. Senator Kennedy disputed these HEW figures and presented Ways and Means with his own cost data: "The increased federal taxes required by my bill would easily be made up by money the taxpayer would save on insurance, hospitals, doctors, and other related items."

The administration plan mandated health insurance for all employed Americans. Employers would be required to provide coverage for employees, either through their own insurance plans or private health insurance policies. Employers eventually would pay 75 percent of premiums. Private health insurers would provide most of the coverage, under federal standards. Delivery of efficient, less costly care by health maintenance organizations (HMOs)–comprehensive, prepaid group practices like the California-based Kaiser Permanente Plan, would save funding requirements.

Mills sought a compromise between Kennedy and Nixon with a complex plan, entertaining national health insurance plans advocated by the American Medical Association, the health insurance industry, the American Hospital Association, and the American Nursing Home Association. Mills declined comment on any particular plan, but pushed for stringent cost controls. Having helped design Medicare-Medicaid, Mills was determined to keep the lid on medical costs. Nixon threatened to veto Mills' tax bill. Mills saw this as a "polite way to put on pressure." Senator Long agreed. The House version, shepherded through by Mills, was acceptable to Nixon, but the Senate version added some expensive provisions, such as an $800 personal income tax exemption to parents of college students. Mills, having chaired the conference committee, agreed with the Senate version, and calmly observed that if Nixon vetoed this bill, there would be no tax legislation that year. Nixon signed.

CHAPTER 10

THE PRESIDENTIAL ELECTION
1972

Confined to his home in Kensett during the 1971 Christmas and New Year holidays with painful back trouble, Mills faced a turning point in his career and his life. It was a black omen. Mills described his increasing physical pain, "The doctors call it a muscle spasm. It is painful when it happens to you and it takes a little time to get over it. I am much better now, but I still am not free of all pain."[1] Mills was treated at Searcy's White County Memorial Hospital on December 22 and 23, 1971, followed by therapeutic treatments at home. He told everybody he looked forward to a walk downtown or a short drive into the countryside, two of his favorite relaxations. "I may even go to my Searcy office a little bit," he was hoping.[2]

Mills' severe back pain had set in the day before Congress' Christmas recess. Refusing to change his plans, Mills flew home to Arkansas. "I suffered all the way down on the plane."[3] A severe muscle spasm in his back had once before kept him in Washington during the holidays.[4] This time, he was determined to be home in Kensett for Christmas. All four grandchildren were scheduled to come from Connecticut and Maryland.[5] The press wanted to know: How would this untimely and excruciating muscle spasm affect the Draft Mills for President momentum? Mills quashed fears, "It won't have any effect at all. I know I'll be all right in another few days. I have had a sore back before and have lived over it. You know, a fellow sometimes can get too much weight on his shoulders and his back will give way on him."[6] Later that January, though, Mills' administrative assistant and chief of staff, Gene Goss, had to call doctors in Houston to cancel a Mills speech at their conference. They asked, "What will we do?" Goss remembered fondly wanting to tell them: "Take an aspirin and call me in the morning!"

It was during a similar, earlier time of self-imposed convalescence, many pain relievers, and substantial alcohol that Mills was approached by Joe Johnson, Warren Bass, Charles Ward, Dave Parr, and other close friends to urge him to allow his name to be placed on primary ballots in selected states and in nomination at the Miami convention. Mills recalled that they came away believing he had agreed. Parr remembered such a visit and recalled no reservations by Mills. Closest friends sometimes joked about learning from him that "yes" can mean "no" and "no" can mean "yes." Parr even recalled telling Mills once that he was tired of being in first grade. Mills was somewhat bewildered and said, "But look where you are." Mills returned to Congress and the speaking circuit fairly soon after the New Year.

SOCIAL SECURITY

Early in 1972, Mills introduced HR 13320, providing an immediate Social Security benefit increase of 20 percent.[7] The House did not concur right away. After some wrangling, Mills' motion that the House concur with a Senate amendment, granting a 20 percent Social Security benefit increase, as well as annual automatic cost-of-living adjustments, was accepted 302 (108-R, 194-D) to 35 (28-R, 7-D).[8] The Social Security Amendments of 1972, signed into law October 30 by Nixon, had been fashioned and fostered by Mills. Rowland Evans and Robert Novak, nationally syndicated columnists, assessed this effort in light of Mills' brief flirtation with presidential politics: "The highly unusual exchange, opening the closed-door meeting of the House Ways and Means Committee on February 24, showed how rapidly that most prestigious and most important committee of Congress is changing now that its chairman, Rep. Wilbur D. Mills of Arkansas, is an active candidate for president." The column noted that Representative Barber Conable (R-New York) argued with Mills, requesting hearings on Mills' Social Security proposal.

Mills compiled quite a record by raising Old Age Survivors' and Disability Insurance (OASDI) benefits three times from 1969 to 1972 for a 45 percent total increase, more than during any other similar period in history. The 1972 amendments (HR 1), were more far-reaching than any Social Security legislation since 1965, when Medicare was enacted. The 1972 law provided increased benefits for widows and widowers, long a prime goal of Mills. It also increased earnings permitted without a benefits reduction; a reduced waiting period for disability benefits; and an extension of Medicare protection to disabled beneficiaries on Social Security for at least two years. OASDI tax rate increases were scheduled for future years to keep the Social Security Trust Fund actuarially sound. OASI went from a minimal safeguard to an adequate pension during these years. For many years, this had been an objective of the Social Security Administration career staff, led by Commissioner Robert Ball. It had also been an objective of many in Congress. Mills' brilliant strategies made it possible, enhancing his reputation as a living icon for lawyers and businessmen, whose fortunes revolved around the Internal Revenue code. The usual opposition from traditional opponents of Social Security increases in the business world was tempered by fear of offending Mills and of weakening Nixon, who, though deploring certain increases, dared not oppose them openly. After Nixon's re-election, he only dismissed Ball, the Social Security administrator.

TAXATION [9]

In an unprecedented challenge to traditional procedure, causing a little feeling of foreboding, two House members effectively blocked consideration of 18 of 22 minor tax bills called up under the unanimous consent procedure by Mills.[10] Known as "members' bills," these were proposed by House members rather than drafted by committee, and were usually approved with little or no debate. Most bills of this type were intended to correct tax inequities affecting a single company, industry, or interest, and these bills usually proposed authorizing tax breaks, sometimes exempting millions of dollars from federal taxes, to correct alleged inequities.

Wright Patman (D-Texas), chairman of the Banking and Currency Committee, unexpectedly attacked the unanimous consent procedure used by Mills. Under this procedure, bills are passed in a one-step process by voice vote, if no objections are heard. Patman noted that some of the bills involved bank holding companies, his panel's purview. Despite this setback, Mills achieved gradual abolition of 54 tax loopholes or special deductions, including the oil depletion allowance.[11] Senate Majority Leader Mike Mansfield (D-Montana) introduced its Senate companion.[12] Eighteen deductions would die each year, unless re-enacted, with estimated savings of $50 billion by 1974.

Mills saw an ongoing need for orderly and systematic review of all tax laws.[13] He wisely included deliberative discussions with business leaders on the impact of tax policy on their day-to-day decisions affecting the nation's economy.

PRESIDENTIAL POLITICS

There was intense speculation on whether Mills would enter primaries beyond Massachusetts and Rhode Island, especially New York.[14] Mills continued to be welcomed warmly by the press to the presidential sweepstakes: The *Wall Street Journal's* editorial page called Mills "among the first rank of the nation's political minds" and enthused that he "has compiled an awesome record of responsible public service."[15] The *New York Times* welcomed "the addition of such a power as Wilbur D. Mills" to the presidential race. "His mastery of . . . complex subjects has become a legend in the House."[16] Joseph Kraft told Gene Goss the Mills effort was "the most consequential boomlet in progress." The *New Republic,* impressed that Mills was not an embodiment of the antebellum South, ran a sympathetic look at Mills' presidential aspirations by Paul Wieck.

Meanwhile, Senator Ted Kennedy (D-Massachusetts) came to Little Rock to praise Mills at the National Conference for Christians and Jews annual award banquet, calling him, "one of the greatest giants" and "a man whose reputation surpasses that of any other senator or congressman."[17] At that ceremony, the NCCJ named Mills its Humanitarian of the Year.

Consistent in his denial of interest in any higher office, Mills often bluntly denied having any interest in the presidency or speakership, "If I had wanted to be speaker, I had a chance when John McCormack retired. Many Democrats said then that if I wanted it, I could have it. I think they exaggerated the situation but that's what they said. I've never had any interest in it. I'd rather create legislation than be speaker."[18]

LEGISLATIVE ACHIEVEMENTS

The 92nd Congress (1971–1972) was productive for Ways and Means even with Mills distracted with presidential politics throughout. During this time, his suffering from back pain increased. So did his intake of alcohol and pain relievers. Mills' legislative victories included:

- State and Local Fiscal Assistance Act of 1972, Public Law 92-512, a landmark in federal-state-local fiscal relations. The legislation distributed $5.3 billion in revenue sharing to state and local governments in 1972, with larger amounts projected for future years.

- Revenue Act of 1971, Public Law 92-178, provided tax reduction and tax incentives to grow the economy, increase jobs, and relieve the distress inflation placed on those with modest incomes. It also enhanced international trade, restored the 7 percent investment credit, increased the personal exemption, and repealed the excise tax on cars and light trucks.

- Mills' HR 1, the Social Security Amendments of 1972, Public Law 92-603, approved October 30, contained the most far-reaching provisions of any Social Security enactment since 1965, when Medicare was initially approved.

- Medicaid changes included adding coverage for the disabled and for those needing long-term dialysis.

- Under Social Security, it provided new help for the aged, blind, and disabled, so that virtually every aged person would live above the poverty level. Because of Senate action, however, HR 1, as finally enacted, did not contain the family assistance plan Mills' House version had sought.

Mills opposed indexing of Social Security benefits in 1972, as he always had, "[indexing] got us into all that trouble with Social Security, when we got into double-digit inflation. It just wasn't financed for that. The final argument I made was that Congress would never have the opportunity to raise benefits in the future. There's always a lot of political benefit out of raising Social Security benefits. Before indexing, we did it every two years."[19]

FEDERAL DEBT

The *New York Times* and *Congressional Quarterly Almanac* described the debate that spring,[20] when Congress cleared the president's bill (HR 12910–PL 92-250), authorizing a temporary $20 billion rise in the public debt ceiling–to $450 billion–through June 30, 1972. Mills said that the national debt stood above $429.9 billion, dramatically close to the $430 billion limit imposed by Congress in 1971. He refused to attach his tax-reform bill to the bill increasing the federal debt limit. During debt ceiling hearings before Ways and Means, Mills held firm that his tax reform plan would get separate hearings. Doing so added drama and uncertainty to the legislative agenda for the tax-reform bill, debt-ceiling bill, and revenue-sharing bill. Renegade members considered attaching reform proposals to debt ceiling and/or revenue-sharing legislation without Mills' concurrence. This kind of questioning and potential opposition to the chairman was a new development.

Meanwhile, the administration asked that the debt ceiling be increased from its temporary level of $450 billion by $15 billion, necessary for the government to operate through February 1973. This $465 billion request was $15 billion less than the administration's previous projection, made possible by higher-than-expected tax collections. The possibility that Congress might raise the debt ceiling to only $450 billion–permitting the government to operate through October–was raised by Representative Burke, who sometimes reflected Mills' thinking. Burke was serving at the time as chairman of the Draft Mills for President Campaign. Burke's plan would require another increase in the ceiling just before the November presidential election, a rather open political move. When the time came, Mills defected from Democrats in the House and was able to clear HR 12910, authorizing a temporary $20 billion rise in the federal debt ceiling, less than half of Nixon's requested $50 billion. According to Treasury estimates, the $20 billion increase would meet federal borrowing needs until June.[21]

However, the Senate backed Nixon against the House on the debt ceiling, a rare defeat for Mills. The earlier defection on the debt ceiling issue dimmed Mills' chances for any higher position in the House leadership. Now Mills found himself trapped as chairman of Ways and Means, which was the main target of congressional reformers. Mills warned his colleagues: "If we abdicate here any willingness to join in controlling spending ... all... the president has to do is to go before the American people on television and ask for a Congress ... that will cooperate with him in getting control of spending."[22]

In a letter dated February 7, Mills reminded Nixon of his September 1971 promise to submit tax reform proposals to Congress in 1972, saying such a program must be sent to Congress no later than March 15 for action to be completed by adjournment.[23] "To me this matter is most important if there is to be a debt-ceiling increase" for next year, Mills wrote, referring to the extent of House opposition to repeated increases in the debt ceiling without corresponding increases in tax revenues.[24]

CIVIL RIGHTS

In civil rights legislation, Mills was not always a typical Southern congressman. The conservative coalition was a voting majority of Republicans and Southern Democrats who often combined to oppose a voting majority of Democrats from other regions. The House adopted the Erlenborn amendment, a bill to put teeth into court-ordered desegregation (backed by the administration), instead of the comprehensive committee bill, which would have given the Equal Economic Opportunity Commission power to issue cease-and-desist orders. The coalition prevailed by five votes, 200-195, on the first vote, taken by tellers and recorded, and by five votes on the follow-up roll call, 202-197 (R 133-29; ND 6-152; SD 63-16). Two southern votes by Mills and Mendel Davis (D-South Carolina) were cast against the so-called Southern Conservative Coalition and this administration bill.[25]

FAVORITE SON

"The Congressman from Kensett," a 25-minute documentary film was shown to the press. Scenes depicted a contemplative Mills sitting in a yard chair, at his modest Kensett bungalow reminding viewers of his connection to the common man. Other scenes followed "Mister Chairman," the man of action, through the halls of Congress, greeting national political figures. Another tracked him through an Arkansas crowd, displaying his easy knowledge of seemingly every voter present. The work of Draft Mills for President, it also included ringing endorsements given at the Appreciation Rally held August 25, 1971 at Barton Coliseum, in Little Rock. Mills had been interviewed for the film on August 28, 1971, on the front lawn of his wood-frame bungalow, its green roof striking against the clear Kensett sky. Mills spoke of busing, international trade, and reminisced about his rich life among the powerful and famous (such as playing ball with legendary New York Yankee catcher Bill Dickey, also of Kensett). He looked to a bright future for generations of kids and grandkids. William H.

Bowen, the Little Rock banker, and his 13-member Friends of Wilbur Mills Committee, raised money for the film and retained Faulkner and Associates, a Little Rock advertising firm, to produce it. The cost was not disclosed. Burgess Meredith, the grandfatherly motion picture star, narrated, and the background tune was "Brown Shoe," made popular at that time by the Beatles.

The first public showing was at 6:30 p.m. on January 19, 1972, on the ABC affiliate, KATV (Channel 7) in Little Rock, premiering as a public service. Jim Faulkner, president of Faulkner and Associates, made 35 copies, 20 of which were purchased by the Draft Mills for President Committee for showing across the nation. The original copy was presented to Mills.[26]

Mills' name had not been entered in the March 7 New Hampshire primary or March 14 Florida primary, but a very brief write-in campaign was conducted in New Hampshire. Mills was immediately recognized as "a highly popular candidate among conservative Southerners," but his steadfast unwillingness to formally declare for more than a year led most analysts to see him as a less-than-serious candidate and, instead, to see him as too late entering. However, the *New York Times* welcomed him with an editorial that was just short of an endorsement.[27] "Mills saw Massachusetts as a good test of his strength in a state completely and totally removed from Arkansas."[28] Some of his strongest supporters in Massachusetts were friends and family of the late President John F. Kennedy, House Speaker John McCormack, state legislator Michael Dukakis, and New Bedford Tax Assessor Henry Correia, all of whom were close friends. Mills knew television stations in New England served more than one state and that his TV spots in New Hampshire would be seen in Massachusetts and Rhode Island. Boston television stations ran ads for the New Hampshire campaign. Burke estimated that 600 volunteers worked in Mills' Massachusetts campaign. "We will more than likely wind up with 6,000 to 7,000 volunteers before the campaign is over," he predicted.[29]

Before opening the Massachusetts campaign headquarters, Mills met privately at his hotel room with 10 doctors, the "Massachusetts Doctors for Mills Committee." Afterward, Mills said, "They are anxious to help and we discussed ways that they could."[30] In a letter, doctors said they understood that Mills was determined to secure a national health insurance program, and they were reassured he was keeping an open mind about what should go into the bill. Mills saw his support in Massachusetts as crossing "the gamut of the entire economic structure," including labor leaders, the business community, and professionals.

"Yea Wilbur!" became the rousing cry of the Mills for President campaign in Massachusetts. It originated when Mills spoke at Boston College. According to Dick Sullivan of Boston, special events chairman for Mills' Massachusetts campaign, young people shouted "Yea Wilbur!" both at the outset of Mills' address, and again at its conclusion. When Mills rode in the South Boston St. Patrick's Day parade a few days later, people of all ages in the crowd took up the cry, "Yea Wilbur!" White-on-green "Yea Wilbur" bumper stickers and lapel patches appeared and became popular at speaking events nationally and were much in demand at the formal opening of Mills' campaign headquarters in Little Rock.[31]

Mills' lack of name recognition among voters, and the difficulties of House members in achieving nationwide coverage were reflected in his receiving fewer than 20,000 votes in the Massachusetts primary. McGovern, Muskie, Humphrey, and Wallace overwhelmed both Mills and Representative Shirley Chisholm of New York City.[32] Michael Dukakis, then a young Massachusetts state legislator, worked hard in his state and on Congressman Burke's national Draft Mills Steering Committee.[33] Meanwhile, many Tennessee Democrats hoped Mills could unite the fragmented Tennessee Democratic Party in their state's May 4 presidential primary. They wanted to prevent Wallace from winning the Tennessee primary, as he had in Florida. The *New York Times* described the race as the "Southern showdown of Wallace vs. Mills."[34] Four of Tennessee's five Democratic House members urged Mills to make the race. Shortly thereafter, Mills accommodated his colleagues and asked the secretary of state to place his name on the ballot.[35] Wallace won Florida by denouncing busing. He won 42 percent of Florida primary votes, 75 convention delegates, and swept every congressional district except the Miami district, which gave its six delegates to Humphrey.[36]

Tennessee Secretary of State Joe Carr placed all Florida candidates on the ballot in the Volunteer State's first-ever presidential primary. Tennessee state law provided that delegates were to be chosen at the state convention and were to vote on the first two ballots at the national convention for the winner of the primary, after which, they would be released to vote as they pleased. Rep. Richard Fulton (D-Tennessee), a member of Ways and Means and later mayor of Nashville, said that Mills "would do the party a great service" by campaigning actively in Tennessee: "The major problems confronting our country today deal with the areas in which he is an expert—economy, trade, tax reform."[37]

Mills campaigned only briefly in New Hampshire, receiving 4,000 write-in votes in the March 7 primary. Voting machines were new and election officials were just learning how to process write-in votes. In Manchester, where write-in procedures were established, Mills' garnered 28 percent of the vote.[38] Mills was "surprised that I got as many votes as I did. If you don't let people see you, they won't vote for you."[39]

Tennessee's Democratic primary ballot had been expanded to include Senators Jackson, McGovern, and Muskie, Mayor John V. Lindsay of New York City, Representative Chisholm, former Senators Eugene J. McCarthy of

Minnesota and Vance Hartke of Indiana, and Mayor Sam Yorty of Los Angeles. Senator Edward M. Kennedy of Massachusetts, although tentatively placed on the ballot, immediately asked that his name be withdrawn.[40] Mills instructed his campaign staff to seek pledges from uncommitted delegates. He also had his eye on second and subsequent ballot pledges from delegates whose first-ballot votes were committed to other candidates.[41] Mills thought Democrats needed a candidate who could mitigate divisiveness and help heal wounds inflicted in primaries battles. "I believe I could be that man."[42] Mills said, "I've said it's a long shot [to win the nomination]."[43] National analysts continued to say that he had a good chance to defeat President Nixon, if nominated.[44] The *New York Times* ran 93 articles covering Mills' presidential race in 1972, plus hundreds of other articles quoting him on policy positions.[45] He was the most heavily press-covered congressional leader for decades.

In January 1972, Mills and Kennedy requested removal of their names from the candidacy on the March 14 Florida presidential primary ballot. Later, state Democratic Chairman Jon Moyle simply said, "[Mills is] not a candidate."[46]

MIAMI CONVENTION

Mills said he would consider the vice presidential nomination if Senator Edward Kennedy were the nominee,[47] and predicted that McGovern would not win the nomination. He felt a deadlocked convention might turn to Kennedy.

At a press conference in Wichita, Kansas, Shirley Chisholm predicted the only way for Democrats to oust Nixon would be a Kennedy-Mills ticket.[48] Chisholm, the first African-American woman elected to the House, predicted, "... The ticket's going to be Kennedy-Mills. Nixon became president as a result of his Southern strategy, and if Democrats want to win we have to have a Southerner on the ticket–that's basic politics."49 She closed by emphasizing that Mills could pull the South together.50

Mills and Kennedy teamed up on a number of issues, as Mills related almost 20 years later:

> Ted Kennedy and I worked together ... and developed a
> compromise in 1972 that went before the Democratic Party
> platform committee, which, as I remember, adopted our national
> health insurance programs. Labor fell out with Ted about that;
> they thought he'd given in too much to me. My friends fell out
> with me because they thought I'd given in too much to Ted.
> But, what we were trying to do was to work out a program that
> we thought we could pass. Actually, the program was one that I
> think I could have passed in 1974, had I been myself, for I talked
> to President Ford about it and he supported it. I found myself

in committee just unable to bring the committee together, you know, on anything. This was unusual because I'd always been able to in the past. My mind was badly affected at the time and I didn't know it. My idea was this: If you're going to have a national health insurance certainly you're going to need everybody presently engaged in rendering of any kind of service that involves health. You've got to have them. You've got to have insurance companies, you can't wipe them out. You've got to include them all. You're going to need more than you have today in place of less. That was a softening of the relationship between doctor and government. Get somebody in between the agency you deal with and the government that you deal with, such as a doctors' organization, primarily Blue Cross/Blue Shield, something they set up themselves. That would be the intermediary. The whole theory that we had was the more services you make available, the more people you're going to need to provide those services. Don't want to rule any of them out nor wipe them out. Oh, no, this was not done as a sop to anybody, but in recognition of what we thought was a fact. They're all going to be needed. So you've got to work it out on the basis that they will participate. If they won't participate, you haven't got a program.[51]

In early convention action, the Credentials Committee stripped McGovern of 151 delegates from California because that state's "winner-take-all" system violated party rules.[52] When the full convention voted, the vote for seating the California delegates and counting them for McGovern was 1,618.22 for and 1,238.22 against.[53] McGovern found himself facing the first ballot with pledges of 1,485.35 delegates of 1,509 needed. Mills' draft organizers believed Governor John West of South Carolina had not worked several delegations as he had promised.[54] Thus, McGovern lacked only 24 votes for a first-ballot nomination. All hopes of stopping McGovern and, they speculated, of defeating Nixon, appeared dashed.[55] Those with Mills in Miami later reported that his reaction to Edmund Muskie's endorsement of McGovern at this crucial time, killing the "Stop McGovern" movement dead in its tracks, was "I'll be damned."[56]

McGovern later surmised, "I think by the time we had gotten to Miami, Wilbur Mills had given up, although he had considerable support in the business community and throughout the South."[57]

Humphrey, biggest loser in the California decision, immediately gave up and stepped aside. The convention then voted to oust the Illinois delegates, led by Mayor Richard J. Daley, Sr., with far-reaching consequences for the fall election. Daley's delegates were replaced by a group led by Operation Push's chair, the Reverend Jesse Jackson of Chicago.[58]

Larry O'Brien, convention chairman, ruled on two vital procedural questions. First, he allowed the 120 California delegates, representing the California vote McGovern received, to vote on seating 151 delegates who represented votes for other candidates, even though the challenge was to the entire California election process. Then he ruled to lower the figure needed for a majority by the number not being allowed to vote on their own challenge.[59] Had these decisions by O'Brien gone the other way, the majority needed would have been 1,509 and the total McGovern vote, without California voting, would have been 1,498–11 short, possibly changing the outcome.[60] The convention dropped credentials cases affecting delegates from Michigan, Texas, Rhode Island, Washington, Connecticut, and Oklahoma. It also refuted a challenge seeking more women in the South Carolina delegation and the bid of an integrated, diverse group to supplant the pro-Wallace Alabama delegation.[61]

Mills did not come to the convention floor for these votes, spending most of his time in his suite at the Deauville Hotel, 22 blocks from the Arkansas headquarters in the Mimosa. However, he was in close touch with the coalition of candidates seeking an open convention. He also went fishing while in Miami, catching a huge marlin.[62] Meanwhile, Speaker Carl Albert let it be known that he planned to nominate Mills, if asked, vote for him, and deliver 25 of the 28 uncommitted votes in the Oklahoma delegation.[63]

Suddenly, however, Mills withdrew as a candidate.[64] Although his friends in the Arkansas delegation were disappointed, a loyal delegation of longtime friends and admirers gave Mills 25 of its 27 votes and began touting Mills for the vice presidential nomination.[65] The two who did not vote for Mills–Steve Smith of Huntsville and Dewey Stiles of Malvern–were concerned that Jim Johnson, a controversial segregationist, seemed to be an insider in the Mills campaign organization in Miami. "Politically, Jim Johnson and I are poles apart," Smith said. Other delegates reported Mills did not seem especially pleased to have Johnson in his headquarters. "If he can't get rid of Johnson in his camp, he couldn't get rid of him if he was elected president, and that scares me to death," Smith said.[66]

Bumpers and Oklahoma Governor David Hall suggested to McGovern, at a breakfast with four other Southern governors, that he consider Mills for vice president.[67]

POST CONVENTION

Mills continued to solve his district's problems, tackling Little Rock officials' and community leaders' number one concern–getting an expressway extended to the airport and river port.[68] He wrote special language in a bill to fund the linking of two interstate highways with an airport and a river port. It turned out that Little Rock and only one other city could qualify. Interstate 440 would soon link I-30, I-40, I-630, Little Rock National Airport, and the Little Rock Port Authority. Mills was always supportive of extending the interstate system to create jobs and support economic development

In 1972, Arkansas' share of federal outlays, again, reflected Mills' influence and persuasiveness:

- The First Congressional District: $434,950,875;
- Mills' Second District: $641,382,007;
- Third District: $374,379,877; and
- Fourth District: $376,749,410.[69]

Mills' key votes favored revenue sharing, political contribution disclosure, and corporate campaign contributions limitation. He voted against strip mining, Cambodian bombing, opening the highway trust fund to other than highway purposes, limiting farm subsidies, allowing prayer in schools, imposing interest on checking accounts, and ending the House Un-American Activities Committee.[70]

Mills and Representative Hugh Carey of New York (later governor), also on Ways and Means, introduced a bill to authorize aid to public and nonpublic education (HR 16141) to provide a trust fund for elementary and secondary education, and to allow tax credits for tuition paid to private schools, which would have expanded Ways and Means into a new jurisdiction. Mills simultaneously introduced another bill (HR 13495) with James Burke, dealing only with tuition tax credits.

Rebounding from his dark-horse position, Mills supported McGovern, defending him against those who said McGovern was a radical, "Don't be misled by all this talk about somebody being a radical. They told me that Franklin Roosevelt was a radical and that Harry Truman was a radical in some of his proposals. Sometimes a man speaks frankly and comes out so early with his viewpoints that maybe he is ahead of the rest of us and maybe that is true this time." Mills cautioned Arkansans not to "make any bets on Richard Nixon, for this fall," and observed that he "had done more in the conduct of his office to justify his defeat than any other officeholder."[71]

McGovern announced his desire to have Mills as secretary of the Treasury because of his "vast experience in all aspects of tax, fiscal and monetary policies." Wall Street rallied bullishly behind Mills, who coyly commented, "If he's elected and actually offers it to me, I'd have to think about it."[72] McGovern mentioned nominating Mills in a speech before the New York Society of Security Analysts. McGovern's prepared text had not mentioned Mills, but dealt exclusively with his welfare and tax reform proposals. McGovern said, "I realize he cannot give an unqualified commitment now while he is a candidate for re-election." McGovern added that he would not expect Mills to agree with him on every point of fiscal policy.

The press contacted Mills at his home in Kensett. Surprise was his first reaction. Recovering quickly, Mills remembered discussing the post with McGovern, who had "mentioned" the position the week before in a telephone conversation after McGovern's visit to former President Lyndon B. Johnson. A later statement, issued from Mills' Little Rock congressional office, clarified: "I am deeply gratified that Senator McGovern would consider me for such a high position in his cabinet. If Senator McGovern were elected I would certainly have to give it my greatest consideration. I'd have to weigh such a position against the position I have in the House."[73] Arthur M. Moren, Jr., investment officer for Chemical Bank of New York, observed that McGovern's economic proposals did not sit well with business, but his announcement regarding Mills met with great enthusiasm. There is "great respect for Mills in the financial community."[74] The bullish reaction on Wall Street was not a huge surprise.

Mills defended McGovern, encouraged support among those who expressed anxiety about some of his announced positions, and predicted that he would have to change some of his defense and economic postures, once elected, to pass legislation and build programs. "We're not going to disarm this country, unilaterally," Mills said. "Everybody knows that. I've served with a great number of presidents. I haven't known one that hasn't changed his mind on some matters after he was elected and got more information."[75]

Mills accused Republicans of distorting McGovern's views when the Arkansas Committee to Re-elect the President estimated that Arkansans stood to lose 2,600 jobs and $52 million in business because of cuts to the state's defense installations.[76] Mills said that no one could tell where cuts would fall. "I think the Arkansas delegation could see to it that we not lose any [jobs]."[77] He also predicted, "We've not had any cutbacks and I don't estimate we will have any whatsoever under the McGovern program."[78]

Mills continued to fight Nixon, calling for an investigation of his presidential campaign tactics. Fulbright joined Mills at a news conference in which they announced that McGovern would make an appearance at the Little Rock airport on the Saturday evening before the election. At the rally, Senator Fulbright decried "deliberate efforts to destroy the Democratic Party" and said, "It smacks of the same kind of tactics used by the fascists."[79]

Mills called for a post-election committee of either the Senate or House of Representatives to thoroughly investigate efforts to "sabotage" the 1972 Democratic presidential campaign. Mills was upset about numerous disclosures of efforts by President Nixon's re-election campaign to undermine Democratic candidates and of a systematic "Madison Avenue" attempt to give the public a false image of McGovern.[80] Senator Fulbright also condemned Nixon's campaign tactics. He said that although "story after story" had been written disclosing efforts to sabotage the Democratic campaigns, there had been "no serious effort" by the White House to comment on them.[81]

Mills and Fulbright recalled a number of disclosures about the circulation of false letters and statements, telephone impersonations and other acts to disrupt and cause confusion in the campaigns of Democratic presidential candidates.[82] "It all adds up to a concentrated campaign to sow dissension within the Democratic Party," Fulbright said. "This is the type of thing they did in [Nazi] Germany—destroy your opposition."[83] Fulbright and Mills repeatedly said there had been nothing like it in the history of American presidential politics.

The congressional investigation should be "complete and total," Mills said, indicating he personally was aware of more incidents than had been reported publicly. Mills was convinced that persons at the White House were aware as "dirty tricks" unfolded. He said an investigation should determine who directed the operations. He pressed hard in the media, in spite of the apparent sensitivity at the White House. As Mills continued relentlessly, Nixon put him on the White House enemies list.[84] If a Senate committee did not authorize an investigation, Mills promised that a House committee would, saying obviously additional laws were needed to prevent a recurrence of such tactics. Subsequently, the Senate created the Watergate Investigating Committee, chaired by Senator Sam Erwin of North Carolina. Fulbright said he did not think that laws could completely stop such low-handed practices: "The real sanction is in the people themselves. They should defeat the politicians who engage in such practices."[85]

Mills expected "a tremendous crowd" in Little Rock to hear McGovern at the rally at the Central Flying Service hangar on the west side of Adams Field, Little Rock National Airport. Fulbright introduced McGovern at the rally. Mills made strongly supportive remarks, as did several other Democratic officials. McGovern was at the airport for about an hour on his way to a stopover in St. Louis.

The 1972 general election results deeply disappointed Mills. McGovern carried only Massachusetts and the District of Columbia. He lost every county in Arkansas. White County's vote was 8,042 for Nixon and 3,754 for McGovern, a little better than Vice President Hubert Humphrey had run in 1968, when Wallace received 5,064 votes, Nixon 3,888 votes, and Humphrey 3,179. Mills feared 1972 was the Democrats' last chance to win the White House for the foreseeable future. Twenty years later, Mills was delighted when another Arkansan, Bill Clinton, won the presidency. Mills had met Clinton in 1963, and was distinctly impressed during Clinton's days as a Fulbright staffer. Clinton was a student at Georgetown University in the early 1960s, and often stopped by Mills' office to seek advice. (Clinton graduated from Yale University Law School just after that 1972 election, then moved to Fayetteville to teach at the University of Arkansas Law School–at age 26).

As supporters of Carl Albert initiated his drive for re-election as speaker of the House, speculation persisted of a challenge by Mills. Mills denied it. Rumors escalated with Nixon's overwhelming landslide re-election, with some fearing Nixon might run roughshod over Congress. Mills' name was the only one mentioned as a potential replacement, probably because Albert's foes believed Mills the only one capable enough to mount a viable challenge. Traditionally, the majority leader assumed the speakership and served there until death or resignation. Mills had indebted many colleagues by campaigning in their behalf in the fall of 1972, making contributions to several Democrats. The *Arkansas Gazette* quoted a Democratic congressman: "If you wanted Wilbur Mills to help you last fall, all you had to do was pick up the telephone. He's been accumulating debts."[87][86]

Disavowing any interest in the speakership, Mills deflected a raw battle with Albert. Some sources believed Mills hoped that the speaker would step aside as sentiment for Mills mounted. However, Mills said, "I never wanted to be speaker; I only wanted to legislate."[88]

During late November 1972, Mount Pleasant Baptist Church in Little Rock, a congregation established by former slaves in 1875, presented its Human Relations Award to Mills in recognition of his "concern for the poor, the black and the underprivileged." In receiving the award, Mills spoke of a "divisive season" in recent years, along partisan lines, including clashes between races, between classes, and between generations. He observed sadly that a casualty of "heightening of stormy times" had been "the element of trust." From its inception, he said, "the United States has been dependent on people's trust in themselves, in each other, and in mankind, as a reflection of the image of God."[89]

CHAPTER 11

THE TIDE CHANGES
1973-1974

A specialist from HEW relayed in confidence that he and many of his other GS 12–15 staff reported regularly to Mills about department policy and procedures, particularly the problems they perceived. The Treasury Department also harbored informative friends. Mills' antennae were acute, ensuring that his questioning was to the point–sometimes embarrassing to various administrations. He was very close to a host of career employees in various agencies touched by the Ways and Means Committee's work.

Mills' ability to gauge House sentiment stemmed from his warm personal relationships, not only with members but also with their staffs. Every morning when the House opened, like Sam Rayburn before him, Mills would sit in the Speaker's Lobby off the House Chamber "available to members seeking help on projects that only a powerhouse like Mills can give."[1] He could often be found there, working crossword puzzles and puffing on a cigarette or small cigarillo. Each morning, he would check the overnight baseball scores. Baseball remained one of his passions since his days at Harvard, when following the Red Sox became a habit. He followed the New York Yankees during his college-days visits with Bill Dickey. The St. Louis Cardinals became favorites by virtue of being closest to his native Arkansas. Any member could approach him about upcoming legislation. When members did come to talk, he knew who they were, where they came from, their families, and problems in their districts. His uniquely informed, one-on-one relationship with most House members enabled Mills to find out how they stood on a bill he wanted to pass or on a move he wanted to make. All the while, in his head he was counting votes to decide whether or not the time was ripe to move forward with legislation.

In committee, Mills' ability to listen to and understand individual views, coupled with his desire to preserve committee prestige, created a nonpartisan atmosphere and easy consensus. By keeping his own position unclear, Mills remained flexible on policy. His apparent lack of an inflexible personal agenda fostered a cooperative environment. Mills would talk with lobbyists to determine how an upcoming piece of legislation would affect their interest. Every morning he read the *Washington Post*, the *New York Times*, the *Wall Street*

Journal, the *Washington Star,* the Searcy *Daily Citizen,* the *Arkansas Gazette,* and the *Arkansas Democrat.* He read several weekly magazines, and several sports papers. He always worked the *New York Times* crossword puzzle first, for him a task of only 15 to 20 minutes.

About this time, Mills and his wife Polly moved from their longtime apartment on Connecticut Avenue, NW, Washington, D.C., to the Crystal Towers on South Eads Street in the Crystal City section of Arlington, Virginia.

By 1973, the chairman's formal authority was diminishing by the slow tide of change. The "closed rule" was no longer automatic for Ways and Means. Also, the House leadership began to exert more authority over committee assignments. On June 18, 1973, the Ways and Means Committee room was packed with press and public observing the drafting of a foreign trade bill. Nixon administration officials were on hand to testify on sensitive trade negotiations. Heated debate ensued, and the committee voted 15 to 10 to close the hearing, removing all but committee members and those testifying. Later that year, while Mills was recuperating from surgery, the committee agreed for the first time to meet in public, while they were drafting a pension reform bill.

In July 1973, Mills worked on and eventually shepherded through a two-step, 11 percent Social Security benefit increase. He had argued vigorously that an earlier and smaller increase was inadequate to meet unusually rapid inflation, then rampant. Mills personally wrote the bill's conference report, after the Senate passed it, in preparation for the president's signature.

Then, surprising everyone–even himself–in July 1973, Mills announced he would retire at the end of 1974 if his severely painful back condition didn't improve. He had not shared this thinking previously with family, staff, or constituents. He missed the dedication of the Wilbur D. Mills Center for the Study of Social Sciences at Hendrix College at Conway due to back pain, and issued a statement: "The basic requirement of our times includes renewal and expansion of our intellectual capital ... striving for new ideas of man's proper relationship to his fellow man and to his physical and cultural environment. It is the educated person, rather than the specialist who must take initiative in pointing out consequences of increasing knowledge and who must find means for its exploitation to the advantage of all of us."[2]

His public image remained solid. The *Washington Post,* in response to his announcement that he was considering retirement, wrote, "The power of Wilbur Mills is something that goes beyond his formal rank as committee chairman, and something that defies easy definition. It is something in the personality of the man, his calm self-assurance, his firm command of the committee that handles the critical issues that touch all Americans, a feeling that if Mills says the bill is a good one then it is. He is a complex politician. He can be the most cautious of legislators in refusing to take a bill to the floor until he is certain it will pass. He can be the most imperious in making deals with presidents over the opposition of his party leaders, or even negotiating import agreements with other nations when administrations fail."[3]

The *Evening Star* in Washington said that Mills had "few peers in the nation's history as a legislative engineer," and referred to him as "the last of the great wheel horses that included Lyndon Johnson and Sam Rayburn."[4]

Rowland Evans and Robert Novak lamented that Mills' "once majestic authority has dwindled close to mortal dimension" and referred to his tenure as "one of the great legislative careers in history."[5]

But the tide was slowly and quietly turning.

Under medical care, Polly had stopped drinking and was staying out of town with a daughter to rest and recover her health. Not enjoying solitary drinking, Mills began going out in search of drinking companions. Wanting to avoid traveling Arkansas constituents or congressional colleagues, he sought dives.[6]

Mills remained the leading authority on international trade. On TV's "Meet the Press," he declared ". . . We have got to put the president in the position where the United States can take leadership in discussions of monetary policy, trade policies, and all these other things, including military spending abroad."[7] Mills sought viable trade legislation. His work culminated in The Trade Act of 1974. A landmark achievement, it granted the president authority to negotiate agreements and influenced trade policy for decades. The bill zipped through the House. But Mills' lack of attention to the Senate resulted in the failure of both the trade legislation and a Social Security proposal as well. Mills was spending less time working the Senate side, less time in his own office, and more time seeking solace in alcohol. The result was a tangle of loose ends that heretofore he would have handled with care.

Ten days later, Mills left Washington for a rest under doctor's orders, destination not disclosed. Described as the only real vacation of his entire lifetime, it would give him two full weeks of rest and relief from the pressures of office. The plan was to go home to Kensett for two weeks following the respite, and be back in Washington after the Labor Day recess.

Mills went to the island of Antigua in the British Virgin Islands with his friend and neighbor Annabella Battistella, later known as "Fanne Foxe," his friend and former campaign aide Joe Johnson and his secretary Jan Ireland (soon to become Johnson's wife). Polly was still at their daughter's home.

Mills spent his time napping, sunning, reading, and working crossword puzzles. He consumed chilled vodka and chopped steak, preferably with sliced tomatoes and cottage cheese. He called Polly every day. After this longest vacation and only trip out of the U.S., he was ready to return to Kensett, Washington, and Congress. Mills reported that he felt "great." He said he'd have a brief medical checkup and then return to Arkansas.

Ten days later, it was announced that Mills would undergo surgery at Baptist Medical Center in Little Rock for a ruptured spinal disc. Mills was operated on the morning of August 29. Gene Goss reported that he had a lumbar laminectomy to remove excess material before the fourth and fifth lumbar vertebrae. In extreme cases, two vertebrae may sometimes be fused, but Mills' doctors never considered such a fusion. Goss reported that Dr. Thomas Fletcher indicated Mills, after receiving a spinal anesthetic, was awake throughout the two-and-a-half-hour operation, and chatted with doctors and nurses throughout. Dr. Fletcher was assisted by Dr. Austin Grimes of Little Rock, an orthopedist. Dr. Porter Rodgers, Jr., of Searcy, a general surgeon and Mills' personal physician–as well as the son of his longtime friend and physician– led the procedure. Mills returned to Kensett to recover, spending time at Hot Springs, in a house provided by a friend. Mills relaxed in the therapeutic baths, took long walks in the woods, and received visitors, some from Washington, many from Arkansas, and a few from Hollywood. He would gulp down his drinks, never sipping. Those who sipped were "real alcohol abusers," he teased. Visitors noticed that his judgment, memory, and sensory perception became impaired. Concentration was difficult and insight dulled. Sometimes he would become angry and near-violent. The alcohol induced drowsiness, fatigue, frustration, and sometimes even fear.

Nevertheless, in early November 1973, Mills returned to Washington. He said his back "doesn't bother me a bit." His doctors cautioned him against a full schedule. He was careful to not interfere with committee matters because he didn't want to be unfair to fellow members, for several senior members had stepped forward for hearings and decisions on pending legislation. It was agreed, Mills would resume chairing the committee when the next new item was taken up.

Mills was not present at Ways and Means hearings on national health care. He was relying on Valium and Librium to get him through, but he wasn't in his office either of those two days, according to Gene Goss. Though back pain kept Mills from walking many days, he told neither staff nor committee. At home and alone, Mills was drinking vodka from his freezer. On days he went to his office, the urgency upon arriving home was that he would rush to the refrigerator for a first drink before taking off his coat or hat. He would fill an iced-tea glass with vodka from the freezer and guzzle it down in one long series of gulps. Only then he could relax enough to remove his coat and hat and find his favorite chair.

HOUSE POLITICS

Congress was moving toward reform. The seniority system was targeted. Personal and health problems were controlling Mills' private life and increasingly impacting his public performance. Still, few of those around him recognized the degree of his anguish. Congressman Hale Boggs was often quoted as saying, "I sat next to him on Ways and Means for 20 years, and I never knew what he was thinking!"[9] Nor, apparently, how much he was drinking. Outwardly, his life seemed to be so dominated by complicated intricacies of high finance, some Arkansas businessmen joked that Mills was not really born in Arkansas at all. Instead, they mused, he was "issued by a New York bank as a high-yield debenture and was put up by the state as collateral for a government loan."[10]

During this vulnerable time in Mills' life, Kensett Mayor Eugene Walton said that the entire town dearly loved Mills. "This is a Mills town. He was raised here. He went to school here. He might lose a few votes, but he won't ever lose any friends here."[11]

COMMITTEE REFORM

Ways and Means became the chief target for reform. Along with other House committees, Ways and Means was forced to open its hearings and meetings to lobbyists and the public. The Democratic caucus established a procedure to make it easier to get an amendment to a Ways and Means bill considered on the floor. The caucus forced Ways and Means to create five subcommittees, its first since Mills' second term as chair. Ways and Means Democrats were stripped of their committee assignment authority; and the committee was expanded to 37 members. However, Ways and Means escaped major changes in its traditional jurisdiction, despite repeated attempts by House reformers. The major House reform group was the Democratic Study Group. The DSG in 1970 persuaded the party caucus to appoint an 11-member Committee on Organization, Study, and Review to examine the seniority system. Chaired by Julia Butler Hansen (D-Washington), the committee reported two sets of recommendations, one in 1971, and another in 1973. The first set, adopted by the caucus on January 21, 1971, was designed to limit the power of committee chairs. Mills supported all these changes in his many conversations with Hansen, but later regretted the results, feeling they weakened congressional leadership.[11]

When Mills stepped out of his traditional role, by tentatively entering presidential politics, a steady erosion of his enormous House stature began. His uncharacteristic flirtation with higher ambition undercut his classical aura of a powerful senior statesman. The presidential campaign also brought with it huge legal, and allegedly illegal, campaign contributions from many special interests that benefited most from the tax system and special tax legislation for which Mills and his committee were responsible. Allegations arose of illegal contributions from oil companies, milk producers, and others. These were investigated by the Senate Watergate Committee and special prosecutor, as well as by the Public Citizens' Tax Reform Research Group. Attempts were made to connect Mills' campaign contributions with alleged favored tax treatment for those contributors. The committee eventually concluded no wrong doing on Mills part. These and other challenges eroded his mythic aura and authority. With Mills' perceived power declining, the next step was inevitable. A challenge to him from within Ways and Means came in the spring of 1974 over repeal of the controversial oil depletion allowance.

For years Mills had brought committee legislation to the floor under a "closed rule," which barred floor amendments and excluded the other 410 House members, as well as the committee's liberal minority, from any say in tax legislation other than a "yes" or "no" vote on the whole tax package. Congressman William Green (D-Pennsylvania) proposed to completely repeal the depletion allowance, an idea that was rejected by Mills in favor of a three-to-five-year gradual phaseout. Mills, serving notice that he would again seek a closed rule, refused to allow Green's amendment to be voted on by the full House. Green took his fight to the Democratic caucus under a new procedure adopted at the beginning of the 93rd Congress with Mills' approval. An overwhelming majority supported Green's efforts and directed Mills and Rules Committee Democrats to report the bill for floor action, allowing a vote on the Green amendment. Instead of following the caucus instruction, Mills refused to bring the bill to the floor for seven months. His strategy to control tax legislation ensured continued oil company windfall profits–disappointing many congressional Democrats.

Then the congressional reform effort intensified with creation of the House Select Committee on Committees in early 1973. Chaired by Richard Bolling (D-Missouri), the committee held extensive hearings and recommended sweeping changes in procedure and jurisdiction. Bolling was perhaps Mills' only admitted political opponent in the House, despite Mills' early help to Bolling with Rayburn. As Mills recalled it, the speaker originally feared Bolling had communist leanings. Mills went to bat for him, assuring Rayburn of his loyalty and patriotism. Bolling went on to become a regular at Rayburn's "Board of Education Club," along with Mills.

Mills and Bolling served together on the Joint Economic Committee. Mills wanted Bolling on Ways and Means, but Rayburn suggested Rules, so then Bolling went on the Rules Committee, where he made his historic name for congressional reform, authoring two books–*House Out of Order* and *Power in the House*.

Tip O'Neill called Bolling "mean and impatient," indicating that when a congressional witness before the Rules Committee couldn't answer one of his questions, Dick would go through the ceiling. "He'd crush the guy and send him back to his own committee to study the bill further."[12] However, O'Neill went on to say in his book, *Man of the House,* that Mills and Bolling were the two most able members with whom he served.[13] Bolling, though brilliant, sometimes appeared jealous of Mills and seemed to use every opportunity to try to surpass him in congressional power and prestige. Bolling's goal was to become speaker and his perception was that Mills was in his way. Mills largely ignored Bolling and went his own way.

It was not too surprising that Mills' committee was Bolling's principal reform target; the Democratic Study Group concluded:

> The present jurisdiction of the Ways and Means Committee is entirely too broad to permit ongoing and thorough legislative and oversight review. The select committee therefore recommends that the Ways and Means Committee retain its historic jurisdiction over taxes, tariffs, and Social Security and relinquish direct control of other jurisdiction not directly related to those matters.[14]

Specifically, recommendations included transferring:

1. non-tax aspects of health care to a proposed Committee on Commerce and Health,

2. non-tax aspects of unemployment compensation to the Committee on Labor,

3. renegotiation of government contracts to the proposed Committee on Banking, Currency, and Housing,

4. general revenue sharing to the Committee on Government Operations,

5. work incentive (WIN) programs to the Committee on Labor, and

6. trade to the Committee on Foreign Affairs–in terms of Ways and Means' historic jurisdiction, this last item marked the most significant reduction.[15]

The reform plan encountered strong opposition in the House. The Democratic caucus referred it to the Hansen committee, which drafted a substitute proposal, with Mills' support. Under terms of the resulting House Resolution 988 (Committee Reform Amendments of 1974), House Rules were amended to mandate that committees with more than 15 members, specifically Ways and Means, establish at least four subcommittees. Mills was deeply concerned that committee staff members were also increased, sharply raising congressional staff costs. One-third of the staff was guaranteed to the minority, weakening the chairman's control. The Democratic caucus subsequently instituted more reforms.

In 1974's post-Watergate elections, House Democrats gained 52 seats, of a total of 75 new members. Known as the Watergate class, they were generally supportive of congressional reform. At the party caucus' organizational meeting in December 1974, Ways and Means Democrats' role as the party's Committee on Committees was transferred to the party's Steering and Policy Committee. Ways and Means was expanded from 25 to 37 members, and the ratio of majority to minority changed from 15/10 to 25/12, allowing for appointment of more junior and liberal members.[16] These reforms, it was hoped, would liberalize the committee's actions.

LEGAL AND POLITICAL PROBLEMS

In January 1974, William A. Dobrovir, an attorney with Ralph Nader, filed a motion in federal district court requesting White House documents relating to telephone conversations with Mills, Congressman Clark MacGregor of Minnesota, Nixon's campaign director, and Speaker Carl Albert. Dobrovir also requested a memorandum from Treasury Secretary George P. Shultz to John D. Ehrlichman, then Nixon's second top aide. These requests were made regarding Nixon's raising of the support price of milk. A White House statement had indicated the price was raised because the Democratic Congress, presumably Mills and Albert, "put a gun to our heads."[17]

The Select Committee on Presidential Campaign Activities, better known as the Watergate Committee, chaired by Senator Sam J. Ervin, Jr., of North Carolina, began examining all presidential candidacies of 1972, including that of Mills. Charles Ward, chief executive officer of Ward Bus Company of Conway, Arkansas, was the founder of the Draft Mills Movement and subsequent committee in 1971. Ward reported to the Watergate Committee that $200,000 in contributions went to the Draft Mills Committee from July 1971 to February 1972, at which time Mills officially became an exploratory candidate. About 75 persons gave $1,000 or more; only a few donated more than $3,000. In addition, the General Accounting Office records show that receipts, after the new campaign finance law limitations went into effect on April 7, 1972, totaling about $293,000 were received.

The Senate Watergate Committee in June found that the dairy lobby, Associated Milk Producers, Inc., had illegally contributed $75,000 in money and services to Mills' 1972 exploratory presidential campaign and an additional $55,000 to Mills' campaign. Gulf Oil Corporation, which like other oil companies depended on Mills' committee for tax breaks, including oil depletion allowances, also contributed $15,000 illegally, the report said. Other reports showed that Mills' campaign aides accepted campaign contributions on behalf of executives of beer and trucking industries. Mills repaid Gulf Oil Corporation $15,000 by check from his personal bank account at the Bank of Kensett out of concern for his longtime friend Carl Arnold, originally of Batesville, Arkansas, a lobbyist for Gulf.

The Watergate Committee found that Mills, representing an agricultural congressional district, supported legislation favorable to dairy farmers, dairy products, and dairy prices. They also found that dairy trust contributions were made to Mills' campaign. However, Mills had been very supportive throughout his congressional career–and even before as the White County executive and a businessman and lawyer–to dairy and all agricultural interests, which were prominent in his home county, his congressional district, and the whole state of Arkansas. (Just before his death in 1992, this life-long commitment was formally recognized, when he was inducted into the Arkansas Agricultural Hall of Fame, with a tribute by Herschel Friday of the Friday, Eldridge, and Clark Law Firm, founded by William Jennings Bryan Smith, originally called the "Smith Firm" and subsequently the "Friday Firm.")

The Watergate Committee's conclusion was "this limited investigation has not uncovered any direct evidence that Congressman Mills' support of March 1971 diary legislation constituted a specific quid pro quo for money, goods, and services given to him."[18] Farmers, including dairy farmers, had always supported him during his 42 years in public office and he had always supported them. That conclusion should have ended the anguish of a continuing investigation of the exploratory campaign for those three years–not supervised by him, and falling during a time when he was incapable of his traditionally close and careful scrutiny over all his own public and private financial matters.

However, the committee did note that Mills had avoided testifying before it. He was scheduled to testify the day after the Tidal Basin incident, according to George Jernigan. Mostly, he was not sober enough to appear. Some of those involved hoped he would not testify because they feared what he might say. Joseph Johnson, Mills' campaign manager, took the Fifth Amendment when he appeared.[19] Mills probably would not have.

In April 1974, Mills cast the deciding ballot in a 13-12 vote against an amendment aimed at boosting oil industry taxes. Oil companies sought to plow back into exploration and development the funds that would have gone into the federal government Treasury, which would have been collected under a proposed new windfall profits tax.[20][21] The final oil tax reform bill, by Ways and Means, phased out the petroleum depletion allowance and revamped tax treatment of American oil company income earned abroad. Petroleum firms, through the depletion allowance, saved some $2 billion to $3 billion a year at that time in federal taxes.

PERSONAL PROBLEMS

Before and after his 1973 back operation, Mills drank increased amounts of alcoholic beverages, primarily vodka, as a way to find temporary relief from excruciating back pain, and to sleep at night. (During this period, he usually passed out after midnight.)[22]

Years earlier, he would have a drink or two before dinner, which he said was to relax, to whet his appetite, and to perk him up for nightly homework on legislation. During this latter time, he talked about taking as many as 20 25-milligram Librium pills and drinking two quarts of vodka a night—and eating no dinner before passing out. He was still rising the next morning, singing in the shower, breaking out with profuse perspiration, and going to work, but his powers of concentration were lagging and his hands were shaking. His staff secured a signature machine, avoiding the embarrassment of having to sign more than a hundred letters a day in the shaky script of an alcoholic. He explained that he had a problem on his left hand, used for writing his signature, with a pulled tendon. Mills was seeking a plausible explanation to avoid accepting alcoholism as the reason for his difficulty in signing his name.

His younger brother, Roger Mills, was elected regional delegate to the American Hospital Association at its annual convention in Washington during the first week in February.[23] Roger was a longtime member of the board of trustees of White County Memorial Hospital and a longtime local, state, and national leader in health care. While in Washington, he visited with Mills and observed, "You really have yourself in a mess," and urged him to cut back on his drinking. Mills' reaction was characteristically succinct, "Don't tell me what to do. If you came up here to lecture me, you are wasting your time." Roger said, "Okay, I won't ever mention it again, Wilbur."[24]

SECOND HOSPITALIZATION

Back in Washington in February 1974, Mills became frightened by chest and head pains. Convinced he had a brain tumor, Mills once again entered Baptist Medical Center, this time for a general physical checkup and rest. Phone calls and visitors were prohibited. Dr. Fletcher, who had performed surgery on Mills' spinal disc, was attending physician and issued a report that Mills was in "reasonably good health."[25] Fletcher reported that Mills was receiving physical therapy, pedaling on a stationary bicycle and doing leg lifts with 10-pound weights.61 Massive doses of antibiotics were administered for peritonitis and hepatitis. And he was receiving treatment for pancreatitis. All of Mills' symptoms likely resulted from excessive alcohol and insufficient nourishment. The chest pains, it was found, had been caused by a cracked rib. As expected, after a little more than two weeks' hospitalization, Mills called a press conference to announce his plans to run for re-election. The announcement signaled his 21st decision to run, setting a record for all public officials ever to have sought elective office in Arkansas, except for Senator Max Howell of Jacksonville. It was nearly a national record.

OPPOSITION

In early 1974, Mills went to Indiana to help Senator Birch Bayh in his campaign for re-election to the United States Senate. For the first time in his career, Mills drew Republican opposition in the person of Judy Petty of Little Rock, a former member of Governor Rockefeller's staff. In 21 elections, this was his sixth contested race. The press attributed her entry to Mills' appearance in Indiana in behalf of Bayh, whom she referred to as an "ultra left-winged liberal." She also made much of Mills' close relationship to milk producers. Jokes and bumper stickers circulated, saying "Wilbur Milk."

In August, Mills' longtime friend and colleague, Vice President Gerald R. Ford, once House Minority Leader, succeeded to the presidency upon Nixon's resignation under fire of the infamous Watergate controversy and from the resultant threat of impeachment. Mills and Ford at that point had been friends for a quarter century and had what Mills called "a mutual admiration society."[26] Many times, Mills spoke of Ford as "my good friend." In fact, on January 19, 1974, regarding the turmoil caused by the Watergate investigation and controversy, Mills said–long before other members of Congress would speak so candidly–"Under existing circumstances, we would be better off with Jerry Ford as president."[27]

As soon as Ford became president, he called Mills and said, "This is Jerry." Mills answered, "It's awfully hard for me to say, but protocol requires that I call you "Mr. President."[28] Later in the summer of 1974, Mills met with Ford regarding the president's top priority plan to enact a multibillion-dollar national health insurance bill. Mills said, "I would prefer to reconvene following the election. We can't be home during that period of time with the problems we have in this country."[29]

Mills met with Ford on August 21 from 4:15 to 4:45 p.m. in the Oval Office, along with Bill Timmons. Timmons' memo to the president described the importance of Mills and the meeting: "(1) There are probably only five working weeks left before final adjournment. (2) Wilbur Mills is a powerful member of Congress and can be helpful to enactment of the president's program. The president met with Mills' Senate counterpart, Russell Long, last week. (3) The committee is in mark-up on the health bill, has virtually finished consideration of the tax reform package and is holding energy taxes from the floor because Wilbur can't get a closed rule. The chairman will be a conferee on the trade bill when it passes the Senate."[30]

Mills and Ford predicted approval of a national health insurance program. Ford had said, while in Arkansas at Mills' behest to celebrate the new Baptist Medical Center, that he would "go so far as to say that national health insurance, when approved in one form or another, may be remembered in history as one of the most important domestic accomplishments of the decade of the 1970s."[31] This Mills and Ford meeting took place just a few hours after the Ways and Means Committee failed to reach a quick compromise on health insurance. The delay was due to a clash over financing methods—new payroll taxes vs. another tap on general revenues—and over whether the plan should be voluntary or compulsory. A memorandum for President Ford from Caspar W. Weinberger on National Health Insurance, surveys the issues at stake:

> Over the past three days, Chairman Wilbur D. Mills has been discussing with me and department representatives outlines of a compromise proposal.
>
> There are a number of features in the compromise about which Mills seems to be exceedingly flexible and other features which he has thought about very little. This morning in executive session, for example, he seemed to be wavering about cost sharing. Nonetheless, the general framework of the compromise, as we understand it, seems to be quite favorable to the administration position. Attached is a statement of basic elements of the Mills proposal carried to a bit more detail by the department's staff.
>
> While we have not had enough details until yesterday to permit any kind of cost estimating and do not have precise estimates yet, it appears that the federal net cost can be held in about the same range as the $6 billion proposal.[32]

At Mills' suggestion, President Ford met with Republican members of Ways and Means on September 13. Timmons summarized the meeting in a memorandum to the president:

> 1. Ways and Means Committee members are split over three plans: the administration's, the American Medical Association's, and Senator Kennedy's. If Republicans could get together, there is a chance of enacting a compromise plan this year.
>
> 2. Chairman Wilbur Mills has requested the president's assistance with GOP members.[33]

Mills told Ford the outlook was rather bleak, "The membership of the committee is not in a position to come together on any proposal."[34] Mills often said in later years that when he read the account of this meeting in newspapers he could not remember having been at the White House. He also blamed himself for not being able to secure the usual consensus for which he was so widely noted, and believed that "it was the only time, as I look back, that I let alcohol make a difference."

Petty made two basic charges during her campaign against Mills: taxes paid by individuals had risen 300 percent while Mills had been chairman, and corporations with an interest in legislation had contributed to the Draft Mills Committee.[35]

Mills noted that Petty was referring to increases in revenues, rather than tax rates, which reflected economic growth, rather than inequitable tax legislation. Even though his health was marginal and his last congressional campaign in full swing, Mills continued to blaze trails in tax reform, as in September 1974, when Mills predicted that Ways and Means would recommend stringent new tax regulations governing the oil industry:

> I go back to Washington Tuesday night to commence the executive sessions that will result in passage of another tax reform program, which will impose limitations upon those who seem to be very hungry for large profits in the oil industry. We will take from them over a five-year period more than $12 billion of additional taxes if, after 1975, they do not spend all those windfall profits in the development of further reserves of oil and gas.
>
> This will be a tough blow for them. In the past oil firms have only been paying domestically about $800 million in taxes.[36]

FIRST INCIDENT

On Sunday before his scheduled Watergate grand jury appearance, Mills began his day drinking. It started early in Kensett, before he drove to Little Rock's Adams Field to catch a noon flight to National Airport in Washington. George Jernigan visited with Mills at the airport while waiting for his own flight. Jernigan was struck that Mills received numerous calls from a lobbyist friend about Mills' scheduled testimony before the grand jury the next day. In those days, to reach someone by phone at an airport, one had to call the airport or airline to page the person. It was a conspicuous, intricate process, to reach someone there, even a member of Congress.

Back in Washington that evening, Mills dined at the Junkanoo Restaurant, 1629 Connecticut Avenue, NW, and then had a drink at the Silver Slipper.

At 2 a.m., on October 7, 1974–eight hours before he was scheduled to testify before the committee looking into possible campaign improprieties–Mills was a passenger in a car that the U.S. Park Service Police pursued for "traveling at an unreasonable speed with its lights off."[37] The Lincoln Town Car sped south on 17th Street, then westbound on Independence Avenue at Kutz Bridge, near the Jefferson Memorial at the Tidal Basin. The Lincoln was registered to Mills. Arkansas license DOT-003 indicated that the licensee was a member of the

Arkansas congressional delegation.

The driver, Albert G. Capaldi, 39, a one-time, mid-level Nixon aide, could not figure out how to turn on the car's lights. He had worked in the Interior Department from May 1969 to June 1970, first as a consultant, then as a $30,000-a-year assistant to Carl McMurray, a special assistant to Nixon's Interior Secretary Walter Hickel of Alaska. The other occupants were Liliane M. Kassar, 27, a secretary in the World Bank's legal department, the driver's date; Mills' neighbor Annabella Battistella, a 38-year-old native of Argentina, who had danced and stripped under the name "Fanne Foxe, the Argentine Firecracker," at the Gayety Theatre, Champagne Room and Blue Mirror in Washington before the Silver Slipper; Gloria Sanchez, 56, Battistella's cousin; Carmela, Battistella's associate from the Silver Slipper; and Lini, Carmela's roommate. Battistella, sporting two black eyes, jumped or fell into the Tidal Basin to divert attention from Mills. Police officer Larry Brent rescued Battistella from the pool–10 feet deep at that point–handcuffed her and committed her to St. Elizabeth's Hospital for possible mental illness. She was released to Capaldi, the driver, whom she said was her "boyfriend."[38]

Mrs. Mills was at home at the time–at the Crystal City apartment, recovering from a broken foot, the result of tripping over an electrical cord days earlier. Battistella, her husband, Eduardo, and their three children lived in the same apartment building as Mills and his wife. The family had newly immigrated from Argentina. Mrs. Mills had helped Mrs. Battistella select a new Electrolux vacuum cleaner, shopped with her, and often played cards in the Battistella apartment. Polly sometimes accompanied Wilbur and the Battistellas to the Junkanoo Restaurant and the Silver Slipper. One of Mills' daughters also went shopping with Battistella to "keep the lines of communication open" during this difficult time.

The *Washington Post* reported that Mr. Bertran of the Junkanoo Restaurant said Mills came in about 6 p.m. Sunday with a man and three women, and that two additional women later joined the party but left early. He said the Mills party drank a single magnum of champagne and consumed wine and other drinks with their dinner. He said the check came to more than $60 and that Mills paid in cash. The party then ordered another round of drinks and Mills paid the additional $18 in cash.[39]

Edwardo Battistella, Ms. Foxe's husband, told the *Washington Star* he ran an import business in Washington from 1965, and Mrs. Mills was a customer at an interior decoration firm he operated. He said she introduced him and his wife to the congressman. According to Battistella, the Millses visited their apartment in Crystal Towers in Arlington, Virginia, and liked the building. Battistella said he helped Mills find an apartment three floors above their own and, at Polly's request, he decorated it.

At the Tidal Basin scene, Mills was reported to have a cut over his left eye and on his left cheek, a bloody nose, broken glasses, and an intoxicated appearance.[40] Mills later explained that Mrs. Battistella had tried to jump out of the car before it stopped. In the scuffle to restrain her, he had broken his glasses and received the minor injuries.[41] Mills remembered falling out of the car in his effort to visit with a television reporter and falling again on his way back into the car.

However, Sgt. Livesay, a U.S. Park policeman, said Mills was hospitalized at Washington Hospital Center after a second struggle, in which Mills fell over a bush, injuring his back and leg.[42] Larry Krebs, a freelance television photographer and reporter, was there immediately with a video camera. Krebs heard Park Police contact their headquarters on the police frequency with the observation that a car without lights was speeding and it could be kidnapping of a congressman, so he began active pursuit immediately. At the scene, Mills was unable to locate his identification, but he did not impede the officers. In fact, he introduced himself immediately and shook hands with Officer Livesay, just as if he were campaigning.[43]

Two days later, three national television networks ran clips of the shocking events. Gene Wirges, Republican editor of the *Petit Jean Headlight*, was a Rockefeller ally and political enemy of Mills' ally, Conway County Sheriff Marlin Hawkins of Morrilton, Arkansas. Wirges claimed he himself had urged replaying the tape of Mills and Park Police at the Tidal Basin. He ran the story and pictures in his own paper first and then advocated it by phone to Dave Kelly, a national television director. Next, the *Washington Post* carried the story.44

The police incident report did not mention Mills or his car, and listed the incident as an attempted suicide.45 In a few days, Mills issued a statement explaining the incident, apologizing to his supporters, friends, staff, and family, expressing discomfort, embarrassment and humiliation.46 Friends of Mills, as well as objective observers, have raised questions over the years about this tragic event: Was Mills set up? Who would want to set Mills up? Why did a television camera crew arrive so quickly at that time of night? Why did Mrs. Battistella jump into the water: to divert attention away from Mills or perhaps to dramatize the situation? To spotlight Mills? Was the former Nixon administration aide part of a conspiracy? Was there a connection with Mills being scheduled to testify the next day before the Watergate Committee? Was there a connection to phone calls he received at the Little Rock airport? No conclusions have been documented. Mills generally did not spend time thinking about the past, including this incident. He assumed full responsibility himself, pointing to his alcoholism, blackouts, and related problems. He even explained the uncommonly quick appearance of a television crew as simply a regular "night crawler" who heard the U.S. Park Police report. Mills called Battistella's jump in the water a well-meaning gesture and abortive effort to divert press attention away from him. He concluded that he should never have put himself in that position, discounting the suspicions of others. Mills often said, "If I had been in my right mind, I would never have been in a position to be set up, so it doesn't matter in my eyes whether I was or not. In any case, it was my actions and decision that put me there."

Nancy Dickerson, a national television newswoman, opined, "JFK used to say that life is unfair, and indeed it is unfair if history chooses to focus only on the brief period when Wilbur Mills was an alcoholic, instead of on his lifetime of outstanding service to his country."[46]

An essay by William Safire, published on the *New York Times* editorial page on October 17, 1974, questioned the treatment of the Mills incident up to that point: "The Mills story deserved coverage, but not the whoop de do it received; an inside page sufficed, a permanent record that could be consulted if he aspired to a higher office. As a great and wise man put it the other day: 'Who hasn't had a few wild nights?'"[47]

Mills, however, was not as critical. "... By and large I have no complaint of the way I was handled by the press before or after the incident at the Tidal Basin," he said. "It's quite interesting to me that many, many people feel that the press was a part of a scheme to see that I was taken out or injured, but I have never thought so, I have never believed it. I know the press was merely doing what it thought to be its job."[48]

Sander Vanocur quoted Harry Ashmore of Santa Barbara, California. The former editor of the *Arkansas Gazette*, and Pulitzer Prize winner, was asked if he realized that Mills was an alcoholic. Ashmore replied, "No, not until the day he showed up sober."[49]

BACK TO BUSINESS

On October 16, nine days after the incident, Mills made his first public appearance. Back in Arkansas, Mills talked openly and easily with the media.[50] Mills' first public address was to the Little Rock Jaycees on October 17. He told them he was wrong for drinking and praised his relationship with Polly. He also clarified that Mrs. Battistella had received no compensation from him, except for decorating Mills' apartment. He offered some advice to the young men, "Don't go out with foreigners who drink champagne."[51]

One of the Jaycees asked about news reports that the incident had diminished Mills' prestige among his peers and that some might attempt to remove him as chairman of the Ways and Means Committee. Mills' response drew a standing ovation and rousing cheers, "Let me tell you, my friend, I've been in a lot of fights. Do you know of anyone I've lost to yet?"[52] After the meeting, he and his wife were escorted to their car, and Mills drove away, headed for Kensett, saying, "I guess I better turn these lights on, shouldn't I."[53]

In spite of his ability to find humor even in difficulty, Mills was under tremendous emotional strain, noticeable to James Dickenson of the *Washington Star*, "During the benediction by the Jaycees' chaplain, his jaws worked continually and just before the audience finished reciting the Jaycee creed he shivered noticeably."

"Bless us, 0 Lord, as we gather here to hear a man who has a lot on his mind," the chaplain intoned, imparting an unintended double meaning to his blessing.

The Jaycees were generally sympathetic during what was probably Mills' most difficult campaign appearance ever. "It had to be done and he said what had to be said," one listener commented afterward.

Mills was asked in a CBS interview, "Was there anything between you and the young lady?" The congressman replied. "No, I ought to be flattered at my age of 65 for anybody to ask me such a question, but, I know the impression is trying to be created that there was. But she [Mrs. Battistella] said herself that Mrs. Mills was with us whenever we went out except one or two occasions when she was at home with her foot broken, but we were not by ourselves on any of those occasions."[54]

Mills' re-election campaign appearances were often covered by as many as 50 members of the national press. On election eve, he spoke with Walter Cronkite, David Brinkley, John Chancellor and Howard K. Smith, as well as a dozen Arkansas broadcast and print reporters.

Mills had conducted a very effective grassroots campaign, including swings through each of his district's nine counties, plus a final, large rally at the Camelot Hotel in Little Rock. He made three swings through his home county, the last a handshaking tour through shopping centers in east Searcy and the White County Memorial Hospital, talking with constituents primarily about inflation and pledging his efforts "to seek an excess profits tax on oil, sugar, and coffee industries that had shown extremely high profits during inflationary times."[55] He promised to go to work on these excess profits upon his return to Washington.

During the campaign, Mills said he had once facetiously remarked, "If the United States continues to rely on oil from the Middle East, Arab nations will become so economically powerful by the year 2000 that we'll be trading in camel dollars." Mills noted that he was no longer sure that was a joke.

As voters went to the polls on Tuesday, November 5, a partly cloudy day with nippy temperatures, the prediction was that 640,000 would turn out to make their selections from U.S. senator to county committeemen, with major national attention focusing closely on Mills' race for re-election against Judy Petty, a 30-year-old Republican in her first political race.[56] Mills had been provided with opposition research on Ms. Petty, but declined to use it because he did not believe in political mudslinging and personal criticisms, choosing to stick with current issues and his own thinking on them.

Publicity on "the incident" swirled about him throughout the whirlwind campaign. He awkwardly paraphrased an adage of Harry Truman's: "I can take all of that. You have to be able to if you're going to be in politics. If you want the kitchen to stay cool, you'd better not get into politics."[57]

At the campaign's end, he invited Gene Goss and a few campaign staffers to sit with him while he waited for dinner and the election returns. They had drinks in his room at the Camelot Inn in Little Rock. Then, he and Polly, along with Goss, a couple of campaign workers, and North Little Rock officials, went to the Sawmill Restaurant in West Little Rock to have a leisurely steak dinner with red wine. The gathering expanded several times to add more and more close friends and supporters, until Mills found himself buying drinks for everybody in the restaurant. He said, "I don't want anybody to be left out."

Mills gave the maitre d' a significant tip and asked him to keep the wine coming.

During dinner, Mills confided concern about his health. He was 65 at that time and said, "I was in perfect health until I became 60 and then my whole body fell apart. First, I had a miserable case of shingles, which lasted for months. It was caused by my grandchildren's chicken pox. Then, I had a slipped disc, a broken rib, hepatitis, a deviated septum, and a rare skin disease known as bullous pemphigoid." He even suspected a malignant brain tumor, but he did not mention that during the election night celebration. It was obvious to all that his health was basically sound, but stretched to the limit in a workaholic whose routine was characterized by extreme stress, little exercise, and excessive indulgence in alcohol, painkillers, and tobacco.

As results came in, it was apparent his constituents supported his return to Congress:

> His majority in White County, Arkansas' second largest county geographically, was 7-1 in many areas and totaled more than 75 percent, with 8,273 votes to 2,621. His hometown of Kensett overwhelmingly endorsed him 460 to 74.[58]
>
> With 441 precincts reporting, Mills received more than a 59 percent total vote–80,786 to 56,065 votes.[59]

Mills told an election-night victory celebration at the Sheraton Hotel, organized by Governor-elect David Pryor, that he believed he had been damaged by news media reports of his enormous congressional power, causing voters to blame him for inflation and other pressing economic problems: "A reputation for power can be a liability, rather than an asset."

Mills released a prepared statement a couple of days after the election, estimating that his re-election campaign cost between $75,000 and $80,000 for office rental, travel, and advertising.[60]

Mills and Polly remained at the Camelot Hotel in Little Rock for several days after the election, resting, visiting friends, drinking and sleeping. They returned to Washington over the weekend.

BACK TO CONGRESS

Mills forged forward on several tax reforms. Congress, he said, would not wait another year to phase out the oil depletion allowance.[61] Mills had an agenda for the post-election congressional session on the Monday following election:

- Increase the minimum standard deduction for individual income tax returns for calendar 1974 income from $1,300 to $1,500.

- Apply individual income a maximum standard deduction of 17.5 percent with a limit of $2,500, to calendar 1975, and perhaps 1974.

- Impose an 85 percent windfall profits tax on oil companies for profits they earn in calendar 1974 and 1975.

- Urge President Ford to ask Congress for a wage and price commission.

- Prohibit future price and wage increases beyond cost-of-living increases for workers or materials for manufacturers.

On November 18, 1974, Mills remembered telling Speaker Albert he was very tired and did not plan to seek re-election as chairman of Ways and Means. The speaker encouraged him to hang tight. Mills developed the Energy Tax Act of 1974, the first major bill he was asked to submit to an open rule.

Meanwhile, personal challenges mounted. The press reported that Mills, Polly, and Annabella Battistella appeared at a well-known nightclub. Mrs. Battistella's husband joined the group shortly after they sat down. Mills, fresh from re-election to his House seat, appeared to enjoy himself, dancing many times with Mrs. Battistella, autographing cocktail napkins and, at one point, hugging a row of girls from George Washington University at the club for a pledge dance. Mills did not dance with Polly. He reported that she recently had broken her foot. Mrs. Mills appeared to be limping that night as she entered the club.

That night, Mills reappeared at the Junkanoo, where he was a regular patron. During the evening he was helped to a men's room by Mrs. Battistella, who had her arm around his shoulder. In the men's room, he was greeted by graffiti that read: "Help, I'm a prisoner here, Wilbur Mills."[63]

By the end of November, Mills yielded to another reform effort and asked the Democratic caucus to increase Ways and Means' size by six members.[64]

Speaker Albert predicted that a move to expand the committee would be made at the caucus' organizational meeting on December 2.[65]

There were 15 Democrats and 10 Republicans on the committee. It would be increased to 21 Democrats and 10 Republicans.[66] The committee, which had been the smallest in Congress, now faced an expansion that was expected to liberalize it, reflecting the House's new political character.[67] Mills tried to see the larger size as a possible plus for achieving a consensus in committee that could hold in the House, "They always said I was a consensus man. The whole purpose of the committee to me was to develop the idea in a way, dress it up in such a way, that it would be attractive to a majority of the members of the House. Otherwise, why waste your time?"[68]

SECOND INCIDENT:
WAKING UP IN HIS OWN NIGHTMARE

On November 28, 1974, the day after Thanksgiving, Mills made an ill-fated trip to Boston, at the urging of Eduardo Battistella, Annabella's husband. He flew in a private jet owned by Executive Air and flown by his favorite pilot, Jim Thomas. Mills appeared on stage at the Pilgrim Theatre, a burlesque house, with Annabella Battistella. Henry Correia, Mills' longtime friend and an assessor from New Bedford, Massachusetts, blamed himself. Correia had planned to dine with Mills that evening at Anthony's Pier 4 along Boston Harbor. It was Mills' favorite restaurant in Boston. Correia had to cancel because of a conflict, leaving Mills in a vulnerable position. Correia was a mutual friend of Mills, former Speaker John McCormack, and Representative Jimmy Burke.[69] Mills blamed his own ego, saying that, when Battistella's husband suggested that if he would go to Boston, it would help Annabella's career, Mills wanted to help. Mills said, "I did what any good congressman does, go to help a person with their career."[70]

Mills telephoned Polly five times during his Boston visit.[71] He explained his reasons for making the trip:

"I went up there to be seen," Mills said. He said this was not the way a man would behave if he had a clandestine relationship with a woman. As for rumors that Mills and his wife might be considering ending their 40-year marriage, Mills said, "Certainly not." He said he and Mrs. Mills "must have played bridge with the Battistellas a hundred times."[72]

After returning from Boston on Sunday, the news hit Washington. Mills had no memory of the weekend. On Monday, he went to his congressional office and chaired a committee meeting. Then, on Tuesday, he was on the floor, requesting recognition from the speaker. There had been storm damage in West Virginia and Pennsylvania, with $5,000 grants given to those with less than $15,000 net worth. The IRS was contending that disaster grant recipients owed taxes on that money. Mills was adamant: "That was not Congress' intent." He got the committee to pass a bill specifically exempting the recipients from those taxes. The bill passed both Houses, but President Ford vetoed it. So, Mills was requesting recognition to ask his colleagues to override the president's veto. Congressman Charles Bennett of Florida asked him if there was not someone else on the committee who could handle it. He said, "Of course not, no one can handle it as well as I can." Bennett insisted. Someone else did handle it, and the House declined to override Ford's veto, just as Mills feared. Mills, while on the House floor that day, told a close friend, "I just can't do it."[73]

Charlie Bennett observed that Mills looked sick. Mills said, "I'm not only sick, I am dying!" So, his congressional colleagues called Admiral Carey, the Capitol physician, to come quickly. Carey advised Mills to go immediately to Bethesda Naval Hospital because his blood pressure was dangerously high, both above and below the line, and he was a very high risk for a heart attack or a stroke. Mills reportedly conferred with his Ways and Means protégé, Dan Rostenkowski of Illinois, who advised him that the caucus was turning against him. He should seek medical help.

Shortly after, he entered Bethesda Naval Medical Center for much-needed treatment. "They took me out to the hospital sometime around four o'clock," he said. "Now, I know I was in a blackout or I would never have gone to the hospital. I had gone to the Naval Hospital in Bethesda a number of times before. I would come to around three or four o'clock in the morning and would call someone, usually Walter Little, to come and get me. I wouldn't even spend the night there; I know I must have been in a blackout or I would have never stayed there, but this time I entered and stayed at the hospital."[74]

Meanwhile, the Democratic caucus voted to enlarge Ways and Means from 25 to 37 members and to remove its power to assign party members to other committees.[75] Starting in January, these assignments would be parceled out by the Democratic Steering and Policy Committee.[76] Mills received support from liberal Representative Phil Burton of California, newly elected chairman of the Democratic caucus, who said he "wouldn't vote to unseat Mr. Mills as chairman."[77]

Many sharp contrasts and paradoxes appeared in the media commentary about Mills: "Steering wheel of the House" [1962], "single most powerful man in Congress" [1971], "second most powerful man in America" [1972]. "Was. Has been, used to be ... today the cropped black hair is gray and rakishly long, the owlish eyeglasses are swingingly mod; the inscrutable Puritan is a baffling night-clubber–and the power is fast draining away."[78]

When Speaker Albert was asked to comment, he said: "I don't think he's feeling well, I really don't. I don't think Wilbur Mills has fully recovered. You know he's been sick a lot. I think it has had an impact on his whole system."[79] And then the next day he said: "We don't want to hurt a man who has done so much for Congress for 36 years. He has a great record. He is one of the greatest congressmen of our generation, but he is a sick man. I don't want to comment further until we hear from the doctors."[80]

Representative James H. Scheur of New York began openly speaking of censuring Mills for his conduct.[81] Capitol observers talked about seeing personality changes in him that year. The usually formal Mills became friendly with many persons he had stood back from in the past.[82] The *Washington Post* reported, "But the original mixed mood of both anger and humor directed against Mills, turned more to empathy and concern. Speaker Albert said he felt 'sorry' for Mills. Another committee member said, 'It's always sad to see a giant fall so hard ... This place can be pretty rough.'"[83]

Meanwhile, Dr. Bohan requested that Nona B., a member of Alcoholics Anonymous, take Mills to a meeting. One of the great relationships in all of AA history resulted from that night. Mills met the man who was to become his AA sponsor, recovery mentor, and great friend for the rest of their lives–Buck Doyle, a national stalwart in the recovery movement for more than 30 years. Mills eventually became obsessed with going to meetings, almost as much as he once was obsessed with work and then with drinking. He attended as many as 22 a week. However, at first, he could see little purpose. Once, Buck called him and Mills said, "I can't go. My sister-in-law is here from Arkansas." Twenty minutes later, he heard a knock at his apartment door, and it was Buck. Mills said, "I thought I told you I couldn't go to a meeting tonight." Buck replied, "I didn't come here to take you to a meeting. I came to meet your sister-in-law." No sister-in-law appeared, so they went to a meeting together. Mills would say, "Buck Doyle always told me that I should only go to alcohol-related meetings on two occasions–when I wanted to and when I didn't want to."

On December 10, Congressman Joe Waggoner of Louisiana, a close friend of Mills, went to visit him. Later, at Mills' request, Waggoner called Speaker Albert to tell him, once again, that Mills would not seek reappointment as chairman of Ways and Means, more than a month before the designation would be made at the convening of the new Congress on January 14, 1975.[84] On a later date, Waggoner was authorized, by House Resolution 8, to go to Bethesda Naval Hospital and administer the oath of office to Mills for the new term to which he had been re-elected in November.

The following day, Mills was quoted simply as saying, "I am bone tired and I want out!"[85] He had served longer than any other chairman of Ways and Means, and he had also served on the committee longer than any other member, records that still stand. During his time as chairman, Mills increased Social Security benefits five times, a cumulative increase totaling 64 percent. Mills' tenure as chairman was often called the liberal era of progressive tax legislation, with repeal of unpopular excise taxes, cuts in personal rates, closing of loopholes, and creating a minimum tax in 1969 aimed at rich people who were avoiding taxes entirely. If Mills' tax code had been in effect when President Clinton took office, the richest 1 percent of Americans would have been paying another $70 billion in taxes per year, according to Robert McIntyre of Citizens for Tax Justice.[86]

On December 29, 1974, Mills issued a full statement that he had dictated to his AA sponsor Buck Doyle, former Senator Harold Hughes of Iowa (his sobriety mentor), and Jeremiah O'Leary of the *Washington Times*, Doyle's partners in assisting Mills in coming to grips with his need to stay on the recovery process. Mills once again apologized to his family, staff, friends, constituents, and congressional colleagues, said he would remain in Congress, and work on recovering from his acute case of chronic alcoholism, committing himself to total abstinence.[87] O'Leary believed that Mills went ahead with this statement, although it is discouraged by the 12-Step program, not only because he was a politician needing to communicate publicly with voters, but as a challenged man needing to box himself in to stick to his resolution for recovery.[88]

Mills explained, "Perhaps the easier path would have been to resign my seat and disappear from public life and public scrutiny. I have never been one to quit in face of adversity and I will not be a quitter now. I know what it is I have to fight and I am resolved to do so."[89]

Medical experts all agreed that the most important factor favoring Mills was   that he recognized alcoholism to be his problem, admitted it openly, and accepted total abstinence as the only cure.

CHAPTER 12

FINDING SOBRIETY AND SLIPPING INTO LEGEND
1975-1992

He began 1975 at Bethesda Naval Medical Center, being treated for acute alcoholism. At the same time, he had nose surgery to correct a deviated septum, a sinus problem.[1] His grandchildren put a sign on his door: "Take Good Care of Granddaddy." President Ford called him.[2] Rose Kennedy called him. The *New York Times* praised him editorially.[3] At the hospital, U.S. Representative Joe Waggoner (D-Louisiana) swore him in for his 19th congressional term.[4] The House chaplain came by to visit him every morning. On January 27, he was released after 57 days of hospitalization. For two months, Mills' world had been contained to the 10th floor at Bethesda. His stay had provided him medical attention, time to think, rest and relaxation, and ready access to AA meetings. But that was a marked, even miraculous change, from his attitude and experience early in his convalescence, in his own words:

> Everything that happened to me in that hospital was an insult.
> There was a woman there, Nona B., that came in one night to tell
> me that a group of people with AA had come in from the Eastern
> Shore of Maryland, down in Virginia, and the District to see me.
> I said, "Well have them come to the room." She said, "No," they
> wanted to see me down in the conference room, in the basement
> of the hospital. She said she was going to take me there. I told
> her that they weren't taking me anywhere, I was going to sleep.
> I didn't have time to talk to a bunch of people. If they wanted to
> see me, they could come up to my room. I figured they had some
> business or something. She finally said, "Well, if you don't go, I'm
> going to lose my job." She knew I was from the South, she knew
> the proper approach to take with a Southerner. A Southerner
> wouldn't be the cause of a woman losing her job. I couldn't think
> of doing that.

I told her I would go. To add insult to injury, she said she'd have to take me down in a wheelchair. However, I was plenty able to walk, so why did they want me in a wheelchair? Perhaps they were afraid that if I got to the elevator by myself, I would run and leave them. After going down to the basement, I sat there from eight o'clock until eleven o'clock. These folks were telling me all about how much they could drink. Well, all in the world they were doing was convincing me that I could have drunk any one of them under the table.

I set out to prove all of them wrong. One afternoon, early in February 1975, I went to Virginia to a liquor store. I bought two quart bottles of 100-proof vodka to take one drink. As ludicrous as it sounds now, it seemed very logical to me at the time. I was thinking that, if someone came by to see me that night, I wanted to have at least enough to have one drink with them. I know now it was insane. People had quit coming to see me months before. They knew that if they wanted to see me and to talk to me, they would have to do it during the daytime. They knew not to come at night. In fact, even my constituents had quit calling me at night.

When I got home, I put one of the bottles into the icebox to chill a bit. With the other, I filled one of my huge glasses to the top and drank it down. I still wasn't sipping. I knew I could pass the test, because never once in my life had I ever taken a drink because I had to. I always drank because I wanted to. I put the glass down and left the kitchen to go into the living room to read or watch television or something. I had won, I had passed the test, I knew it.

After about five minutes had passed, this awful compulsion to have another drink overtook me. It was unbelievable. I can never remember having had anything like it in my life. I gripped the arms of the chair in which I was sitting in an attempt to fight the temptation. I couldn't overcome the temptation. I nearly carried the chair into the kitchen with me. It was a good thing I had bought those two bottles, and people I had expected to visit me never showed up. I then poured myself another drink, and another and another and another.

But it wasn't just two drinks that I took. I drank both bottles and went out for more. I then decided to go to New York. Hugh Carey had asked me to come up to his swearing in as governor in

January, but this was in February. I was going up to his swearing in, and I really thought I was, even though I would be more than a month late. I called Executive Jet Service, headquartered in Columbus, with an operation in Washington. I went to New York City and ended up passed out at the Waldorf-Astoria.

Buck and my doctor were down at the foot of my bed as I opened my eyes.

Buck asked, "Well, what do you think you are now, Wilbur?"

I said, "Well if it will do you any good, I'll say I'm an alcoholic." He said, "It's not what does me good, it's what does you good; now what are you?" I had tried to pass the test, but it had backfired and I had failed.

I had this awful feeling about myself. Good people just didn't do things like that. I had become the lowest thing that God let live. I was an alcoholic. I didn't want to go through life having to say I was an alcoholic. The stigma was too great; I didn't want to live.

The decision was made for me to go into an alcoholic treatment center. Being winter, I opted for the Palm Beach Institute in Florida.[5]

When Hazelton in Minnesota was recommended, Mills asked, "Isn't there a place I can go that is warmer and has lots of sunshine?"[6]

Throughout his treatment, Mills was in regular contact on economic issues with President Ford, Federal Reserve Chairman Arthur F. Burns, Treasury Secretary William Simon, other senior administration officials, and his colleagues on Ways and Means.[7] On February 14, Mills' office released his statement that he was going to receive intense treatment, "the finest expert care," as well as treatment for his "general mental exhaustion," and that his doctors had advised him not to reveal the location of his stay, so that he would not be disturbed, because seclusion and lack of pressure would enhance his chances for recovery.[8] This date, February 14, Valentine's Day, became the beginning of his new sobriety–a day he celebrated each year thereafter.

Television cameras followed him to the Palm Beach Institute (PBI). To assist with the privacy necessary for his successful treatment, his caretakers moved him to a room where he never had to leave the building. A Miami television executive in treatment at the same time, when she noticed a cameraman there from her station, ordered the cameraman away, but others remained to catch a glimpse of Mills.

Mills described his stay at PBI:

My first days of treatment were very difficult. In the hospital, they were giving me sleeping tablets, but in this treatment facility, they wouldn't even give me an aspirin. My first night there I wanted a sleeping tablet. The woman who was in charge of my building asked me if I had ever known of anyone who had died from lack of sleep. Of course, I hadn't. She told me that I wouldn't die either, when I got sleepy enough, I'd fall asleep. I was up half the night.

I had the desire to stay sober. I had it in my mind, then, for the rest of my life. Being in the company of others who understood what I was going through was certainly a help. Polly and I also came to a better understanding of each other. We had fewer disagreements than we had in many, many years."[9]

The Palm Beach Institute had been founded in 1970 by Dr. Ron Catanzaro, "a very, very smart psychiatrist," whose mother was an alcoholic. His father and two brothers were doctors, but they left the treatment of his mother to him. He had been head of a drug and alcohol program in Missouri for Governor Warren Hearnes, and then for Florida's governor, before founding PBI. His father had practiced medicine in Fort Smith, Arkansas, and Dr. Catanzaro had been born there, Mills found out later. He often told his friends, "No wonder he is so effective; he is a native Arkansan."

On April 1, Mills' personal secretary, Jan Ireland, indicated he would remain at West Palm Beach for an additional four weeks and complete his therapy about May 5.[10] Polly joined him after he had been there for a month. She enrolled in the alcoholic treatment program herself, so he remained until she completed her six-week treatment the first of May. He felt guilty about her becoming an alcoholic, saying he had "made her one" by insisting that she join him in drinks. The recovery profession assured him that addiction is largely genetics and chemistry.

In the meantime, many changes were being made at Ways and Means, under the new chairman, Al Ullman of Oregon. One of the first changes was a 1,500 percent increase in the committee staff budget, from less than $200,000 to $3 million.[11] The staff was increased from 35 persons to 100 and the annual budget increase was for salaries. John M. Martin, Jr., continued as chief counsel. In five years, Ullman became the first Ways and Means chairman in history to lose a re-election bid, largely due to his failure to maintain a home, an office, or phone in his congressional district.[11]

Mills returned to his apartment in Arlington on Friday, May 1, and to Congress on Monday, May 4, 1975, after an absence of five months. He looked fit and tan, and his voice sounded relaxed. Everyone who met him heard his warning about alcoholism. His treatment had cost $395 a week for 10 weeks for him and six weeks for Polly, for a total of $6,320.

Mills made it look easy, but he had tremendous internal pain, as he later explained:

> When I got off the plane at National Airport, I passed a bar in the terminal and it really hit me! I wanted a drink. For the next seven months or so, I wanted a drink every waking moment of every day. I would drink ice water and for about five minutes, it would do, then I would have to have more ice water. It was hell, a living hell, every minute wanting a drink. I got back on Saturday and members began calling me that night and on into Sunday. They wanted me back to work on Monday. I don't think that I have ever been more pleased or surprised as I was with the reception that I received."[12]

His colleagues were delighted to have him return and to see him looking so well. They instantly gave him a touching spontaneous standing ovation.

Mills said he planned to be active in Alcoholics Anonymous, "not as a supportive operation but as a way of life."[13] He said he had "been taught not to set goals for myself, just take each day as it comes. Perhaps that was one of my problems. When I didn't come close to goals, I felt frustrated."[14]

In keeping with advice he received to spend as much time in meetings as he previously spent drinking, Mills recalled at first attending 22 alcohol recovery meetings a week for the first five or six years, including breakfast, lunch and evening meetings every day, plus Saturday midnight meetings, with sometimes as many as six or seven meetings on Saturdays and Sundays.[15]

The next day, May 5, his second day back, Mills attended his first committee meeting of the year, was applauded by his Ways and Means colleagues, and sat next to the new chairman, who said, "We look forward to your participation. We have lots of problems and we need your expertise."[16]

Mills told the committee: "You have no reason to miss me. You have performed magnificently. I take a bit of credit for contributing to your training."[17] Mills also said he was leaning toward not running for re-election, but that he could change his mind.[18] In a conversation with Gene Goss, Dan Rostenkowski, later chairman of Ways and Means, characterized Mills at that time–after he resigned from the chairmanship–as being "like Socrates, the great teacher and peripatetic adviser."

Soon after Mills returned to Congress, he went to bat for Riceland Foods of Stuttgart, Arkansas, requesting that the White House provide it adequate time to respond to a *Federal Register* announcement regarding Commodity Credit Corporation's loan maturity dates on rice.[47] The White House granted Mills' request to put off the decision and announcement.

Mills began planning to return to his home in Kensett for a week to visit with constituents and to celebrate his 66th birthday.[20] He made those plans public by phone in a conversation with Dr. Billy Ray Cox of Harding College, who in turn called the local daily newspaper. Meanwhile, Mills announced a $251,000 grant for community development to the City of Searcy under his lifelong friend Mayor Leslie Carmichael.[21]

On his first return to his district after his 20th successful re-election campaign and his subsequent treatment for alcoholism, Mills predicted that he would now be able to better serve.

> I think I will be more help to the district in the present arrangement. I never said this while I was chairman, but that position took 75 to 80 percent of my time. Now I can devote my full attention to my constituents' interests as groups and as individuals.[22]

Mills' reaction to the vast press coverage of his problems was straightforward:

> Whatever opinion one may have with respect to a public figure's private life remaining private—there is no such thing as a private life for one in the public eye. Certainly any of us who follow a life in public have to realize that everything we do, everything we think, everything we say may be fully developed, fully disclosed because it's thought by those who are in the press that the public would be interested in whatever we do, whether this is right or wrong.[23]

Mills also sent a letter supporting local efforts to oust three members of the Arkansas Highway Commission, allegedly appointed unconstitutionally. Mills said that someone from the Second District could have been appointed on three occasions.[24] It was not characteristic of Mills to intervene in state matters, and the letter, apparently written by Max Allison, his longtime supporter, was the first time he had taken direct action in the state since his re-election.

Governor David Pryor appointed Patsy Thomasson, a former staffer of Mills, a native of Rison in South Arkansas who was then residing in Little Rock.

Even in 1975, just after his treatment for alcoholism, Mills received early campaign contributions. He accepted the encouragement and was grateful, but returned the funds.[25] Where some would have returned to the committee with bitterness or not at all, Mills came back as a gentleman. He showed up religiously and took his place alongside Ullman. He took little part in committee discussion and seldom voted.[26] He sat there quietly.[27] His friends knew it was a decision made "in deference to Al."

"No, I don't miss it," Mills said. "I've been tired for a long, long time. It's good not to have all that responsibility for a change.[28] I attend the committee meetings when I want to," he said. "And when I don't feel like it, I don't. After all, I've been over all this stuff many, many times before. I've heard it all."[29] Instead, Mills typically slipped into one of the seats behind the chairman, generally reserved for top committee staff members.[30]

Mills soon announced his opposition to the energy tax bill formulated during his absence by Ways and Mean. He called the bill a short-term approach to a long-term problem. Mills did not take the lead in opposing the measure because it would have been awkward to oppose the first major bill of his immediate successor as chairman. However, in several private discussions, Mills made it clear that he was displeased with the legislation that created a 23-cents-per-gallon increase in the federal gasoline tax. [31]

Mills was disturbed by the Federal Home Loan Mortgage Corporation's vote to close its Little Rock office and move it to Dallas, as a part of consolidation of 12 district offices into five area offices. Mills was joined in his effort to stop the move by presidents of all the area banks and savings and loans. He had his staff call the White House, resulting in a series of memos and conversations in which the White House indicated it was reluctant to intervene and the result was foregone.[32] Mills pushed forward with the president personally and the office was kept open for the remainder of his term, until 1983.

Mills wrote a letter on September 19, 1975, proposing that rice be excluded from the temporary moratorium on the sale of grain to the Soviet Union. The White House responded with positive but noncommittal replies.[33] Mills, in collaboration with New York Governor Hugh Carey, formerly a congressman on Ways and Means, sponsored a bill, HR 10221, to provide an approach to financial problems such as New York City's, extending the Revenue Sharing Act for four years, and allowing distribution of funds directly to cities and counties, rather than having them go through state governments.[34] Under Mills' proposal, cities could issue tax-exempt bonds, with principal being guaranteed by the federal government. Interest on these bonds would be guaranteed by state governments, or other authorized agencies.

Mills sent a telegram to President Ford[35] and issued a statement supporting more aggressive reducing of taxes and federal spending to stimulate the economy:

> What I propose today is an amendment to the individual
> tax reduction section of the bill greater than that which the
> committee has tentatively agreed upon. But that reduction is

coupled with an automatic surtax that will be implemented in stages as federal spending increases above a fixed level. It is a mechanism that for the first time will create a relationship between spending and taxes that must be paid. It is a proposal that will force the Congress to choose between spending and taxing and allow the voters to judge them on that choice.[36]

Nevertheless, Ways and Means on October 23, 1975, approved a $12.7 billion personal tax cut extension, after turning down efforts to tie reductions to federal spending restraints. By a 21-16 margin, the panel then passed Ullman's $12.7 billion plan into a wide-ranging tax revision bill. All 12 Republicans opposed the proposal, joined by four Democrats–Waggoner, Mills, Omar Burleson of Texas and Andy Jacobs, Jr., of Indiana.[37] Mills voted in early December to recommit the tax bill, HR 10612, to Ways and Means, seeking inclusion of a $395 billion spending ceiling for fiscal year 1977.[38] In this, he supported the president and opposed Ways and Means, a first.

Even though Mills faithfully remained sober for the first tough months after his last drink and his successful return to Capitol Hill, he was very down on himself and depressed. He felt great remorse. He felt worthless, hopeless, and useless. He was full of self-condemnation, calling himself "the lowest creature that God let live." A fellow alcoholic recognized the problem and told him, "Wilbur, you are not happy because you have not accepted the fact that alcoholism is a disease. You have not forgiven yourself for being an alcoholic. Repeat to yourself a thousand or two thousand times a day, 'Alcoholism is not a disgrace. Alcoholism is not a stigma. Alcoholism is a disease.' If you say that every day, thousands of times, in time you'll come to believe it."[39]

Then, almost miraculously in December 1975, when asked by friends how he was doing, instead of saying, as he had for many months, "No good" and nervously rubbing his hand, he said, "Fine," and said he did not crave a drink anymore, that he did not remember when he had last craved one. He went to a Christmas party where sangria was served. He didn't drink. He offered to bar tend. He was relaxed and seemed to enjoy visiting with all the guests.

Friends and staff tried to get him to run for Congress again and showed him a poll, admittedly unscientific, with 20 potential candidates indicating he would poll 60 percent. This was about the same percentage he had received after the first incident. He was grateful and inclined to believe it. He jokingly said, "I knew if they would elect me drunk, they might possibly elect me sober."[40]

On March 5, 1976, Mills sent word to President Ford that he would not seek re-election. His longtime friend responded:[41]

Dear Wilbur:

Your decision to retire from the Congress after so many years of distinguished service must have been a difficult one for you to reach. I want you to know that I share the regret of your colleagues and friends that you will not be a member when the 95th Congress convenes in 1977.

During the many years of our association, I have felt that your knowledge and expertise in handling legislation before the Committee on Ways and Means added an invaluable dimension to your service in the Congress. Your record of achievement is one you can view with pride.

You have my best wishes for your years of retirement, which I am certain, will be filled with continued endeavors on behalf of your fellow men.

With warmest personal regards,

Sincerely,

Gerald R. Ford

Representative James Corman of California, later chosen to chair the Ways and Means' Subcommittee on Public Assistance and Unemployment Compensation, once said, "If I've learned anything since I've been here on how to develop a consensus on complex legislation, I learned it from Wilbur Mills."[42] On Tuesday, September 28, from 6 to 8 p.m., Ways and Means hosted a reception to honor its departing members, including Mills, Herman Schneebeli, Phil Landrum, Bill Green and Joe Karth, totaling 112 years of congressional service, and Mills had 38 of them. As Mills retired, his congressional colleagues gave lengthy and laudatory tributes to his extraordinary characteristics of heart and mind, especially his deep care and concern for his constituents.[43]

He reminisced from time to time in those last months, "Beginning with Harry Truman, they were all in here [his office].Cabinet officers, diplomats, ambassadors. They always came by. The ambassador from Bulgaria ... the steel industry people from Japan ... the Common Market secretary ... the minister from Franco's government. One fella wrote once in a column that I'd never traveled, but that I didn't need to. They all came to see me."[44]

Although he had served in Congress for 38 years, Mills said his most significant accomplishment may have come while he was White County judge during the Great Depression[45] when he initiated a medical care program that provided hospital care and medicine to the needy, "probably the first of its kind in the nation."[46] Mills became the member with the longest service on Ways and Means since its inception–35 years–the longest continuous tenure as chairman, and the longest list of major impact legislation.

Mills' concern for those of lowest income levels and for small businesses led to a plethora of laws:

- Tax Legislation, 1954-1975
- Internal Revenue Code of 1954
- Tax Rate Extension Acts of 1955, 1956, 1957, 1958, 1959, and 1960
- Technical Amendments Act of 1958
- Life Insurance Company Income Tax Act of 1959
- Tax Rate Extension Acts of 1961, 1962, and 1963
- Revenue Act of 1962
- Revenue Act of 1964
- Excise Tax Rate Extension Act of 1964
- Excise Tax Reduction Act of 1965
- Interest Equalization Tax Act of 1964, Extensions in 1965, 1967, and 1969
- Tax Adjustment Act of 1966
- Federal Tax Lien Act of 1966
- Foreign Investors Tax Act of 1966
- Revenue and Expenditure Control Act of 1968
- Tax Reform Act of 1969
- Tax Reduction Act of 1971
- Tax Reduction Act of 1975

Mills' major Social Security and international trade accomplishments:

- Social Security Amendments of 1960
- Social Security Amendments of 1961
- Trade Expansion Act of 1962
- Medicare Act of 1965
- Social Security Amendments of 1967

- Social Security Amendments of 1972
- Trade Act of 1974

Mills sought to keep the standard of living high after WWII to increase productivity and to keep tax revenues up and equitable. He always bought American-made cars, usually manufactured by Ford Motor Company and often commented: "You know, Henry Ford was a Democrat." Ford came to Little Rock, at Mills' invitation, to speak to the Economic Council, founded by Mills' close friend Dr. Bessie B. Moore.

Mills worked hard throughout his tenure to keep Social Security on an actuarially sound basis as he implemented increases in benefits and expansions in coverage. To accomplish this, Mills spent his entire congressional career on Social Security, designing it as a nationwide system of social insurance under which workers, their employers, and the self-employed pay Social Security taxes, helping insure workers, their survivors, and their dependents against loss of earnings due to the worker's retirement, death, or disability.

He thought there was no single program—public or private—that had protected the financial well-being of as many Americans as Social Security. Mills' closest aide through all these years was Walter Little, an African-American member of the Ways and Means staff from Mills' earliest days on the committee. He was the consummate aide de camp, chauffeur, "gofer," bodyguard, protector, promoter, clerk, coordinator, facilitator, implementer. He was born in 1917, in Clinton, South Carolina, and died unexpectedly in 1984, in Washington, D.C. Little retired from the Ways and Means staff when Mills retired from Congress in 1977, and continued to work for Mills personally until his death seven years later. Little had 40 years on the committee staff, including Mills' 35 years on the committee. Little's brother, Tim, took his place on the committee staff and served until retirement.

Favorite activities in retirement for Mills included going to recovery functions, keeping up with politics, watching TV mystery shows and sports events, local, state and national news at noon, evening and night, working crossword puzzles and word-search puzzles for relaxation, and taking scenic afternoon drives to Mount Vernon or Manassas, as well as throughout the counties which had at one time or another been in his congressional district in Arkansas.

As Mills left Congress, he had been sober for 23 months. In his view, stopping drinking was "the hardest thing I ever had to do."[47] Eventually, he did not even regret having become an alcoholic:

> I have often said that I would not undo the fact that I became
> an alcoholic after reaching the age of 65. My ongoing recovery
> from alcoholism has taught me so much about myself. There was

a time when I felt that I couldn't make a mistake; if I did, the country would go to rack and ruin. I was making myself a god. Human beings make mistakes, but I thought I couldn't make a mistake. Therefore, I didn't let myself be a human being. That kind of internal pressure is more than the human system can sustain. Here I was doing it to myself consistently. Now, I very deliberately, though only occasionally, make a mistake in dictating a letter or something just to show my secretary that I'm not always perfect.

The primary reason that I wouldn't undo the course my life has taken, including alcoholism, is the relationship that I have developed with my "higher power" that I call God. I have heard people talk about being able to get into a partnership with God. Mine is not a partnership, but a fellowship. For the first time in my life, I'm not lonesome, never, anymore.

I used to be lonesome all the time, even among 10,000 people. I don't remember any time when I didn't feel lonesome. I never feel that way now. I can be driving in Washington traffic and just as I begin to lose my patience, I feel something tapping my shoulder. "Calm down, Wilbur, remember, you can't control anybody but yourself. You just drive your car and let them drive theirs."

Before I got sober I was told that I had the patience of Job; I didn't. I wouldn't show my impatience, just smother it within me. But now, my patience comes from higher up, my God. I carry on a conversation with my "higher power" a dozen times a day, two dozen times a day, three dozen times a day. No matter what I'm involved with, I'm in contact with him, even if it's only in my mind. It is great.

I believed in my mother's God and the church's God, but I never used him the proper way. I tried to make deals with him. He is the hardest fellow in the world to make a deal with, he wouldn't make a deal with me. I've had to learn to communicate with him. Now I communicate, instead of asking him to solve all my problems. If his will is for me to have problems, I'm not going to be able to do much about those problems except to do as he sees fit. I'm not going to burden him with those problems that I think he wants me to solve.[48]

Although *Time* magazine labeled his changing status as "one of the steepest falls from power in congressional history,"[49] Mills indicated he would not miss the power, but he would miss the people he worked with:

> I've served with as fine a cross section of Americans as I think you could find anywhere. I've made many warm friendships over the years, and the members have been very friendly and cooperative. Even in my hours of trouble they were all pulling for me.
>
> I haven't felt anything different today, but I guess I've begun to feel a little remorse these last few days of my congressional career. I'll miss it, and I hope I'll not be regretful of my decision.
>
> They claim they will miss me here. I know they won't miss me as much as I'll miss them.[50]
>
> I enjoy life more now. It's just great to be a human being. In the chairmanship of the Ways and Means Committee, I was more of a machine than a man. I'm happier now than at any time in my life.[51]

Mills on his calling:

> My sobriety was given to me by God. It is a sacred trust that he has reposed in me. I preserve that trust by association with other alcoholics. But there is no pressure on me to perform. There is something that I am supposed to do. There is a challenge in awakening America to problems of alcohol. I know I go too much, but I can't say no to invitations to speak on alcoholism. I have a message I try to take:
>
> 1. I want people of the world to know that alcoholism is a disease.
>
> 2. Alcoholism can be treated.
>
> 3. An alcoholic can be happier sober than when drinking.

His longtime friend, David Parr of North Little Rock, finally figured him out and put it this way: "He programmed those close to him so that they would, in turn, program him."[52] To this day, practically every longtime family in his district has a special story of Mills' legendary care, concern, and help, passed on from generation to generation.

Mills used his personal time during the remaining 15 years and four months of his life after Congress to help others afflicted by the disease of alcoholism.

After leaving Congress, Mills was asked for tax policy advice by Larry Woodworth, who had served as a staffer for Mills on the Joint Committee on Internal Revenue Taxation. In 1977, Woodworth retired, along with Mills, and he was appointed assistant secretary of the Treasury for tax policy. Unfortunately,

Woodworth collapsed and died during a speech on taxation at Williamsburg, Virginia, during the first year of the new administration. Stuart Eisenstadt of the new White House Domestic Policy Office sought Mills out for advice, just as Mills was arriving for a speech at Palm Springs, California. Mills cancelled the speech and returned immediately to the White House. Later, Mills said his advice wasn't followed.

Friends of his at the prominent New York law firm of Shea and Gould, including William Shea of the New York Mets' Shea Stadium fame, invited him to come to New York and recruited him to join as Of Counsel for their Washington, D.C., office at 1637 K Street, NW, and later 1800 Pennsylvania Avenue. During Mills' first meeting with his future law partners in New York, he advised them they probably should not hire him, because he had lost a case before a jury, all of whom he had given jobs. The jury didn't like his client, but made sure Mills had already obtained his fee before deciding against his client. His future partners were amused and charmed by that story. Mills advised clients on tax matters and on strategy with regard to Congress, the White House, and the U.S. Supreme Court. He didn't return to Capitol Hill very often, except as a speaker at special events. He missed Congress very much and rarely returned "because I don't want to start missing it more."

He also would say, "You won't believe how much money I am making." This had never been a priority or even a thought with him. However, he came to enjoy it and to see it as a way in which he could accumulate some wealth to pass along to his grandchildren. The increasing cost of housing concerned Mills. He could not imagine his grandchildren having to pay hundreds of thousands of dollars for a "starter" home. In contrast, Mills often recalled how, when he was starting out, his father bought a house in Kensett for $5,000 and gave it to him. His father then moved the house next door to his own home. It remained Mills' permanent residence for the next 58 years until the day he passed away there. He had never had a mortgage or any monthly payments. Mills' great niece and family now live in that home. Mills' parents' home next door belongs to Mills' nephew, William "Bill" Mills, a retired attorney, chancery judge and state representative, now a Methodist minister, and his wife Treva, formerly his legal assistant and now a Methodist minister. It was Treva who called 911 and administered CPR to Mills on his last day.

In the autumn of 1977 and again in 1985, Mills came back to participate in an Arkansas Highway and Transportation Department ground breaking for Interstate 630, named in his honor, the Wilbur D. Mills Freeway. Its route is an east–west expressway from Interstate 30 to the Interstate 430 bypass of Little Rock, connecting Interstates 30 and 40. Baptist Medical Center, the University of Arkansas for Medical Sciences, and other hospitals became more accessible when I-630 was completed. Community leaders like BMC board chairman

Brick Lile, future Little Rock Mayor Charles Bussey, Herschel Friday, William J. Smith, Bill Bowen, and Buddy Villines believed I-630 would support city and county growth and improve health services.

In 1977, Senator John L. McClellan of Arkansas died. His longtime Senate seat became open over a year before an election would be held. In Arkansas, the governor, then David Pryor, appointed his replacement. There was a draft movement for Mills to serve in that capacity. Mills had a close relationship with Pryor. In fact, Mills had secured him a seat on the House Appropriations Committee, when Pryor was first elected to Congress in 1966. Mills said he was not interested. Pryor appointed Kaneaster Hodges of Newport, who served with quiet distinction.

Mills was shocked that President Carter and Governor Bill Clinton lost their re-election bids in 1980. He never imagined that either would lose and he was deeply saddened, especially with Clinton's defeat. He had known Clinton from his freshman days as a student in international affairs at Georgetown University, beginning in 1964. Clinton, then working two part-time Foreign Relations Committee staff positions for Senator J. William Fulbright, impressed Mills with his penetrating questions—and his habit of listening closely to answers. After the stinging defeat, Mills advised everybody, "Just keep working for Bill, because he will be elected next time. The voters aren't mad at him; they just had their high expectations disappointed."

In 1982, Mills returned to his undergraduate alma mater, appearing at the invitation of Hendrix College, where the Wilbur D. Mills Center contains his congressional papers and a replica of his congressional office. Mills delivered a state-of-the-union-type speech on the economy and future prospects of the country and the world.

In 1983, he returned to cut the ribbon for a new Wilbur D. Mills Treatment Center in Searcy by the Health Resources of Arkansas Corporation, headed by Bill Huddleston of Batesville, as well as to celebrate the 20th Anniversary of President Kennedy coming to Arkansas to dedicate Greers Ferry Dam and Park.

In 1984, the whole Mills family and close friends gathered in White County for the celebration of Mills' and Polly's 50th wedding anniversary. The next year they gathered again to celebrate his brother Roger and Virginia Mills' 50th. Roger and Virginia had met when students at Hendrix College. She was from Conway, the daughter of Rubin Robbins, associate justice of the Arkansas State Supreme Court.

In 1987, Mills brought Polly to the University of Arkansas for Medical Sciences hospital for hip surgery. Polly had broken her hip in 1986. Surgery in the Washington, D.C., area did not resolve the issue and she continued in great pain. The Arkansas surgery went very well. Mills' reaction was: "That figures! I should have brought her here in the first place!" When he was checking her out of the hospital, he asked the bookkeeper how much he owed and pulled out his checkbook to write a check for it. From the expression on her face, that must have been the first time that had happened.

In 1988, General Douglas McArthur Museum of Arkansas Military History sponsored a tribute to Wilbur D. Mills, organized by Catherine Johnson, wife of Mark Johnson, a former Mills intern. Mr. and Mrs. Mills returned for this event to raise funds for the museum. Others participating included then-Governor Bill Clinton, Speaker of the House Jim Wright, Senators Dale Bumpers and David Pryor, as well as then-Vice President George H. W. Bush, who spoke by video.

In 1990, the Baptist Medical System honored Mills with a luncheon to thank him for all of the help he had given them through the years and the leadership role he had played nationally from his time as White County judge to chairman of the Ways and Means Committee. They were especially grateful that Mills had invited then-Vice President Gerald Ford to Little Rock to dedicate the new Baptist Medical System Hospital.

In May 1991, Mills and Polly returned to Arkansas to live day to day in Kensett, after maintaining an apartment in the Washington, D.C., area for 52 years. In October 1991, Mills participated in ground breaking for the new and

Mills talks with his friend, Senator Edward "Teddy" Kennedy, during a conference recess, March 1988. Photo courtesy United States Senate.

larger Wilbur D. Mills Treatment Center for Alcoholism and Drug Abuse in Searcy. Mills called the event "the highlight of his retirement." He celebrated by buying a new 1992 Lincoln Town Car from his favorite car dealer, Dwane Treat, manager of Capps Motor Company in Searcy.

He worked closely with the University of Arkansas for Medical Sciences in launching and advertising the two endowed chairs in medical education and addiction treatment–the Wilbur D. Mills Chairs in Alcohol and Drug Abuse Treatment. Mills was particularly pleased that the first and subsequent Mills chairs and professorships were given to a pharmacologist or drug specialist, rather than a psychiatrist, saying, "Alcohol and drug addiction is a disease, not a disgrace or a character flaw."

He also assisted with the statewide Masonic Lodges' fundraising efforts. Frank Whitbeck asked him to chair the campaign and he agreed. Mills was a Grand Cross, the highest honor in Masonry. He took that position very seriously, especially since being named the first Arkansan to achieve Grand Cross status in 1972.

Mills later returned to Greers Ferry to speak on Earth Day in 1992, along with former Congressman Bill Alexander. Mills recalled his time there with President Kennedy. It was his last public speech.

In May 1992, Mills and Polly were preparing to celebrate his 83rd birthday, her 85th birthday, and their 58th wedding anniversary. On the morning of May 2, Mills collapsed at his home in Kensett. Treva, the wife of his nephew Bill Mills, who lived next door, called 911 and administered CPR. EMTs responded and continued working on him in the ambulance all the way to White County Regional Hospital, with his breathing repeatedly re-started only to stop a few minutes later. At the hospital, Mills was pronounced dead. One doctor believed it to be a heart attack; another thought his body might have been in shock.

The calls of sympathy started coming in to the Mills home, the first one from President George H. W. Bush, who had served under Mills' tutelage on the House Ways and Means Committee from 1966 to 1971. When Mrs. Mills thanked him, she asked him to give her best to Barbara. He responded, "I will do better than that, I will put her on the phone so that you can tell her yourself. Here she is." Mrs. Mills was surprised and grateful.

Mills' funeral was held on May 5 at Kensett Methodist Church, which was filled with hundreds of family and friends, as were the grounds surrounding the church. Loud speakers carried the service to the throng outside. The eulogies were led by David Dixon, Mills' oldest grandson, who said to some understanding and laughter, "I never thought my grandfather's heart would fail; I did suspect that perhaps his driving would." Governor Bill Clinton, out on the presidential campaign trail, called Roger Mills the day of the service. The mayor of Norman, Arkansas, flew the flag at half-staff for the whole summer.

Mills is buried in Kensett Cemetery in the Mills family plot. A memorial service was held in First United Methodist Church, Little Rock, where Professor Robert Meriwether of Hendrix College said, "Mr. Chairman, the committee of your friends and supporters will never adjourn."

Another memorial service was held later in the summer at Washington, D.C., in the House of Representatives Committee on Ways and Means. Dozens of his congressional colleagues spoke and hundreds of his friends, former staff, and family attended. His historic social programs such as Social Security and Medicare, as well as addiction recovery centers, which he supported nationwide, continue to help millions of Americans.

Many memorials to Wilbur Mills are located throughout Arkansas. Memorial busts by Hank Kaminsky of Fayetteville are located at the Arkansas State Capital, Hendrix College, the Wilbur D. Mills Treatment Center in Searcy, John F. Kennedy Park at Greers Ferry, and the Wilbur D. Mills University Studies High School in Sweet Home. Other memorials include Wilbur D. Mills Education Services Cooperative in Beebe, Wilbur D. Mills Avenue in Kensett, Mills Street in Walnut Ridge, Wilbur D. Mills Freeway in Little Rock, the Wilbur D. Mills Center on Hendrix College campus, the Wilbur D. Mills Court Building in Searcy, the Wilbur D. Mills Dam in Desha County, the Wilbur D. Mills Campground at Tichnor, and two Endowed Wilbur D. Mills Chairs on Alcoholism and Drug Abuse at the University of Arkansas Medical Sciences Campus.

Endnotes

Author's Note

1. Robert McIntyre, Citizens for Tax Justice, Director, *Arkansas Democrat-Gazette*, March 23, 1993, page J1.
2. Richard Fenno, *Carl Albert Congressional Research and Studies Center Magazine*, pp. 4-

Chapter 1 Endnotes

1. Interview with Wilbur D. Mills, December 3, 1987.
2. Roger Q. Mills, Sr., May 5, 1988.
3. Wilbur D. Mills, September 10, 1989.
4. Ibid.
5. Ibid.
6. Ibid.
7. Ibid.
8. Hendrix Bulldog, 1926.
9. Wilbur D. Mills Speech, Union Rescue Mission Event, June 29, 1980.
10. Hendrix Bulldog, May 27, 1927.
11. Ibid., April 13, 1928.
12. Wilbur D. Mills, April 12, 1992.
13. Ibid.
14. Hendrix Bulldog, November 9, 1928.
15. Roger Q. Mills, Sr., May 5, 1988.
16. Ibid.
17. Hendrix Bulldog, December 13, 1929.
18. Roger Q. Mills, Sr., May 5, 1988.
19. Hendrix Bulldog, February 7, 1930.
20. Wilbur D. Mills, August 7, 1991.
21. Ibid.
22. Ibid.
23. Newsweek, January 14, 1963, 17.
24. Wilbur D. Mills, September 10, 1991.
25. Ibid.
26. Ibid.
27. The Congressman from Kensett, documentary, interview with Mills, 1971.
28. Wilbur D. Mills, September 10, 1991.
29. Ibid.
30. Ibid.
31. Ibid.

Chapter 2 Endnotes

1. Herbert Hoover Presidential Library website, homepage, www. herberthooverpresidentiallibrary.org.
2. Oral history interview with Wilbur D. Mills by Charles Morrissey, June 5, 1979.
3. Searcy: A Frontier Town Grows Up by R. C. Munsey, 265.
4. Searcy Daily Citizen, July 7, 1934.
5. Interview with Ewing Orr, at Judsonia, Arkansas, October 13, 1987.
6. Interview with Wilbur D. Mills, August 7, 1991.
7. Searcy Daily Citizen, May 24, 1934.
8. Ibid.
9. Wilbur D. Mills, September 29, 1987.
10. Ibid., December 20, 1987.
11. Ibid.
12. Mills Campaign literature, 1934.
13. Wilbur D. Mills, August 7, 1991.
14. Ewing Orr, October 13, 1987.
15. Wilbur D. Mills, September 13, 1989.
16. Ibid.
17. New York Times, August 15, 1967.
18. Wilbur D. Mills, December 26, 1988.
19. Ibid.
20. Ibid.
21. Ibid.
22. Ibid.
23. Ibid.
24. Ibid.
25. Ibid.
26. Ibid.
27. Ibid.
28. Interview with Floyd Bradberry, October 13, 1987.
29. Wilbur D. Mills, September 13, 1988.
30. Ibid.
31. Searcy Daily Citizen, May 15, 1935, 2.
32. Ibid., January 6, 1936.
33. Ibid., January 8, 1936.
34. Ibid.
35. White County Court Order, January 7, 1935, signed by Judge Mills.
36. Searcy Daily Citizen, January 8, 1936.
37. Ibid., January 6, 1936.
38. Ibid.
39. Ibid.
40. Ibid., June 4, 1936.
41. Wilbur D. Mills, December 24, 1987.
42. Ibid.
43. Searcy Daily Citizen, June 8, 1936.

44. Searcy Daily Citizen, July 15, 1936.
45. Ibid., March 24, 1938.
46. Ibid., November 10, 1936, front page.
47. Ibid.
48. White County Court Order, signed by Judge Mills, January 4, 1937.
49. Ewing Orr Interview, October 13, 1987.
50. Searcy Daily Citizen, May 6, 1937.
51. Wilbur D. Mills, April 22, 1992.
52. Interview with Forest Waller, November 18, 1987.
53. Arkansas Gazette, article by C. P. Lee, Jr., April 27, 1936.
54. Ibid.
55. Conversation with Perrin Jones, November 18, 1987.
56. Interview with Charles Yingling, November 18, 1987.
57. Interview with Pangburn City Clerk Ernest Everett, July 21, 1993.
58. Time magazine, January 25, 1962, 19.
59. Panel Presentation by Dr. Steven Neuse, then Director of Public Administration, Department of Political Science, University of Arkansas, Fayetteville, at Arkansas Political Science Association, March 1, 1991

Chapter 3 Endnotes

1. Wilbur D. Mills, August 7, 1991.
2. Arkansas Gazette, October 19, 1937.
3. Searcy Daily Citizen, October 20, 1937.
4. Interview with Jerry Screeton, September 5, 1982.
5. Ibid.
6. Searcy Daily Citizen, December 2, 1937.
7. Ibid., June 15, 1938.
8. Ibid., July 15, 1938.
9. Ibid.
10. Wilbur D. Mills, August 7, 1991.
11. Searcy Daily Citizen, July 14, 1938.
12. Wilbur D. Mills, August 7, 1991.
13. Mills Campaign Literature, 1938.
14. Wilbur D. Mills, August 7, 1991.
15. Interview with Ewing Orr, October 13, 1987.
16. Ibid.
17. Ibid.
18. Wilbur D. Mills, December 24, 1988.
19. Searcy Daily Citizen, August 11, 1938.
20. Ibid., August 15, 1938.
21. Wilbur D. Mills, June 7, 1991.
22. Ibid.
23. Ibid.
24. Roger Q. Mills, Sr., September 10, 1992.
25. Wilbur D. Mills, November 5, 1987.
26. Ibid.
27. Ibid.
28. Ibid.
29. Ibid.
30. Ibid.
31. Ibid.
32. Ibid.
33. Ibid.
34. Ibid.
35. Ibid.
36. Ibid.
37. Ibid., September 19, 1991.
38. Wilbur D. Mills, March 4, 1992.
39. Searcy Daily Citizen, March 29, 1939.
40. Ibid., April 21, 1939.
41. Ibid.
42. Ibid.
43. Ibid., August 8, 1939.
44. Wilbur D. Mills, March 4, 1992.
45. Searcy Daily Citizen, August 11, 1939.
46. Ibid.
47. Ibid.
48. Wilbur D. Mills, March 5, 1988.
49. Ibid., April 4, 1991.
50. Ibid.
51. Ibid., May 28, 1991, upon full-time move back to Arkansas.
52. Ibid., June 17, 1991.
53. Ibid.
54. Ibid.
55. Ibid.
56. Ibid.
57. Ibid.
58. Ibid.
59. Ibid.
60. Ibid.
61. Ibid.
62. Ibid. and Searcy Daily Citizen, December 8, 1941.
63. Searcy Daily Citizen, December 9, 1941.
64. Ibid., February 9, 1942.
65. Ibid., March 28, 1942.
66. Ibid.
67. Ibid.
68. Wilbur D. Mills, August 7, 1991.
69. Ibid.
70. Ibid.
71. Ibid.
72. Searcy Daily Citizen, April 24, 1942.

73. Wilbur D. Mills, August 7, 1991.
74. Searcy Daily Citizen, August 12, 1942.
75. Wilbur D. Mills, August 7, 1991.
76. Ibid.
77. Ibid.

Chapter 4 Endnotes

1. St. Louis Post-Dispatch, August 1, 1942, Report from Capitol Hill, quoting Leon Henderson, Director, U.S. Office of Price Administration.
2. Arkansas Gazette, October 15, 1990, 7.
3. Wilbur D. Mills, August 7, 1991.
4. Ibid.
5. Ibid.
6. Ibid.
7. Ways and Means Committee Print Number 2, 1942.
8. Minutes of Ways and Means Committee, House of Representatives, 1941-1942, 77th Congress, December 2, 1942.
9. Message, President Roosevelt, Document Number 882, 77th Congress, 2nd Session, 2.
10. Searcy Daily Citizen, March 1, 1944.
11. Ibid.
12. Ibid.
13. Ibid.
14. Wilbur D. Mills, August 7, 1991.
15. Minutes of Ways and Means Committee, House of Representatives, March 9, 1943, 29.
16. Ibid., March 16, 1943, 37.
17. Ibid., June 21, 1943.
18. Searcy Daily Citizen, November 9, 1945, front page.
19. Ibid., February 3, 1947, front page.
20. Ibid., May 24, 1947, front page.
21. Minutes of Ways and Means Committee, House of Representatives, March 9, 1943, 113.
22. Searcy Daily Citizen, July 22, 1943, front page.
23. Ibid., August 11, 1943, front page.
24. Replica on display at Sam Rayburn Library and Museum, Bonham, Texas.
25. Wilbur D. Mills, August 7, 1991.
26. Ibid., April 1, 1991.
27. Ibid.
28. Ibid.
29. William Miller: Fishbait, Random House, 1978, 34.

30. Arkansas Democrat-Gazette, June 23, 1992, 7A.
31. Ibid., "America At War, 1941-1945," May 9, 1992, 10A.
32. Searcy Daily Citizen, May 5, 1943, front page.
33. Ibid., August 28, 1946.
34. Ibid., April 6, 1947, front page.
35. Ibid.,
36. Ibid., September 10, 1947, front page.
37. Wilbur D. Mills, August 7, 1991.
38. Arkansas Democrat, August 14, 1943.
39. Searcy Daily Citizen, March 31, 1944, front page.
40. Wilbur D. Mills, August 7, 1991.
41. Letters from Wilbur D. Mills, March 11, 1946, Harry S. Truman Presidential Library, Public Papers of President Truman.
42. Searcy Daily Citizen, June 11, 1947, front page.
43. Ibid., February 12, 1945.
44. Ibid., June 11, 1945.
45. Ibid.
46. Minutes of the Ways and Means Committee, House of Representatives, 1948, 38.
47. Searcy Daily Citizen, January 27, 1945.
48. February 17, 1945, front page.
49. Wilbur D. Mills, August 7, 1991.
50. Searcy Daily Citizen, September 2, 1943, front page.
51. Ibid.
52. Ibid., July 26, 1944, front page.
53. Wilbur D. Mills, August 7, 1991.
54. Interview with Wilbur D. Mills, by Tony Champagne, March 13, 1986, 7-8.

Chapter 5 Endnotes

1. Arkansas Gazette, June 26, 1977, 5A.
2. Ibid.
3. Wilbur D. Mills, May 24, 1988.
4. Business Week, November 6, 1954, 27.
5. Robert K. Walsh, Oral History Interview by Jerry N. Hess, Harry S. Truman Presidential Library, January, 1972, 118.
6. Wilbur D. Mills, September 25, 1989.
7. Searcy Daily Citizen, February 14, 1949, front page.
8. Oral History Project with former Congressman Walter Judd, Former Members of Congress Association, Inc.,

by Charles Morrissey, January 26, 1976, 27.

9. Paul Bursey, March 30, 1993.

10. Searcy Daily Citizen, May 27, 1949, front page.

11. U.S. News and World Report, March 11, 1949.

12. Ibid., June 15, 1956, 143.

13. Interview with Capital Hill Journalist Doug Smith, National Press Club, April 13, 1991.

14. Searcy Daily Citizen, July 31, 1950, front page.

15. Ibid.

16. Ibid., June 2, 1953, front page.

17. Ibid., September 18, 1957, front page.

18. Ibid., March 3, 1955, front page.

19. Ibid., March 15, 1955, front page.

20. Ibid., May 20, 1955, front page.

21. Congressional Quarterly, 1955, lists the signers, in addition to Mills, as Senators Paul Douglas of Illinois, John Sparkman of Alabama, Joseph O'Mahoney of Wyoming; Representatives Wright Patman of Texas, Richard Bolling of Missouri, and Augustine Kelly of Pennsylvania.

22. Ibid.

23. Searcy Daily Citizen, January 10, 1957, front page.

24. U.S. News and World Report, January 11, 1957, 30.

25. Searcy Daily Citizen, November 27, 1957, front page.

26. Minutes of the Ways and Means Committee, U.S. House of Representatives, 1955, 344.

27. Ibid., 1953-1954, 204-205.

28. Ibid., 633.

29. U.S. News and World Report, January 11, 1957, 131.

30. Wilbur D. Mills, April 4, 1991.

31. Business Week, May 25, 1955, 31.

32. Grover Ensley Oral History Interview, Senate Historical Office, November 1, 1955.

33. Searcy Daily Citizen, April 8, 1952, front page.

34. Ibid., April 9, 1952, front page.

35. Ibid., November 17, 1949, front page.

36. Ibid.

37. Congressional Digest, April, 1951, 117-119.

38. Searcy Daily Citizen, May 25, 1953, front page.

39. Ibid., May 24, 1949, front page.

40. HR 4133, 1954.

41. Searcy Daily Citizen, November 19, 1954, front page.

42. Ibid., August 18, 1956, front page.

43. Ibid., July 23, 1951, front page.

44. Ibid.

45. Ibid.

46. Ibid., November 20, 1949, front page.

47. Ibid., October 18, 1957, front page.

48. Ibid.

49. Ibid., December 16, 1957, front page.

50. Ibid., June 29, 1957, front page.

51. Ibid., July 1, 1957, front page.

52. Ibid.

53. Ibid.

54. Ibid., August 24, 1956, front page.

55. Ibid., January 10, 1956.

56. Oral History Interview with Wilbur D. Mills by Charles Morrissey, June 5, 1979.

57. Wilbur D. Mills, December 20, 1987.

58. Congressional Quarterly, Weekly Report, October 20, 1990, 3501.

59. Searcy Daily Citizen, November 27, 1957, front page.

60. Arkansas Democrat, Associated Press story, Michael Landsberg, June 16, 1991, 1H.

61. Lester Thurow, Investing in America, Economic Policy Institute, October 21, 1991.

62. Congressional Record, January 8, 1951.

63. Ibid., January 5, 1955.

64. Wilbur D. Mills, August 7, 1991.

65. Oral History Interview, Wilbur D. Mills by Charles Morrisey, June 5, 1979.

66. Wilbur D. Mills, August 7, 1991.

67. Congressional Almanac, 1956, 222.

68. Ibid., 1957, 348.

69. Wilbur D. Mills, August 7, 1991.

70. Searcy Daily Citizen, October 30, 1954, front page.

71. Ibid.

72. Wilbur D. Mills, September 25, 1989.

73. American Hospital Association Library, Oral History Interview: In the First Person, Wilbur D. Mills, conducted by Editor Lewis E. Weeks.

74. Searcy Daily Citizen, December 19, 1957, front page.

75. Letter from Mrs. Mary Roosevelt, February 2, 1991.

76. Nation's Business, March, 1956, 35.
77. Ibid.
78. New York Times, December 20, 1957, 20.
79. Wall Street Journal, December 20, 1957, 5.
80. Washington Evening Star, December 20, 1957, A8.
81. Searcy Daily Citizen, July 27, 1956, front page.
82. Nation's Business, February, 1957, 109.
83. Ibid., 108.

Chapter 6 Endnotes

1. Quoted in Searcy Daily Citizen, March 24, 1958, front page.
2. Ibid.
3. Ibid.
4. Dignity by Sherry David, Greenwood Press, 1985.
5. Conversation with Sander Vanocur, November 6, 1992.
6. Conversation with Gene Goss, Mills' Chief of Staff, May 2, 1990.
7. Time magazine, February 2, 1959, 11.
8. Business Week, January 13, 1962, 27.
9. U.S. News and World Report, January 15, 1962, 37.
10. Arkansas Democrat, October 6, 1961, front page.
11. Arkansas Gazette, New York Times News Service, "Man in the News," January 9, 1962.
12. Washington Post, Joseph Alsop, January 8,1962, A13.
13. Creation of Income by Taxation, Joshua Clapp Hubbard, 236.
14. Power in Washington by Douglas Cater, published by Random House, New York, New York, 1964, 148.
15. Ibid.
16. Forge of Democracy: The House of Representatives, Neil McNeil, 1963, 334-35.
17. Washington Evening Star, October 26, 1976.
18. Searcy Daily Citizen, October 20, 1961, front page.
19. Arkansas Gazette, November 11, 1962, 3E.
20. Ibid., October 6, 1961, front page.
21. Ibid., November 23, 1961, front page.
22. Ibid.
23. Arkansas Gazette, March 28, 1962, 3E.
24. Ibid., November 23, 1961, front page.
25. Ibid.
26. Ibid.
27. Ibid.
28. No Final Victories by Lawrence F. O'Brien, 5.
29. Oral history interview with Mills by Michael Gillette, Lyndon B. Johnson Presidential Library, Interview II, 63.
30. Searcy Daily Citizen, December 1, 1961, front page.
31. Arkansas Democrat, January 3, 1990, 5B.
32. Ibid.
33. Searcy Daily Citizen, October 26, 1961, front page.
34. Ibid., September 20, 1958, front page.
35. Ibid., May 27, 1959, front page.
36. Ibid.
37. Ibid., October 26, 1959, front page.
38. Ibid.
39. Arkansas Gazette, November 23, 1961, front page.
40. Ibid., November 16, 1961, 2A.
41. Ibid.
42. Congressional Quarterly Almanac, 1961, 280.
43. Ibid., 281.
44. Congressional Quarterly Almanac, 1960, 153.
45. Ibid., 148.
46. Ibid.
47. Ibid.
48. Ibid.
49. Congressional Quarterly Almanac, Volume 3, 1961-1962, 263.
50. Ibid.
51. Ibid.
52. Ibid., 264.
53. Ibid.
54. Ibid., 191.
55. Ibid., 195.
56. Nation's Business, November, 1959, 7.
57. Business Week, March 22, 1958, 60.
58. U.S. News and World Report, December 12, 1958, 112.
59. Life magazine, November 23, 1957, 51.
60. Ibid., 60.
61. Congressional Quarterly Almanac, 201, discussion of passage of HR 7523, Section 86:75.
62. Ibid., 1958, 146.
63. Ibid., 1961, 481.

64. Searcy Daily Citizen, April 9, 1958, front page.
65. Ibid., May 27, 1958, front page.
66. Ibid.
67. Ibid., June 10, 1958, front page.
68. Congressional Quarterly, 1959-1960, 673-74.
69. Searcy Daily Citizen, June 13, 1962, front page.
70. Ibid.
71. Ibid.
72. Oral history interview, Wilbur D. Mills by Charles Morrissey, June 5, 1979.
73. Ibid.
74. Congressional Quarterly, 1962, 509.
75. Letter from John F. Kennedy to Wilbur D. Mills, reprinted in the New York Times, March 23, 1961.
76. C-SPAN coverage of Bicentennial Celebration of the Creation of the Ways and Means Committee, Roundtable of Former and Current Members, 1989, available from C-SPAN Library.
77. Party Leaders in the House of Representatives, by Randall Ripley.
78. Arkansas Democrat-Gazette, Editorial Page, July 28, 1992, 4B.
79. Kenneth P. O'Donnell and David F. Powers, Johnny, We Hardly Knew You, Little Brown and Company, 1972, 278-79.
80. Oral history interview, Wilbur D. Mills by Charles Morrissey, June 5, 1979.
81. Wilbur D. Mills, September 25, 1989.
82. Public Papers of the Presidents, John F. Kennedy, 1962, 488, Government Printing Office, Washington, D.C.
83. Home Place: The Story of the U.S. House of Representatives by William S. White, Houghton Mifflin Company, Boston, 1965.
84. As quoted by Neil McNeil, Forge of Democracy: The House of Representatives, David McKay Company, New York, 1963, 334.
85. Public Papers of Presidents, John F. Kennedy, 1962, Government Printing Office, Washington, D.C., 361.
86. Wilbur D. Mills, January 1, 1992.
87. Ernest Everett, Pangburn City Hall, July 21, 1993.
88. Wilbur D. Mills, January 1, 1992.
89. Roger Q. Mills, Sr., August 28, 1985.
90. Wilbur D. Mills, December 21, 1990.
91. New York Times, January 8, 1962, 18.
92. Newsweek, January 14, 1963, 14.

Chapter 7 Endnotes

1. Time, January 11, 1963, 19.
2. Memorial Services for Wilbur D. Mills, U.S. House of Representatives Ways and Means Hearing Room, Longworth House Office Building, Remarks by former Congressman Barber Conable, June 29, 1992.
3. Memorial Services, Remarks by New York Governor Hugh L. Carey, June 29, 1992.
4. Wilbur D. Mills, August 7, 1991.
5. Interview with Paul Geffert, CEO, Ventus Group, Bethesda, Maryland, January 10, 1993.
6. Congress and The Income Tax, Barber B. Conable, Jr., and Arthur L. Singleton, Norman, Oklahoma: University of Oklahoma Press, 1989, 17.
7. Wilbur D. Mills Speech, Mills Tribute Dinner, Little Rock, Arkansas, March 4, 1988.
8. Newsweek, January 14, 1963, 13-18.
9. Time, January 11, 1963.
10. Newsweek, January 14, 1963, 15.
11. Searcy Daily Citizen, July 19, 1963, front page.
12. Ibid.
13. Wilbur D. Mills, August 7, 1991.
14. An excerpt from speech by President John F. Kennedy, October 3, 1963, at Greers Ferry Dam and Park Dedication, included in documentary film, "The Congressman from Kensett," produced by Jim Faulkner and Associates, Little Rock, 1971.
15. Wilbur D. Mills, September 25, 1989.
16. Oral History Interview with Wilbur D. Mills by Joe B. Franz, November 2, 1971, 10.
17. Ibid.
18. Searcy Daily Citizen, November 4, 1964, front page.
19. U.S. House of Representatives Report on HR 8464, 438.
20. HR 15202.
21. House Report, 1966, 714.
22. Ibid.
23. Ibid.
24. Ibid.
25. Ways and Means Committee Minutes, Volume 1961-1962, 17.

26. Newsweek, January 14, 1963, 15.
27. Wilbur D. Mills, September 25, 1989.
28. Searcy Daily Citizen, April 10, 1963, 15.
29. Time, January 11, 1963, 20.
30. Business Week, January 5, 1963, 15.
31. Newcomb Stillwell, "This Is Strange Coming From Me," Forbes, April 13, 1981, 56.
32. U.S. News and World Report, December 13, 1965, 107.
33. Nation's Business, December, 1965, 50.
34. Wilbur D. Mills, September 25, 1989.
35. Public Papers of Presidents, John F. Kennedy, Government Printing Office, Washington, DC, 27-29, 119.
36. Forbes, December 15, 1964, 15.
37. The Politics of Finance: The House Ways and Means Committee, John Manley, 27-29, 119.
38. Congressional Quarterly, Second Session, Volume 1, 1963-1964, 317; Fortune, June, 1965, 168.
39. Joe Franz Interview of Wilbur D. Mills, 15.
40. Wilbur D. Mills, November 5, 1987.
41. Sheri David, With Dignity, 108.
42. Wilbur D. Mills, September 25, 1989.
43. Congress and Nation, Volume II, 752.
44. Ibid.
45. Ibid.
46. Mike Manatos to Jack Valenti, October 1, 1964, Manatos file, LBJ Papers, Box 4, General Legislative files, Lyndon B. Johnson Library.
47. Manatos to Lawrence O'Brien, September 21, 1964, Johnson Presidential Library.
48. New York Times, October 2, 1964, 16.
49. Ibid., October 3, 1964, 28.
50. Gene Goss, October 10, 1981.
51. Wilbur J. Cohen conversation with Gene Goss, Washington, D.C., October 14, 1974.
52. Fortune, June, 1965, 196.
53. Randall B. Ripley, Congress: Process and Policy, W. W. Norton and Company, 1975, 105.
54. Alton Frye, A Responsible Congress: The Politics of National Security, McGraw Hill Book Company, 1975, 175.
55. Barbara Hinckley, The Seniority System, Indiana University Press, 1971, 91.
56. Gene Goss, October 10, 1974.
57. Ibid.
58. Lyndon B. Johnson, The Vantage Point,
215-16.
59. Conversation with Doris Kearns Goodwin, Kennedy School of Government, April 6, 1991.
60. Wilbur D. Mills, August 7, 1991.
61. Ibid.
62. Fortune, June, 1965, 267-76.
63. Congressional Quarterly Service, Congressional Quarterly Almanac, 87th Congress, 2nd Session, Washington, DC, 1965, 21:252.
64. Congress and Nation, Volume II, 753.
65. Wilbur D. Mills, September 25, 1989.
66. Searcy Daily Citizen, July 28, 1965, front page.
67. Joe Franz Interview of Wilbur D. Mills, 26.
68. Searcy Daily Citizen, April 5, 1964, front page.
69. Wilbur D. Mills, July 7, 1982.
70. Searcy Daily Citizen, August 12, 1965, front page.
71. Ibid.
72. Documentary film, "The Congressman from Kensett," 1971.
73. Searcy Daily Citizen, January 4, 1966, front page.
74. Ibid., April 27, 1966, front page.

Chapter 8 Endnotes

1. Congress vs. President, by Harvey Mansfield, Praeger Publishers, 1975, 4.
2. Vogue, November 15, 1969, 107-108.
3. Boston Evening Globe, June 1, 1968.
4. Fortune, June, 1968.
5. Washington Monthly, December, 1974, and Searcy Daily Citizen, December 15, 1969, front page.
6. The Little Giant, by Carl Albert, University of Oklahoma Press, 1990, 267.
7. Nation's Business, February, 1968, 50.
8. Catherine Rudder, "Fiscal Responsibility and Revenue Committees," Congress Reconsidered, edited by Lawrence Dodd and Bruce Oppenheimer, Congressional Quarterly Press, 1985, 213.
9. I. M. Destler, "Executive-Congressional Conflict in Foreign Policy," Ibid., 353.
10. Steven Smith and Christopher Deering, Committees in Congress, Congressional Quarterly Press, 1984, 95.
11. John Manley, The Committee and the House, 101.

12. Ibid.
13. New York Times Magazine, June, 1968.
14. Wilbur D. Mills, November 5, 1987.
15. Then-Vice President George H. W. Bush in taped message on occasion of Wilbur D. Mills Tribute, March 4, 1988, Little Rock, Arkansas.
16. Fitzhugh Green, George Bush: An Intimate Portrait, 101.
17. Ibid.
18. Robert S. McCord, quoting Sam Walton, Arkansas Gazette, October, 1990, 8.
19. Searcy Daily Citizen, January 28, 1971, front page.
20. Congressional Quarterly Almanac, 1967, 893.
21. Congressional Quarterly Almanac, 1967, 916.
22. Wilbur D. Mills, July 4, 1991.
23. U.S. News and World Report, December 23, 1968, 34.
24. Wilbur D. Mills, September 23, 1988.
25. Congressional Quarterly Almanac, 1969, 840.
26. Ibid.
27. Ibid.
28. Ibid.
29. Joseph Califano, The Triumph and Tragedy of Lyndon Johnson, 1988, 247.
30. Wilbur D. Mills, November 26, 1987.
31. Congressional Quarterly Almanac, 1967, discussion of HR 4765, 1005.
32. Mills' Interview with Joe B. Frantz, 28.
33. Ibid.
34. Arkansas Gazette, January 7, 1968, E1.
35. Mills Interview with Joe B. Frantz, 49.
36. Washington Star, June 16, 1968.
37. U.S. News and World Report, October 9, 1967, 5.
38. Oral history interview of Mills by Michael Gillette, May, 1987, Lyndon B. Johnson Presidential Library, Interview II, 26-28.
39. Congressional Quarterly Almanac, 1967, 653.
40. Arkansas Gazette, January 7, 1968, E1.
41. Wilbur D. Mills, January 3, 1973.
42. U.S. News and World Report, May 6, 1968, 101.
43. Oral history interview with Mills by Michael Gillette, Lyndon B. Johnson Presidential

Library, May, 1987, 4.
44. Searcy Daily Citizen, October 6, 1967, front page.
45. Ibid.
46. Time, February 9, 1968, 17.
47. Ibid.
48. Washington Star, June 3, 1968.
49. Ibid.
50. Joe B. Frantz Interview of Mills, 22.
51. Searcy Daily Citizen November 21, 1967, front page.
52. Wilbur D. Mills, January 3, 1973.
53. Ibid.
54. Ibid.
55. Time, February 9, 1968.
56. Ibid.
57. Joe B. Frantz Interview of Mills, 36.
58. Washington Star, June 16, 1968, front page.
59. Ibid., A10.
60. Ibid., January 7, 1968, E13.
61. Wilbur D. Mills, January 3, 1973.
62. Ibid.
63. Joe B. Frantz Interview of Mills, 14.
64. The Vantage Point, Lyndon B. Johnson, 442.
65. Oral history interview, Charles Morrissey, April 5, 1979.
66. Forbes, Newcomb Stillwell, "This Is Strange Coming From Me," April 13, 1981, 56.
67. Congressional Record, March 7, 1969, S 2449.
68. American Survey, January 4, 1969, 29.
69. Washington Star, June 9, 1971.
70. Wilbur D. Mills, January 3, 1973.
71. U.S. News and World Report, May 26, 1969, 42-43.
72. Fortune, September, 1969, 55.
73. Congressional Quarterly Almanac, 1969, 610.
74. John Kingdom, Congressmen's Voting Decisions, Harper and Rowe, New York, 1973, 130.
75. Ibid.
76. Washington Star, September 10, 1969.
77. Congressional Quarterly Almanac, 1969.
78. Business Week, December 27, 1969, 71.
79. Ibid.

80. Ibid.
81. Wilbur D. Mills, August 9, 1991.
82. Congressional Record, March 10, 1969.
83. Ibid.
84. Ibid.
85. Ibid., 173.
86. Ibid., 1968, 789.
87. Ibid., 1969, 173.
88. History of Ways and Means Committee, Introduction, Government Printing Office, 1.
89. Ibid.
90. Wilbur D. Mills, June 26, 1990.
91. Shirley Chisholm, Unbought and Unbossed, 1971, 81.
92. Ibid.
93. Ibid., 84.
94. Ibid., 85.
95. The History of The House, Congressional Quarterly, Inc., 155.
96. Ibid., 156.
97. Ibid.
98. Ibid.
99. Wilbur D. Mills, June 15, 1980.
100. Forbes, April 1, 1969, 51.
101. Almanac of American Politics, 1972, 34-39.
102. Congressional Quarterly Almanac, 1970, 604.

Chapter 9 Endnotes

1. Congressional Quarterly, July 30, 1971, 1617.
2. Washington Star, March 3, 1971 and New York Times, March 20, 1971, 31.
3. Business Week, May 8, 1971.
4. Reader's Digest, January, 1971, 101-05.
5. Life, February 19, 1971.
6. Conversation with Charles Zuver, Willard Hotel, Washington, D.C., January 21, 1993.
7. Life, Marshall Frady, July 16, 1971, 52.
8. Newsweek, February 15, 1971, 26.
9. Paul Wieck, "Wilbur Mills' Non-candidacy," The New Republic, 18.
10. Los Angeles Times, June 11, 1971.
11. Washington Star, May 2, 1971, C3.
12. Letter from Attorney Bill Penix, Jonesboro, Arkansas, October 2, 1989.
13. New York Times, June 20, 1971, 45.
14. Ibid.
15. Ibid.
16. Ibid.
17. Ibid.
18. Ibid.
19. Searcy Daily Citizen, March 22, 1971, front page.
20. Wilbur D. Mills, July 4, 1981.
21. Business Week, September 11, 1971, 66.
22. Ibid.
23. Ibid.
24. Ibid.
25. Interview by George Herman, Face the Nation, June 4, 1971.
26. The Catholic Worker, June-July, 1993, 1.
27. Searcy Daily Citizen, January 8, 1971, front page.
28. U.S. News and World Report, March 15, 1971, 43.
29. Congressional Record, March 12, 1971, Senate, 6374.
30. Ibid., Roll Call No. 23, not voting 20, 6390.
31. P.L. 91-510.
32. Congressional Quarterly Almanac, 1971, 423.
33. Ibid.
34. Congressional Record, March 16, 1971, House Roll Call No. 20, 6741-42.
35. Ibid., Roll Call No. 24, P 6688.
36. U.S. News and World Report, March 15, 1971, 43.
37. Robert J. Samuelson, "Busting the U.S. Budget – The Cost of an Aging America," National Journal, February 18, 1978, 256.
38. Congressional Record, June 22, 1971, House, Roll Call No. 157, not voting 13, 21463.
39. Ibid., October 5, 1972, Senate, Roll Call, No. 536, not voting 27, 33995.
40. Ibid., October 17, 1972, Senate, Roll Call No. 45, not voting 122, 36936.
41. Ibid., Roll Call No. 567, not voting 39, 36825.
42. Searcy Daily Citizen, July 20, 1972, front page.
43. U.S. News and World Report, March 15, 1971, 42.
44. Business Week, February 26, 1972, 66.
45. Searcy Daily Citizen, July 20, 1972, front page.
46. HR 10947 – PL 92 – 178.
47. Congressional Quarterly Almanac, 1971, 430.
48. Ibid.
49. Ibid.

50. Ibid.
51. Oral history interview with Mills by Michael Gillette, Interview III, 18-19, May 1987, Johnson Presidential Library.
52. Ibid.
53. Time, March 22, 1971, 70.
54. Wilbur D. Mills, October 10, 1981.
55. Ibid.
56. Congressional Quarterly, July 30, 1971, 1615.
57. Searcy Daily Citizen, May 21, 1971, front page.
58. Ibid.
59. Los Angeles Times, June 11, 1971.
60. Ibid.
61. Washington Post, October 1, 1971.
62. Ibid.
63. "Meet the Press," NBC News, March 20, 1971.
64. Ibid.
65. Chicago Tribune, June 2, 1971, 10.
66. Searcy Daily Citizen, July 2, 1971, front page.
67. "Meet the Press," NBC News, June 6, 1971.
68. Speech by Wilbur D. Mills, Ogden, Utah, June 1971.
69. Ibid.
70. Ibid.
71. Ibid.
72. Ibid.
73. Ibid.
74. Searcy Daily Citizen, September 28, 1971, front page.
75. Ibid.
76. Chicago Tribune, July 20, 1971.
77. Searcy Daily Citizen, August 16, 1971, front page.
78. Gene Goss, January 12, 1981.
79. Ibid.
80. Ibid.
81. Wilbur D. Mills, September 10, 1983.
82. Ibid.
83. American Federationist, AFL-CIO, August 1971, 29.
84. Des Moines Sunday Register, October 3, 1971, 4B.
85. Ibid., March 25, 1974, 9.
86. Searcy Daily Citizen, November 11, 1971, front page.
87. Nation's Business, November 1971, 71.
88. Wilbur D. Mills, "Congressman from Kensett," documentary, 1971.
89. Business Week, October 16, 1971, 25.
90. Ibid.
91. Ibid.
92. Ibid.
93. Ibid.
94. Ibid.
95. Ibid.
96. Ibid.
97. Ibid.
98. Ibid.
99. Ibid.

Chapter 10 Endnotes

1. Arkansas Gazette, January 5, 1972, 3A.
2. Ibid.
3. Ibid.
4. Ibid.
5. Ibid.
6. Ibid.
7. Congressional Record, February 23, 1972, HR 13320.
8. Ibid., June 30, 1972, House Roll Call, No. 259, not voting 95, 23738; Roll Call No. 260, 237338-39.
9. Syndicated Evans and Novak Column, July 2, 1972.
10. Thinking in Time, by Richard E. Newstadt and Ernest R. May, "Second Success," The Free Press, 1986, 19.
11. Searcy Daily Citizen, June 1, 1972, front page.
12. Ibid.
13. Ibid., April 13, 1972, front page.
14. Ibid.
15. Wall Street Journal, April 10, 1972.
16. New York Times, April 9, 1972.
17. Searcy Daily Citizen, April 21, 1972, front page.
18. Wilbur D. Mills, January 3, 1973.
19. "Wilbur Mills on Taxes and Other Choice Subjects," Barron's, September 22, 1986, 22.
20. New York Times, June 6, 1972, and Congressional Quarterly, 1972.
21. Ibid.
22. Congressional Quarterly Almanac, 1972, 316.
23. Ibid., 317.
24. Ibid.
25. Arkansas Gazette, March 23, 1972, 10A.
26. Ibid., February 12, 1972, front page.
27. New York Times, February 17, 1972.

28. Arkansas Gazette, February 24, 1972.
29. Ibid.
30. Searcy Daily Citizen, April 21, 1972, front page.
31. Ibid.
32. Ibid., April 26, 1972, front page.
33. Conversation with New Bedford Assessor, Henry Correia, March 4, 1988.
34. Arkansas Gazette, March 21, 1972, 1A.
35. Ibid.
36. Ibid.
37. Ibid.
38. Searcy Daily Citizen, March 8, 1972, front page.
39. Ibid.
40. Arkansas Gazette, March 21, 1972, front page.
41. Business Week, February 26, 1972, 68.
42. Ibid.
43. Ibid.
44. Ibid.
45. Index of New York Times, 1972.
46. Searcy Daily Citizen, January 19, 1972, front page.
47. Gene Goss, August 7, 1986.
48. Searcy Daily Citizen, June 27, 1972.
49. Ibid.
50. Ibid.
51. Wilbur D. Mills, July 7, 1984.
52. Searcy Daily Citizen, July 11, 1972, front page.
53. Ibid.
54. Wilbur D. Mills, November 22, 1987.
55. Searcy Daily Citizen, July 11, 1972, front page.
56. Robert J. Casey, Esquire, Special Memorial Services for Mills, Washington, D.C., June 29, 1992.
57. George McGovern, C-SPAN Interview, July 11, 1992.
58. Ibid.
59. Ibid.
60. Searcy Daily Citizen, July 19, 1972, front page.
61. Ibid., July 11, 1972, front page.
62. Wilbur D. Mills, September 26, 1989.
63. Searcy Daily Citizen, July 12, 1972, front page.
64. Ibid., July 13, 1972.
65. Ibid.
66. Ibid.
67. Ibid.
68. Searcy Daily Citizen, August 23, 1972, front page.
69. Congressional Quarterly Almanac, 1972.
70. Gene Goss, August 7, 1983.
71. Searcy Daily Citizen, August 23, 1972.
72. Arkansas Gazette, 30, 1972, 1A.
73. Gene Goss, August 7, 1983.
74. Ibid.
75. Searcy Daily Citizen, October 24, 1972, front page.
76. Ibid.
77. Ibid.
78. Ibid.
79. Ibid., November 2, 1972, front page.
80. Ibid.
81. Ibid.
82. Ibid.
83. Ibid.
84. Ibid.
85. Ibid.
86. Arkansas Gazette, November 17, 1972, 1A.
87. Ibid.
88. Wilbur D. Mills, Speech at Baptist Medical Center, Tribute Luncheon, November 8, 1990.
89. Arkansas Gazette, November 27, 1972, and Wilbur D. Mills, November 26, 1972.

Chapter 11 Endnotes

1. Gene Goss, August 7, 1981.
2. Arkansas Gazette, November 11, 1973, 4E.
3. Washington Post, July 11, 1973.
4. Washington Evening Star, July 11, 1973.
5. Rowland and Evans syndicated column, July 12, 1973.
6. Wilbur D. Mills Speech, Union Rescue Mission, October 18, 1981.
7. "Meet the Press," NBC News, from files of White House Communications Agency, VTR No. 6185, March 18, 1973.
8. Gene Goss, August 7, 1981.
9. Ibid.
10. Ibid.
11. Roger Q. Mills, Sr., May 5, 1992.
12. Interview, Wilbur D. Mills, by Kelly Luker, Sober Times, February 7, 1992.
13. Man of the House: The Life and Political Memories of Speaker Tip O'Neill, Random House, New York, 1987, 137.
14. House Select Committee on Committees, Briefing Book: Committee Reform

Amendment of 1974, 1974, 76.
15. Ibid.
16. Steven Smith and Christopher J. Deering, Committees in Congress, 1984, 26.
17. Arkansas Gazette, January 13, 1974, front page.
18. Draft Final Report of Select Committee on Presidential Campaign Activities, U.S. Senate for 93rd Congress, Part 2, U.S. Government Printing Office, July 1974, 799.
19. Gene Goss, August 7, 1981.
20. Searcy Daily Citizen, April 9, 1974, front page.
21. Ibid.
22. Wilbur D. Mills, 28, 1990.
23. Searcy Daily Citizen, February 7, 1974, front page.
24. Ibid., February 20, 1974, front page.
25. Ibid.
26. Ibid., August 16, 1974, front page.
27. Ibid.
28. Ibid., August 9, 1974, front page.
29. Ibid., August 22, 1974, front page.
30. Bill Timmons Memo, Gerald R. Ford Presidential Library.
31. Searcy Daily Citizen, January 13, 1974.
32. Casper Weinberger Memo, Gerald R. Ford Presidential Library.
33. Photocopy from Gerald R. Ford Presidential Library, August 28, 1974.
34. Searcy Daily Citizen, January 13, 1974, front page.
35. Ibid.
36. Ibid., September 6, 1974, front page.
37. Ibid., October 9, 1974, front page.
38. Washington Post, October 9, 1974.
39. Ibid., October 11, 1974.
40. Searcy Daily Citizen, October 10, 1974, front page.
41. Ibid., October 11, 1974.
42. Washington Post, October 9, 1974.
43. New York Daily News, October 10, 1974, 2.
44. Gene Wirges, Conflict of Interest: The Gene Wirges Story, 229.
45. Copy of Incident Report on file at Gerald R. Ford Presidential Library.
46. Arkansas Gazette, excerpting Nancy Dickerson's book, Among Those Present, November 14, 1976, 6E.
47. New York Times, October 17, 1974.
48. Karen McDougall, Wilbur D. Mills: Media Treatment of Events Leading Up to and Beyond His Acknowledgment of Alcoholism, Chapter 5, quoting letter from Mills to Karen on his reaction to press coverage.
49. Sander Vanocur Conversation, November 9, 1992.
50. Searcy Daily Citizen, October10, 1974.
51. Ibid.
52. Ibid.
53. Ibid.
54. Washington Star News, October 18, 1974.
55. Searcy Daily Citizen, October 31, 1974.
56. Ibid., November 5, 1974, front page.
57. Benton Courier, October 25, 1974, front page.
58. Ibid.
59. Ibid.
60. Gene Goss, November 7, 1974.
61. Searcy Daily Citizen, November 13, 1974, front page.
62. Wilbur D. Mills, August 7, 1991.
63. Baltimore Sun, November 17, 1974.
64. Searcy Daily Citizen, November 27, 1974, front page.
65. Ibid.
66. Ibid.
67. Ibid.
68. Wilbur D. Mills, November 4, 1974.
69. Henry Correia, May 5, 1992.
70. Wilbur D. Mills, May 6, 1975.
71. Washington Post, December 3, 1974.
72. Baltimore Sun, December 3, 1974.
73. Searcy Daily Citizen, December 4, 1974, front page.
74. Wilbur D. Mills, October 22, 1987.
75. Searcy Daily Citizen, December 4, 1974, front page.
76. Wall Street Journal, December 3, 1974.
77. Gene Goss, August 7, 1981.
78. Christian Science Monitor, December 4, 1974.
79. Washington Star News, December 3, 1974.
80. Searcy Daily Citizen, December 5, 1974, front page.
81. New York Times, December 3, 1974.
82. Ibid., December 4, 1974.
83. Washington Post, December 4, 1974.
84. Ibid., December 10, 1974.
85. Ibid., December 11, 1974.
86. Robert McIntyre, Citizens for Tax Justice, Director, quoted in Arkansas Democrat-

Gazette, March 21, 1993, J1.
87. Searcy Daily Citizen, December 30, 1974, front page.
88. Jeremiah O'Leary, Washington Times, May 3, 1992.
89. Searcy Daily Citizen, December 30, 1974, front page.
90. New York Times, December 31, 1974.

Chapter 12 Endnotes

1. Searcy Daily Citizen, February 10, 1975.
2. New York Times, January 4, 1975, 15.
3. Ibid.; 22.
4. Ibid., January 15, 1975, 14.
5. Wilbur D. Mills, August 7, 1990.
6. Ibid., May 5, 1975.
7. Searcy Daily Citizen, February 13, 1975, front page.
8. Ibid., February 25, 1975, front page.
9. Wilbur D. Mills, May 26, 1975.
10. Searcy Daily Citizen, March 18, 1975.
11. Ibid., March 10, 1975.
12. Wilbur D. Mills, May 26, 1975.
13. Ibid.
14. Ibid.
15. Ibid.
16. Searcy Daily Citizen, May 6, 1975.
17. Ibid.
18. Ibid., May 16, 1975.
19. Ibid.
20. Ibid.
21. Ibid.
22. Ibid., May 26, 1975.
23. Karen McDougall, Wilbur D. Mills: The Media Coverage of His Alcoholism, University of Rhode Island, 1979, excerpted from Mills letter to McDougall.
24. Searcy Daily Citizen, May 30, 1975.
25. Letter from Mills to Mr. and Mrs. Jack C. Miller of Leslie and Des Arc, July 10, 1975.
26. Chicago Tribune, September 5, 1975.
27. Ibid.
28. Arkansas Gazette, May 15, 1975.
29. Ibid.
30. Ibid.
31. Gene Goss, September 10, 1975.
32. File on Wilbur Mills, September 1975, Gerald R. Ford Presidential Library.
33. Ibid., Marsh Letter, October 17, 1975.
34. Searcy Daily Citizen, October 21, 1975.
35. Telegram from Mills to President Ford, December 3, 1975, Ford Library.
36. Press Release, Office of Congressman Wilbur D. Mills, Ford Library.
37. Congressional Quarterly Almanac, 1975, 138.
38. Letter from President Ford to Mills, December 9, 1975, Ford Library.
39. Wilbur D. Mills, December 19, 1975.
40. Mills Speech, Kansas State Alcoholism Conference, October 4, 1980.
41. File on memos, letters, and phone calls during April, 1976, by President Ford, Ford Library.
42. National Journal, "Corman of California," by Linda Demkovich, October 1, 1977, 1523.
43. Congressional Record, October 19, 1976.
44. Washington Star, October 31, 1976, E1.
45. Searcy Daily Citizen, October 20, 1976.
46. Ibid.
47. Arkansas Democrat, June 13, 1988, 3A.
48. Wilbur D. Mills, from regular inspirational speeches to alcohol recovery groups.
49. Time, "The Fall," December 16, 1974.
50. Arkansas Gazette, October 2, 1976, 1A, 3A.
51. Searcy Daily Citizen, October 29, 1976.
52. Dave Parr, 1993.

INDEX